School of the

The Highland Cattle-raiding
Tradition

by

Stuart McHardy

Birlinn

First published in 2004 by
Birlinn Limited
West Newington House
10 Newington Road
Edinburgh EH9 1QS

www.birlinn.co.uk

ISBN 1 84158 300 6

British Library Cataloguing-in-Publication Data
A catalogue record for this book is
available from the British Library

Typeset by Hewer Text, Edinburgh
Printed and bound by
MPG Books, Bodmin

This book is dedicated to storytellers everywhere

Contents

One time the famous Cateran known as the Halkit Stirk was wounded in a skirmish in Strathspey and was left in the care of a family of Stewarts who were foresters at Glenmore. One day he said to his hostess, 'That's a fine manly son you have there. I would say he was ready for the school. How old is he?' She replied, 'He's twelve and he has been going to the school at Ruthven for two years now.' The reply came, 'Cha neill e Sgoille a phaipear ghaeall bhami ciallachadh, ach sgoille-na-geallaich' [It is not the School of the White Paper I am thinking of, but the School of the Moon]. The School of the Moon where the subject was cattle raiding and the classroom set in the moonlit nights of autumn. It was little wonder that the autumn moon was known in parts of Scotland as 'Mac-Pherson's Lantern', for it was by its light that the MacPhersons and so many other clans made their way through the wild country of Scotland to 'lift' the cattle of other clans and head off back home with them. There was also a saying that Highland chiefs counted out their daughters' tochers [dowries] by the light of the Michaelmas moon.

Preface

This book presents both stories derived from traditional sources and historical information regarding one of the central activities of the warriors of the Scottish Highland clans – cattle raiding. Which collecting traditional tales about this ancient activity I began to realise that quite a few of the stories that told of events in the 18th century concerned identifiable historical characters. The contemporary records, some of which, like the Cantonment Registers of the British army – the records of the locations and activities of the army – are still unpublished, and tell a remarkable story. In the years after the last Jacobite battle on Drumossie Moor that we now call Culloden, the British Army was involved in what we would now consider ethnic cleansing. The widespread brutality – much of it perpetrated by Scotsmen of both Highland and Lowland origin – is well documented in a remarkable and heart-rending book called *The Lyon in Mourning*. The evidence from the period confirms that the Jacobite rebellions are best understood as Civil Wars, driven by a complex set of ideas.

What has not been documented is the extent of the Army occupation of Scotland throughout the 1740s and 1750s. There was hardly a town or glen that did not have its own garrison, and the ostensible reason for this was the fact that some of these historical characters, like Iain Dubh Cameron, the Serjeant Mor, took to cattle raiding as a means of survival. The records clearly suggest that what was going on was a form of guerrilla warfare in which scattered bands of Jacobite Highlanders continued to 'stay out' – i.e., they refused to give up their battle with the British Army, even though it must have been clear, to some of them at least, that they had no long-term chance of success, or even survival. In their reliance on cattle raiding these last Jacobites were continuing a practice of inter-tribal activity that had been part of clan life for many centuries, and may have had its origins as far back as the Iron Age.

So this book combines both traditional tales and historical information in an attempt to come to terms with the real story of the last years of the ancient Celtic-speaking warrior society that had survived in the Scottish Highlands from time immemorial into the modern age.

Introduction

For centuries the Highlands of Scotland, like the Border marches and the hills of Galloway were seen by central government as lawless, dangerous places, populated by battle-hardened thieves who came down from their hills and carried off the cattle of farmers in many parts of the Lowlands. In the Highlands these so-called thieves were simply men of the clan, all trained as warriors and keen to show their skill and judgement in raids on others' cattle . . .

A story told by Edward Burt in *Letters to a Gentleman from the North of Scotland*, written in the 1730s, gives a clear example of how the Highlanders themselves viewed the activity of 'cattle-lifting'.

A Highlander had been arrested after taking a considerable number of cattle and was brought to trial. The punishment, if found guilty, was death by hanging. The indictment was read setting forth that 'as a common thief he had lain in wait', etc. On hearing the accusation the Highlander burst forth in a torrent of indignation, 'Common thief, common thief! One cow, two cows that be common thief! Lift a hundred cows that be gentleman drovers.'

If executed, such men were seen as martyrs by their peers, for to them it was not stealing. What they were doing was following an honourable tradition of inter-clan cattle-raiding that had probably been going on since the Iron Age, if not earlier. The clans (the Gaelic word *clann* means children), were a society totally different from Lowland society in Scotland and England.

3

The clan was a tribe formed from the descendants – the children – of a shared common ancestor and all the men were warriors. And these warriors went by the name of *cateran*, which seems originally to have meant a band of armed men. It seems likely that the reference to raiding parties as caterans arose from the fact that this was a regular, if not an integral part of clan society.

Like their counterparts in the Borders and Galloway the Highlanders' society was defined by kin-group – the family. Loyalty to the clan was paramount. Although by the 18th century the clans held title-deeds to their lands, in the main these charters were given in recognition of the fact that they had held these lands since time immemorial, *a ghlaive* – by the sword. This does not mean that they had come in and taken the land by force, but that they were a warrior race who held their lands against all incomers through their bravery and skill at arms. Surrounded by their kin, they were as tied to the land as the animals and birds that lived in the Highlands: this was their territory. And to hold that territory they had developed a society in which every able-bodied male was trained as a warrior. Taught as children how to fight with sticks, as young men they learned to handle the sword and the bow – later the gun – the shield and that ubiquitous weapon/tool – the dirk.

Much has been written over the years about the unswerving loyalty of the clansmen to their chief. Such loyalty was pre-dicated on a complex network of duties and obligations between chief and clansmen, a strict code of honour being observed in all things. All members of the clan were subject to the rules of clan society, and the widespread view that the chiefs were all-power-ful despots is unrealistic. The reality was that the chief was the focus of a whole society in which everyone man, woman and child, was his relation, either by blood or marriage. The loyalty of the people to the chief was based on the fact that he was the direct descendant of the ancestor from whom they all claimed descent, and later we shall consider exactly how this system worked. Another excerpt from Burt's *Letters* features a story of how the relationship between the chief and his clansmen stood in the 1730s:

> . . . and as the meanest among them pretend to be his Relations by Consanguinity, they insist upon the Privilege of taking him by the Hand whenever they meet him. Concerning this last, I once saw a Number of very discontented Countenances when a certain Lord, one of the Chiefs, endeavoured to evade this Ceremony. It was in Presence of an English Gentleman in high station, from whom he would have willingly have concealed the Knowledge of such seeming Familiarity with slaves of so wretched Appearance, and thinking it, I suppose, as a kind of Contradiction to what he had often boasted at other Times, viz., his despotic Power over his Clan.

It is noticeable that he says that it is the member of the clan insisting on *his* right to shake his Chief's hand. While this does not mean that the two were absolute equals it does show that within the tribal/clan set-up there was a social system totally unlike that of England where there were aristocracy, gentry and effectively, serfs, or as Burt puts it here – slaves.

The following description of how the average clansmen saw himself is taken from Stewart's *Sketches of the Highlanders* (1822), p. 48:

> He [the clansman] believed himself well born, and was taught to respect himself in the respect which he showed to his chief; and thus, instead of complaining of the difference of station and fortune, he felt convinced he was supporting his own honour [and that of family and clan] in showing his gratitude and duty to the generous head of his family.

A little later, on page 51, Stewart goes on to describe how justice itself was dispensed within the clan system and he points out how the kin-based system was the direct opposite of the feudal ideas which some scholars have suggested were the basis of clan society.

Freemen could be tried by none but their peers. The vassals [sic] were bound to attend the courts of their chiefs [by mutual obligation not force; and the courts are of the clan not the chief], and amongst other things, to assist in the trials of delinquents. When they assembled on such occasions they established among themselves such regulations as, in their opinion, tended to the welfare of the community, and whenever it became necessary, they voluntarily granted such supplies as they thought the necessity of their superiors required. Their generosity was particularly shown in the marriage of the chief, and in the portioning of his daughters and younger sons. These last, when settled in life, frequently found themselves supplied with the essential necessaries of a family, and particularly with a stock of cattle, which . . . constituted the principal riches of the country. The land was held on behalf of the clan and apart from the generosity of his table and his personal dress and weaponry, which were often of very high quality, the chief had few more personal possessions than his clansfolk, though his household did have to support a sometimes extensive retinue. Apart from his weapons the warrior owned little. Until its later years money does not seem to have been of importance in the day-to-day life of the clan system. The economy was basically one of self-sufficiency, much of it based on the rearing of cattle. Thus a successful *creach*, or raid, would obviously be of significance within the immediate clan economy.

There is clearly a level of egalitarianism that not only contradicts but has no obvious precursors in feudalism. The supposed absolute power of the Scottish chief over his clansmen does not fit in with these accounts. In essence, to command the loyalty of the rest of the clan, the chiefs were required to show their bravery and skill at arms. The Highlander's sense of honour and martial traditions meant that he would only follow someone in whom he had faith. Before being totally accepted as leader the young chief had to prove himself to the warriors of the clan. In the book *A Description of the Western Islands of Scotland, circa 1695* Martin Martin tells us of this practice (1934 edn. p. 101):

> Every heir, or young chieftain of a tribe, was obliged in honour to give a public specimen of his valour before he was owned or declared governor or leader of his people . . . It was usual for the captain to lead them, to make a desperate incursion upon some neighbour or other . . . and they were obliged to bring the cattle they found on the lands they attacked, or to die in the attempt.

The same point is made by Browne in *A History of the Highlands* (1851 edn, p. 129):

> If they failed in their attempts, they were not respected; and if they appeared disinclined to engage in hostile rencontres, they were despised.

As we shall see, the raids or *creachs* in which the young chief participated to prove his valour were an integral part of Highland society and the focus of a great deal of activity, on the part of the men at least. They had their own rules and procedures and there were elaborate customs to be followed as the raiders drove their prey through the lands of other clans. This was necessary as these raids were often the cause of retribution, and raiding one's near neighbours would have meant constant battle and feud. The standard practice was generally to travel a considerable distance and there are instances of Highlanders regularly raiding as far south as Galloway. The raids were virtually always to 'lift' cattle, for many centuries the main form of moveable wealth in the Highlands.

The general plan and procedure of the raid or *creach* was to come into your victim's land stealthily before dawn and gather up the livestock with as little noise as possible, leading them off on the chosen path before the locals were awake. This obviously meant that an extensive survey was required in order that the cateran might know both the whereabouts of the cattle and the route by which they intended moving them. A great deal of skill in dealing with the animals was essential, and the most successful *creach* would be one where the cattle were gathered, taken away and brought back home with no interference from the clan that had been raided. Fighting was an expected part of the raiding process but it does not seem to have been the reason for it. The underlying idea seems to have been to show the skill and bravery of the cateran involved. As has been noted, such cattle-raiding was generally undertaken a good distance away from the clan's homelands. Raiding nearby clans would make little sense as it would probably lead to continuing warfare, and though there were what amounted to established rules of combat amongst the Highland clans, there was always the possibility of a blood feud when one act of revenge would provoke another in an ongoing cycle of killing. Because the raids were undertaken at a distance, this meant that the raiders had to cross the territory of other clans between their home and that of their victims. It was standard practice for raiders to give up some of their booty to the clan whose lands they crossed, and this was known as 'a road-collop'. Disputes could arise as to what was a suitable amount and in one instance a group of cateran from the Munro clan fell out with Mackintoshes in Strathardle when they offered what was deemed an insulting number of cattle; this in turn led to an open battle at Clachnaharry. In this instance the Munros escaped with most of their cattle but this illustrates how easy it could be for permanently armed men to turn to battle, on what we would nowadays consider a flimsy pretext.

Because of the nature of the Civil Wars of the 18th century we have strangely few eye-witness accounts of cateran raids other than through the traditional tales. The early histories of the Highlands all emphasise the bloodiness and savagery of clan life and appear to have been driven by ideas developed by the British establishment to justify their actions against the clans. This is particularly true as regards the Highland warrior's sense of honour, about which most of our knowledge is decidedly second-hand. No contemporary historian ever seems to have addressed this directly.

Given the well-documented brutality in the period immediately after Culloden, which clearly represents how the 'modern' British establishment wished to deal with the Highland problem, this is perhaps unsurprising. However, there are recurring examples in stores of cattle-raiding where pursuing clansmen caught up with the cateran, the next event being a one-to-one sword fight to decide who shiuld have the cattle. This illustrates that the *cothrom na Feinne*, the fair play of the Fianna, was an inherent part of the Highland warrior tradition. This was an idea rooted in the ancient heroic tales of Finn MacCoul and the warriors of the Fianna, common to the Gaelic traditions of Scotland and Ireland. A comparison might be the well-attested behaviour amongst the Plains tribes of North America and their practice of counting coup. Here an experienced warrior would go into battle on horseback, with his lance or spear tied back in the shape of a shepherd's crook, without its spearhead, and then he would go into the fighting, strike his chosen opponent and ride away without receiving any injury. This showed both bravery and skill and was intended to enhance a warrior's status by demeaning his opponent or opponents. Although the Highland warriors, like the Plains tribes, fought in groups, they were warriors rather than soldiers.

In many raids, horses and sheep would often be taken along with the cattle, and particularly in later years, as Highland

society began to disintegrate, there are instances of plain robbery, where money, arms and household goods were lifted. Such
behaviour was not unknown in earlier times but may have been
more closely associated with feuds between clans. There were
also those who were simply criminal. The famous James Mac-
Pherson, the subject of the traditional song 'MacPherson's
Rant', was accused of a whole range of criminal activities at
his trial, and there were witnesses to all of them.

The black cattle of the Highlands were a hardy breed and in
later centuries the great cattle droves followed many of the same
paths through the same glens and over the same mountains as
had earlier been taken by caterans driving their booty. The
creachs provided a splendid opportunity for the warriors to
prove themselves: they could keep up their skill at arms and
they had a chance to increase the wealth of the clan. Long after
the money economy was a fact of life for many Highlanders, the
cattle-raids continued and, as we shall see, the last flowering of
Highland warrior traditions showed in the cattle-raiding of the
remnants of the Jacobite Army who 'stayed out' after Culloden.
Faced with death or transportation at best, these Highland
warriors fought in a last vain battle to preserve a way of life
that had lasted for many centuries in the Highlands of Scotland.

In his *Northern Rural Life* (1887) William Alexander has this
to say of the practice of cattle 'lifting', p. 65:

> The practice of cattle lifting came to be a well systematised
> business and the freebooting highlanders had their own code
> of honour in conducting it. When cattle were stolen, one
> means of recovery used was to send an emissary into the
> region where the thief was supposed to be, and offer a reward
> for his discovery. This reward was looked on with great
> abhorrence. With the high-minded Highlander, who scrupled
> not to rob his Lowland neighbours' byres and girnals, *tascal*
> *money* as it was called was the 'unclean thing' and he and his

fellows would solemnly swear over their drawn dirks that they would never defile their consciences by taking any such reward . . .

Oral transmission

Much of the education and entertainment of the clansfolk came through the tradition of the great epic poems concerning Finn MacCoul and other heroes who had lived long, long ago, but whose lives were echoed in many ways by the lives of the Highlanders. Finn MacCoul's legendary warriors the Fianna, or Fenians, were very like the cateran bands who went raiding for cattle and, like the illustrious warriors of ancient times, the Highland warriors were fond of the hunt and ever ready for battle. Much of the material in this book arises from that same oral tradition, the handing down of traditional tales by word of mouth. Many commentators on the ancient story traditions of the Celtic-speaking peoples of Britain have considered that the material, believed to have come from the eighth century CE and before, in some way represented only a faded reflection of a way of life that had long died out. What we know of Highland society suggests that such ancient warrior society adapted and lived on. Just because the written word, originally the Bible, arrived, did not mean that the oral tradition had died out. Even today in Scotland, we cannot boast 100 per cent literacy. With us, the storytelling tradition itself has never disappeared, and is in fact currently undergoing a revival.

This storytelling tradition covers a long period. In *Australian Dreaming, 40,000 years of Aboriginal History*, Jennifer Isaacs has shown that oral tradition can carry stories that contain ascertainable facts over tens of thousands of years.

The historian's general disdain for oral tradition serves us ill. It was through following up traditional stories from various parts of Scotland that I was able to discover just how extensive the military occupation of Scotland was in the period following Culloden and that what was going on in the guise of a 'police action', was actually the suppression of a guerrilla war. Many of the stories here have come originally from the oral tradition and have little or no precise historical worth, in that they do not concern identifiable individuals and actions. This does not diminish their value.

Collectors of folk tales since the 19th century have often commented upon the prodigious memories of tradition-bearers, many of them carrying remarkable amounts of remembered material. As an illustration of the tenacity of the oral tradition I can think of no better instance than the tale of 'Jack and the Seven Magic Islands' in Dr Sheila Douglas's book *The King of the Black Art and other Tales.* This story, which Dr Douglas got from the traveller, James Stewart in the 1980s is a previously uncollected variant of the 'Voyage of Brendan', a tale which originated no later than the 8th century.

Battle, not War

Though their distant Caledonian ancestors had united against the invading Romans in the first century, the normal life of the clans, although involving regular *creachs* and resulting battles, seems rarely to have been interrupted by war. Their battles, if not exactly ritualistic, were fought along clearly organised lines and often involved equal numbers of men chosen from both sides in a battle with the overall victory, and any spoils thereof, going to the winning side. Probably the most famous instance of this type of structured battle was the Battle of the Inch at Perth in 1396 where thirty men from two clans, who appear to have been the MacPhersons and the Davidsons, fought before king Robert III, the MacPhersons taking the day. Cattle-raiding was endemic amongst the Highland tribes: it was how the warriors fulfilled their role in society, but as the ancient tribal way of Highland life began to break down the cateran increasingly raided the Lowlands. Effectively two different societies, the Gaelic-speaking warrior pastoralists and the Scots-speaking modern agriculturalists increasingly came into conflict. The Lowland saying, 'Show me a Highlander, and I will show you a thief', was matched by the Highlander's, 'show me a Southron and I will show you a glutton'.

Although the demarcation between the two societies along the Highland Line of Scotland was never like a modern border – there was interaction between the two language groups and Highland and Lowland families regularly inter-married – there is no doubt that we have here two societies whose beliefs and mores were so different that in many instances they were incapable of understanding each other.

Another Lowland saying describes the 'lifting' of the Lowlanders' cattle in interesting domestic terms: 'Highland lairds tell out their daughters' tochers [dowries] by the light of the Michaelmas Moon'. A tocher is a dowry, and as the Highlanders counted their wealth in cattle, the raiding made sound business sense. It was under the light of the autumn moon, after the harvest was in, that the cateran went on their raids. This is from Carlo Ginsburg's *Ecstasies* (1992) and gives a recognisable context for the beliefs and practices surrounding the 'School of the Moon' (p. 236):

> In the legendary biography of the young hero, the theft of livestock carried out in league with their contemporaries was an obligatory stage, virtually an initiation ritual. It respected a very ancient mythical model, amply documented in the Indo-European cultural milieu: the journey to the beyond to steal the livestock of monstrous being.

Such mythical journeys obviously arose out of very ancient practice indeed, and in Scotland this ancient practice was still being followed in the 18th century. Probably the most remarkable story about the cateran originates from that period. Initially, in following the stories of the cattle-raiders, I came across reference to one Serjeant Mor, a cateran who was not captured, and hung, till 1753. According to folk tradition he had 'stayed out' after the defeat of the Jacobites at Culloden in 1746, leading a group of cateran, and in effect carrying on a kind of guerrilla campaign.

It was subsequently gratifying to find the details of the British Army occupation of the Highlands through the late 1740s and into the 1750s. Ostensibly the garrisons in every glen were there to stop cattle-thieving. And indeed this was how Serjeant Mor and his companions lived, by lifting cattle. But they were a group of Jacobite rebels who never surrendered, and fortunately, though there are no separate British Army casualty figures for Scotland in this period, we do have some of the situation reports sent in by junior officers on the ground. Among these young officers was one who would rise to fame as General Wolfe, and another – the man who finally captured Serjeant Mor – became a great hero of the Indian campaigns of the 18th century, General Sir Hector Munro. Serjeant Mor and perhaps as many as 400 others 'stayed out', and in order to survive in an occupied country they turned to their traditional practice of cattle-raiding, and for the last time utilised the skills that were learnt in the School of the Moon.

The Background – Tribal Scotland

The first written records concerning Scotland come from the Romans. Ptolemy's 2nd-century map shows Scotland being occupied by a series of tribes. In the north he tells us there were the Caerini, Carnonacae, Cornavii, Decantae and Lugi; further south the Creones and Caledones; to the east the Taexali and Venicones; with the Epidii in Kintyre, the Damnonae in Strathclyde, the Novantae in Galloway, the Selgovae in the

central borders and the Votadini on the east from the Forth
south. Only a few of these names survived in later Roman texts,
particularly the Caledonians and the Votadini, in whom we see
the people later known as the Gododdin. In a poem entitled 'The
Gododdin', written in an early form of Welsh from the early 7th
century, we can make out something of how early tribal warrior
society functioned. Welsh, like the Gaelic of the Highlanders, is a
Celtic language and is referred to as P-Celtic while Gaelic is Q-
Celtic. The 'p' sound replaced the 'c' sound at some time in the
far distant past, e.g., the Gaelic *Mac* [son of] is *Map* in Welsh,
while *ceann* [head] is *peann*. An easy way to understand the
difference is to think of a Scot, 'Ewan MacEwan' and his Welsh
cousin 'Owen Map Owen'. The 'p' sound has replaced the 'c'
sound and there are vowel changes, but the underlying similarity
of the names is still obvious.

It is generally accepted that the tribes of what we now think of
as Southern Scotland were predominantly P-Celtic speakers and
that the Picts had a similar language. At the time the Romans
arrived it is more than likely that there were Gaelic-speaking
Scots living in Argyll, and on the east coast, through contact with
continental Europe across the North Sea, the sound of Germanic languages would not be unknown. As far back as Megalithic
times, when the great monuments of Maes Howe on Orkney,
Calanais on Lewis, New Grange in Ireland and Stonehenge in
England were erected, Scotland was part of an extensive cultural
world. It is the descendants of the megalith builders who were
the ancestors of the Highlanders, and of us modern Scots. The
isolation of the Highland clans over much of Scottish history
perhaps owed as much to their retaining the ancient tribal way of
life as to geography, though until the building of General Wade's
roads in the 1730s travel in the Highlands was difficult and slow.

Later Roman sources refer to tribes like the Caledones, the
Dicalydones, the Maetae and the Verturiones. While many
scholars have attempted to define the precise areas that were

inhabited by these people it is clear that we are dealing with essentially tribal societies. There were no great cities, though there were substantial areas of building on many hill-tops. These have always been interpreted as defensive military structures, but many of the hill-top sites featured prominently in communal rituals on the great feast days of Beltane (1 May) and Samhain (1 November) – the modern Hallowe'en. This suggests that while there may indeed have been some military aspect to many of these locations, they also had a social, or perhaps a religious function. In fact such imposing sites would provide a very handy central focus for social activities among the small scattered family groups within their immediate locality.

The ongoing resistance of the Highland clans to centralised control was rooted deep in their history. Within the clan system, loyalty to one's kin was absolute, and particularly to the chief as the social, political, and originally perhaps, sacred focus of the entire tribe. The Highlanders saw themselves as answerable to no one but themselves, though in times of particular trouble they could ally themselves not only with their neighbours, but with other clans with whom they were often at odds. As early as the Battle of Mons Graupius, circa AD 80 we have Tacitus putting these words into the mouth of Calgacus, the Leader (not the King) of the Caledonians. It is in Tacitus's *Agricola* (1948 edn,) p. 31:

> Whenever I consider why we are fighting and how we have reached this crisis, I have a strong sense that this day of your splendid rally may mean the dawn of liberty for the whole of Britain. You have mustered to a man and to a man you are free . . . We, the last men on earth, the last of the free, have been shielded till today by the very remoteness and seclusion for which we are famed . . . Brigands of the world they have exhausted the land by their indiscriminate plunder, and now they ransack the sea . . . Robbery, butchery, rapine, the liars call Empire; they create a desolation and call it peace.

This passage is perhaps nothing more than Tacitus (enhancing the reputation of Agricola, his father-in-law), presenting Calgacus as an honourable and worthy opponent, but it does strike a chord that echoes down the centuries. The name Calgacus, thought to mean 'The Swordsman', is fitting for someone whose function was to lead the allied tribes against the invaders. It might be that this is echoed in later clan practice when the chief was known simply as 'The MacPherson' or 'The Macdonald'.

The Roman writer Xiphilinus told of the Severan campaign of 208 CE, as given in Watson's *Celtic Place Names of Scotland*, pp. 56–7:

> . . . the two most important tribes of the Britons (in the North) are the Caledonians and the Maetae; the names of all the tribes have been practically absorbed in these. The Maetae dwell close to the wall which divides the island into two parts and the Caledonians next to them. Each of the two inhabit rugged hills with swamps between possessing neither walled towns nor cultivated lands, but living by pastoral pursuits and by hunting and on certain kinds of hard-shelled fruits. They eat no fish, though their waters teem with all kinds of them. They live in tents, naked and shoeless: they have their women in common, and rear all their offspring. Their government is democratic, and they take the utmost delight in forays for plunder. They fight from chariots, and have small swift horses. Their infantry are extremely swift of foot and enduring. Their weapons are a shield and short spear with a knob of brass on the end of the butt . . . they have also daggers. They can endure hunger and thirst and every kind of hardship. They plunge into marshes, and last out many days with only their heads above water, and in the woods they live on bark and roots, and above all they prepare a certain food such that, if they

eat only the bulk of a bean of it, they suffer neither hunger nor thirst.

This remarkable passage raises several interesting points. His comment that all the names of all the tribes have been absorbed into just two is a little strange. Given that we know the people were living in small kin-groups, with no walled towns, it seems unlikely that the earlier tribes had merged into much bigger polities. Perhaps he is referring to a practice akin to later clan times when different clans shared allegiance within larger federations such as Clan Chattan and Siol Alpin. The reference to the hardiness of the natives is something that is echoed by many later commentators in describing Highland troops who seem to have retained their ancestor's physical durability.

The reference to having their women in common has been seen by more than a few commentators as an outsider's view of a society in which women actually had considerable status. One suggestion is that it was women who were free to pick any man they chose and that the children of different fathers were brought up together. Looking at this from the viewpoint of a patriarchal society, such as the Roman, it would be easy to misinterpret what was being seen. Xiphilinus, who was abridging an earlier writer, Dio Cassius, had no first-hand knowledge of Scotland and could hardly have been expected to understand modern ideas of tribal anthropology. The reference to weaponry mentions daggers and it is a notable fact that most complaints about the Disarming Act of 1746 were about the banning of the dirk – a very handy tool as well as a murderous weapon. The miraculous food he refers to, I am assured by Dr Brian Moffat of Edinburgh University, is a tiny tuber that grows on the roots of the Bitter Vetch and which contains an amazing array of concentrated sugars – enough in fact to do just what Xiphilinus tells us. The reference to democratic government can be understood as meaning the regular discussions that take place within all types of tribal society regarding practical, political and military matters. Tribes are social organisations that develop from familial relationships within given territories, and are never the result of the despotic endeavours of any individual.

Nearly thirteen hundred years later than Mons Graupius we have the remarkable Declaration of Arbroath in which the Scottish people gave voice (this is the translation from Professor Ted Cowan's *For Freedom Alone* (2003, pp. 145–46)):

> But from these countless evils we have been set free, by the help of Him, who though He afflicts yet heals and restores, by our most valiant prince, king and lord, the lord Robert, who, that his people and heritage might be delivered out of the hands of enemies, bore cheerfully toil and fatigue, hunger and danger, like another Maccabeus or Joshua. Divine providence, the succession to his right according to our laws and customs which we shall maintain to the death, and the due consent and assent of all of us, have made him our prince and king. We are bound to him for the maintaining of our freedom both by his rights and merits, as to him by whom salvation has been wrought unto our people, and by him, come what may, we mean to stand. Yet if he should give up what he has begun, seeking to make us or our kingdom subject to the king of England or to the English, we would strive at once to drive him out as our enemy and a subverter of his own right an ours, and we would make some other man who was able to defend us our king. For as long as a hundred of us remain alive, we will never on any conditions be subjected to the lordship of the English. For we fight nor for glory nor riches nor honours, but for freedom alone, which no good man gives up except with is life.

Each of these statements speaks of a form of governance which is anything but the despotic rule of a single individual. In the first instance we are told that Calgacus is the leader of the massed tribes, not their king or supreme chief; the Roman Xiphilinus calls them democratic; and over a thousand years later, in Christian Scotland, it is clear that even the king is answerable to the people. He is the King of the Scots, not King of Scotland, a distinction of great importance because it underlines that without the consent of the ruled there is no ruler. And if the ruled are unsatisfied with their ruler, they will find themselves a new one. This is clearly not feudal.

We cannot be sure that Tacitus was doing anything other than presenting an idealised form of a suitable opponent in the panegyric to his father-in-law but it is remarkable that we have statements over such a period that have the same sense of egalitarianism. It is also worth noting that in the modern world such a fundamentally important document as the American Declaration of Independence was modelled to some extent on the 1320 Declaration.

Even in the latter, declining years of Highland Gaelic society, when most chiefs had accepted paper deeds for lands that they and theirs had held for centuries, and were on the way to becoming Lairds, sole owners of what had been the much loved lands of entire societies, society in all of Scotland was never as feudal or class-ridden as it was south of the border. An instance of this occurred when a chief, educated and living away from the clan, offended the clan members on his return to take his place as their head. The situation was thus described by Logan in *The Scottish Gael* (1876), p. 195:

The anecdote of the young chief of Clanranald is well known. On his return to take possession of his estate, observing the profuse quantity of cattle that had been slaughtered to cele-brate his arrival, he very unfortunately remarked that a few hens might have answered the purpose. This exposure of a narrow mind, and inconsiderate display of indifference to the feeling of his people, were fatal.' We will have nothing to do with a hen chief,' said the indignant clansmen, and immediately raised one of his brothers to the dignity.

We can be pretty sure that part of the reaction to the 'Hen Chief's' ignorance and disdain of his own clan's traditions resulted from the fact that a feast greeting a new chief would have been considered a momentous occasion in clan life, and the excuse for a good party for the entire clan. The handing of power to his brother echoes ancient practice in Scotland where a brother was considered to be closer to the original founder of the clan than the chief's son, who was a further generation removed. This was perhaps the reason why Malcolm Canmore's sons succeeded each other to the throne in the eleventh century. The chief's role however was absolutely central to the functioning of the tribe. This is from Skene's *The Highlanders of Scotland* (1902), p. 102:

The chief exercises an arbitrary authority over his vassals, determines all differences and disputes that happen among them and levies taxes upon extraordinary occasions, such as the marriage of a daughter, building a house, or some pretence for his support or the honour of the name, and if anyone should refuse to contribute to the best of his ability, he is sure of severe treatment, and if he persists in his obstinacy, he would be cast out of his tribe by general consent. This power of the chief is not supported by interest as they are landlords but as lineally descended from the old patriarchs or fathers of the families, for they hold the same authority when they have lost their estates. On the other hand, the chief, even against the laws, is to protect his followers, as they are sometimes called, be they never so criminal. He is their leader in clan quarrels, must free the necessitous from their arrears of rent, and maintain such who by accidents are fallen to total decay.

21

Clearly chief and clan were bound together by age-old mutual duties and privileges. The clansfolk of the medieval period and later appear to have lived much like their remote ancestors in the Dark Ages, living in the same glens, practising a form of subsistence agriculture, hunting, fishing and enjoying the occasional raid to lift other clans' cattle. Certainly by the medieval period they had become Christians and soon had access to more sophisticated weaponry in the form of firearms, but there seems to be much in their way of life that was just the same as in Pictish times. In this regard we should remember that many of the clans claim descent from the Picts. In his book *The Scottish People*, James Rennie suggested that as much as forty per cent of the clans were Pictish in origin. As late as the 14th century there is a record of Highlanders being referred to as 'Picts' or 'Redshanks'.

We should perhaps think of the tribes of Dark Age Scotland as extended families banding together with neighbours to form tribes within defined territories when necessary, but spending much of their lives living in small, scattered kin-groups.

When the Romans first arrived in Britain it seems clear that the population was essentially tribal. The people were living in close-linked kin-groups, in what was essentially a subsistence economy. This does not mean there were no luxuries. It simply means that the people lived in small groups and effectively fended for themselves, without centralised city states and their political appurtenances. They were pastoralists, much of whose energy was focused on the raising of cattle, but hunting and foraging were an everyday part of their lives. Recent archaeological thinking is that the old picture of the past in which such tribal peoples were constantly in fear of invasion and attack and whose lives were nasty, brutish and short contains very little substance. Much of such thinking seems to have arisen from the essentially Victorian idea of progress wherein humanity was presented as growing steadily from a primitive and barbaric state towards ever more technologically advanced civilization.

Given today's problems with the subsequent pollution and climate change, this idea of progress has lost some of its attraction. However the instances of death in childbirth and the incidence of child mortality were much higher than would be acceptable today, and life was in general considerably more dangerous then.

The clan system is itself a development from these earlier tribal times and is differentiated to a great degree by the use of the patronymic – the name of the original father of the clan. Thus the MacLeods are descended from Leod, son of Somerled, Lord of the Isles, just as the MacAlpines claim original descent from Alpin, King of Scots and father of the first king of the Picts and Scots, Kenneth Macalpin. It is worth keeping in mind that Somerled, who had control of the Western Islands and some of the west coast was of mixed descent – Norse and Gaelic.

The attitude of the rest of Britain towards the Highlands in the centuries before Culloden was essentially one of fear. To a great extent it was fear of difference – different language, different social structure and fear of a people who still considered skill at arms the greatest masculine attribute. Such skills always needed to be practised and used. This difference led to the situation where the British government could garrison almost the whole of the Highlands in the period after Culloden under the guise of preventing cattle theft. In the introduction to *Burt's Letters* (p. xviii), the editor, Jamieson, tells of the Lowland attitude towards the Highland warriors:

> Of all their virtues, courage was the only respectable quality conceded to them, and this out of compliment to the best disciplined troops of the day, whom, with less than equal numbers, they had so often routed; but even their courage was disparaged, being represented as mere ferocity, arising from ignorance, and a blind and slavish submission to their chiefs.

It is understandable that many writers have tended to concentrate on the military skills of the Highland warriors and these skills were fundamental to the practice of cattle-raiding. Battle was central to their existence but it had to be fought according to the rules. Later we will look at remarkable instances of this sense of honour – the sense of honour, based on traditional practice, that led the Highlander mentioned above to react with such fury to being called a thief. By Lowland lights he was a thief, by his own, an honourable warrior pursing the way of life of his ancestors. Given the pride that was also a hallmark of the Highland warrior it is little wonder that they frightened many of their Lowland neighbours. In this context it is interesting to note that the arrangements between Lowland farmers and Highlanders, to protect their cattle from other Highlanders, and known as 'Blackmail', were not only regularised, but were put down in the form of contracts. Was Blackmail originally a form of insurance? It would certainly appear to be one way of reading the evidence (See Appendix).

However, we should resist seeing the Highlanders as essentially some kind of noble savages. Certainly they held on to an ancient way of life into modern times, but they were not living in a vacuum and there were advantages to the clan, or tribal system, for many of its members apart from the guaranteed support and care that arose from being a member of the clan. Jamieson notes the following, again in the Introduction to *Burt's Letters*, p. xxiv:

> This advantage of conversing freely with their superiors, the peasantry of no other country in Europe enjoyed, and the consequence was, that in 1745 the Scottish Highlanders, of all descriptions, had more of that polish of mind and sentiment which constitutes real civilization than in general inhabited any other country we know of, not even excepting Ireland . . . most of the gentlemen spoke Gaelic, English, Latin and

French and many of them Spanish, having access to all the
information of which these languages were the vehicles.

He has left out the fact that so many of them would have also
spoken Scots, the language of the Lowlands. Jamieson here is
interpreting clan society by a model that is fundamentally
flawed. Although there were undoubted gradations of wealth
and status within the clan system they were never as rigid as the
class distinctions of English (and British) society that had arisen
out of feudalism. Referring to someone who would happily stand
shoulder to shoulder with his chief in battle against any odds,
and willingly lay down his life in doing so, as a peasant, is simply
wrong. Also many chiefs from the Middle Ages onwards sent
their sons to be educated at Continental universities and they
were usually accompanied by other young men of the clan,
sometimes their foster brothers – in whose family they had been
brought up. These were not primitive people in any sense and
though their way of life may have seemed harsh to outsiders, it
was the only way of life they knew.

Even with the growth of the money economy people in the
Highlands continued to live in a basically subsistence economy
into the 18th century. Great changes came about as a result of
the Government's road-building programme in the Highlands
from the 1730s, but before that many areas had maintained the
traditional way of life. We should remember that the Scottish
governments had problems controlling the areas of Galloway
and the Borders till at least the 16th century. Probably because
the kin-groups here spoke Scots, a Germanic relation of English,
they have been seen as totally different from the Highland clans.
In fact in their lifestyles, kin-group arrangements and commitment to raiding, they were very similar, and it is possible they
were also the direct descendants of earlier tribal systems. They
too had long resisted any authority other than that of their own
families, and the subjugation of these areas was at times as

bloody as anything that went on in the Highlands, until Culloden, at least.

All of these groups were fiercely independent and generally opposed to any kind of central control, but they could be incredibly loyal to any cause they espoused. It is difficult to know at this distance in time what exactly the reasons were for so many of the clans to come out in favour of Prince Charles Edward Stewart in 1745. For centuries their ancestors had been resisting the centralising tendencies of the Stewart dynasty. Religion clearly played a part: the Highlands were mainly Catholic and Episcopalian and the British establishment was decidedly Protestant, and in Scotland, Presbyterian. There can be little doubt that many of the Highlanders realised their ancient way of life was under threat in the fast-changing 18th century – they only had to see the Wade roads to know that. In a victory for Prince Charlie they perhaps saw some hope of their being able to continue to live as their ancestors had done. Many would follow because their chiefs, in consultation with clan councils, had decided to support the Pretender. But many must have seen it as an opportunity to go on a gigantic raid, attacking their traditional enemies and lifting spoil on the way. There has been a persistent rumour that the Jacobite army turned back north at Derby in December 1745 because the Highlanders wanted to get back home. Whether this is true or not it does illustrate that the Highland warriors were fundamentally attached to their own way of life and possibly thought that their involvement in a dynastic struggle was unlikely to affect them much. If so, they were wrong. Their basic commitment was to family and land and their warrior's code of honour. Tellingly, they were warriors, not soldiers – warriors tied to an understanding of the world that was about to be shattered for ever on the bloody field of Drumossie Moor. No matter how brutal and sadistic Cumberland and his troops were after Culloden, they were effectively carrying out what had been the policy of Scottish governments for centuries. At last the power of the clans, the ancient warrior tribes of the Highlands, was broken for good.

It was after this catastrophic defeat and the quasi-genocidal behaviour of the Redcoat army, with Lowland and loyal government Scots well to the fore, that some of these warriors, faced with certain death if captured, continued a last vain struggle against overwhelming odds by utilising the skills and techniques they had all learned at the School of the Moon.

> He has felt from his early youth all the privations to which he can be exposed on almost any circumstances of war. He has been accustomed to scanty fare, to rude and often wet clothing, to cold and damp houses, to sleep often in the open air or in the most uncomfortable beds, to cross dangerous rivers, to march a number of miles without stopping and with but little nourishment, and to be perpetually exposed to the attacks of a stormy atmosphere. A warrior, thus trained, suffers no inconvenience from what others would consider to be the greatest possible hardships, and has an evident superiority over the native of a delicious climate, bred to every indulgence of food, dress and habitation and who is accustomed to marching and fatigue.

This is the description of the Highland warrior from *The Analysis of the Statistical Account,* p. 106, Sir John Sinclair's commentary on his great project of the 1790s, *The Statistical Account of Scotland.* It sounds like the kind of training British SAS troops might be subjected to nowadays! The Highlanders have long been known for their hardiness and no wonder. Their physical fortitude, like their knowledge of their landscape and their way of life could hardly have made them more different from the people of the rest of Britain. It is as if we had an Iron Age tribal society living alongside the modern world. This is in fact as good a description as we can hope to have of the situation – the tribal

Highlanders were still living in social, and to large extent physical conditions that had disappeared many centuries earlier in other parts of the British Isles, with the possible exceptions of the Borders and Galloway.

Storytelling

The role of storytelling in pre-literate societies is a complex one. As the means of transmission of cultural heritage, moral education and practical knowledge, stories were central to such societies. There was no sense of what we now call historical accuracy – the point of the story was what mattered, and while the protagonists and location were often important, the need for definitive statements as to time and place were not part of the tradition. This continued very late and is part of storytelling tradition to this day. This might account for what appear to be anomalies in stories like 'The Rose of Glenesk', where one of the main protagonists is said to have fought with General Wolfe on the Heights of Abraham in the late 1750s. This would mean that a cateran raid was taking place after the time when it is generally believed the Highlands had been totally pacified, but is not impossible. Only recently I have been told of a current tradition that the people of the adjoining glen, (Glen Clova), held Highland Games secretly on the high plateau, in the years after Culloden.

Within Highland society by the 17th and 18th centuries, although literacy had been long known, the main book that people read, as in the Lowland Protestant areas of Scotland, was the Bible. Certainly the sons of chiefs and other members of the clan were educated, and some had quite extensive libraries, but book-reading was not a particularly important part of daily life. The very survival of folktales concerning the period after Culloden in 1746 shows that even in decline, oral transmission continued in Highland society. This was paralleled in Lowland society, where again the availability of books before the Industrial Revolution was extremely limited. People still sat around the hearth fires in winter, telling and repeating their traditional tales. Also, in both Gaelic- and Scots-speaking communities there were great singing traditions, the great Gaelic epic tales being paralleled by Scots ballads. Historians have long been reluctant to put much faith in such material – at least written material can be both located and dated, to a certain extent – while stories are by their very nature apparently transient. The situation is further complicated by the attitudes towards stories within predominantly oral societies. What matters is the reality of the story and what it means to the audience, not when the specific action took place, or even necessarily where.

Some stories survive in almost identical forms but are told in different areas. While this tends to be true of the epic tales – stories of the Fianna were told throughout Scotland and Ireland in locations which were known to the audience just as the Arthurian tales were told in locations in Scotland, Wales, Cornwall and Brittany amongst the P-Celtic speaking peoples. The truth of story is not bound by historical precision. As long as a story continues to mean something to the teller and to the audience, it will be told. It is also possible within storytelling for an actual heroic figure to replace an earlier perhaps mythological one: what matters is the relevance of the tale, its moral force and its entertainment value, particularly within closed tribal societies. So perhaps in this tale the fact of Rose's father having fought with Wolfe was added later, to give some extra colour to the tale. After all, if he had fought alongside Wolfe on the Heights of Abraham in 1759, this would place the events, at the earliest, in the mid to late 1770s which seems unlikely. By then it would have been very unusual for James Cameron and Ronald Maclean to be carrying weapons. After the Disarming Act of 1746 there were only a few people still allowed to carry weapons in Scotland, though, tellingly, some of these were cattle drovers who were still prey to the practices of the School of the Moon to some extent.

However this adaptation, or modification of the story does not detract from the story itself or stop it being a pretty fair representation of an actual cateran raid. What is clearly based on known behaviour is the careful spying out of the land, the use of a well-known pipe tune to serve as an alarm – and bagpipes are loud – and perhaps even the attempted abduction of Flora herself. Such rough wooing was not uncommon in Scotland, as elsewhere, although in many instances from the 18th century onwards it was a staged re-creation of such an abduction that took place. In reality, in olden times in many societies the stealing of brides was far from unknown and was even customary.

The capacity of stories to survive is incredible and it may be that what we have in 'The Rose of Glenesk' is a tale from a much earlier period brought up to date for a more modern audience by the addition of detail with which they would be familiar. However, in the main thrust of the tale and in its brutal dénouement we are presented with a story that is clearly part of the traditions associated with the students of the School of the Moon.

Terminology

The term *cateran* was used of both individual Highland warriors and groups. It really just means 'warriors' but had become associated specifically with the activity of inter-clan cattle-raiding by the 17th century. Variations that occur in printed sources include *kern* and *keithrin*. Clearly those defending themselves against raiders would at other times be raiders themselves, given the centrality of cattle-raiding to clan society. The terms for their raids include the Gaelic *creach* and the Scots *spulzie*, both meaning a raid or depredation.

Tracking

One of the legal resorts employed by the government against cattle-raiding was 'tracking'. Complainants could come before the Commissioners of the Justiciary and lay claim that they had tracked the stolen cattle to the lands of a particular clan and call upon them for compensation. As many clans were in the habit of charging the raiders 'tasgal' money for allowing them to cross their lands this was in effect a clever way of attacking the very structure of cattle-raiding by attacking the tradition of letting cattle raiders cross other clans' lands. This could lead to complications though.

In 1701 Thomas Fraser of Shewglie in Glen Urquhart had several horses stolen by persons unknown. A man of some skill himself he tracked the horses over the river Enrick and on to Comarkirktown in Strathglass, on Chisholm land. Now the Chisholms were unable to show that the tracks of the stolen beasts went on over their lands, so Fraser had them taken before the Commissioners of Justiciary. This august body was in no way concerned that the Chisholms were innocent of the theft and ordered them to pay 'ane hundred and nyntie merks' to Fraser as compensation. Chisholm, realising he would be fined the one hundred and ninety merks himself, unless he could pass the blame on, followed the trail to Lundie in Glenmoriston, the property of one James Grant who had been under suspicion a few times before this. The Grants were unable to show that the horses had gone beyond their lands, and in May 1702 the Chisholms had another summons served on them for the amounts they had been found liable by the Chamberlain of Urquhart. The Commissioners sat in the tollbooth of Inverness on the 26th and the Grants hired a lawyer to put their defence. His name was John Taylor and he tore holes in the evidence and had the Chisholms' case thrown out of court! The use of the law in dealing with cattle- raiding does not seem to have been much use in this case, and the Chisholms paid for the crime of some unknown cateran, who might perhaps have been a Grant!

Until the second half of the 18th century the efforts of succeeding monarchs and governments had failed to curtail the power and the activities of the Highland clans. However, the slaughter at Culloden and the subsequent actions of the government troops in Scotland finished off the way of life of the Scottish clans and no more would young lads be taught the ways of the School of the Moon.

THE STORIES

Gilderoy

<hr/>

The following ballad was very popular in the 18th century and tells the story of Patrick Gilroy McGregor, known as Gilderoy, from the perspective of his sweetheart. While many of the facts in the ballad are correct the tone presents him in a heroic light. Where his sweetheart refers to him when he 'bauldy bare away the gear, Of many a lawland town' we are seeing the attitude of the cateran themselves, in that they saw the raiding of the Lowlands as perfectly acceptable behaviour, in the same way they saw the raiding of other clans. Gilderoy, however, was brought to justice by the Scottish government in the end:

Gilderoy

Gilderoy was a bonny boy,
Had roses tae his shoone,
His stockings were of silken foy,
Wi garters hangin doun;
It was, I weene, a comlie sight,
To see sae trim a boy;
He was my joy and heart's delight,
My handsome Gilderoy.

Oh! sik twa charmin een he had,
A breath as sweet as rose,
He never ware a Highland plaid,
But costly silken clothes;

School of the Moon

He gain'd the luve of ladies gay,
Nane eer tae him was coy;
Ah! wae is me! I mourn the day,
For my dear Gilderoy.

My Gilderoy and I were born,
Baith in one toun together,
We scant were seven years before
We gan to luve each other;
Our daddies and our mammies they
Were fill'd wi mickle joy,
To think upon the bridal day
Twixt me and Gilderoy.

For Gilderoy that luve of mine,
Gude faith, I freely bought
A wedding sark of holland fine,
Wi silken flowers wrought:
And he gied me a waddin ring,
Which I receiv'd wi joy,
Nae lad nor lassie eer could sing,
Like my love Gilderoy.

Wi' mickle joy we spent our prime,
Till we were baith sixteen,
And aft we past the langsome time,
Amang the leaves sae green;
Aft on the banks we'd fit us thair,
And sweetly kiss and toy,
Wi garlands gay wad deck my hair,
My handsome Gilderoy.

Oh! that he still had been content
Wi me to lead his life;

34

Gilderoy

But, ah! his manfu' heart was bent
To stir in feats of strife:
And he in many a venturous deed,
His courage bauld wad try,
And now this gars mine heart to bleed
For my dear Gilderoy.

And whan of me his leave he tuik,
The tears they wat mine ee;
I gave tae him a parting luik,
'My benison gang wi' thee!
God speid thee weil, mine ain dear heart,
For gane is all my joy;
My heart is rent sith we maun part,
My handsome Gilderoy.'

My Gilderoy baith far and near,
Was fear'd in evry toun,
And bauldly bare away the gear
Of many a lawland loun;
Nane eer durst meit him man to man,
He was sae brave a boy,
At length wi numbers he was taen,
My winsome Gilderoy.

The Queen of Scots possessed nought
That my love let me want:
For cow and ewe he brought to me,
And e'en when they were skant.
All these did honestly possess,
He never did annoy,
Who never fail'd to pay their cess
To my love Gilderoy.

Wae worth the loun that made the laws
To hang a man for gear,
To reave of life for ox or ass,
For sheep, or horse, or mare;
Had not their laws been made sae strict
I neer had lost my joy,
Wi sorrow neer had wat my cheek
For my dear Gilderoy.

Giff Gilderoy had done amiss
He might hae banisht been,
Ah ! what fair cruelty is this
To hang sik handsome men;
To hang the flower o Scottish land,
Sae sweet and fair a boy;
Nae lady had sae white a hand
As thee, my Gilderoy.

Of Gilderoy sae fraid they were,
They bound him mickle strong,
Tull Edenburrow they led him thair,
And on a gallows hung:
They hung him high aboon the rest,
He was sae trim a boy,
Thair died the youth whom I loued best,
My handsome Gilderoy.

Thus having yielded up his breath,
I bare his corpse away,
Wi tears that trickled for his death,
I washt his comely clay;
And sicker in a grave sae deep
I laid the dear-loued boy,
And now for ever maun I weep
My winsome Gilderoy.

The popularity of this ballad is perhaps accounted for by a general sympathy for those who, like Robin Hood, stood out against centralised authority. There is no doubt however that Partrick Roy McGregor was an historical person. He was brought to trial in Edinburgh in 1636 after having been captured by members of the Grant clan. A year or so earlier Gilderoy had been in Edinburgh when seven of his companions were hung, after which he went straight to Atholl to burn the houses of the Stewarts of Atholl who had initially captured his men. The McGregors were persecuted by the Scottish crown for centuries from around 1500, and particularly by the Campbells who ended up with much of the land that had originally belonged to the Gregorach. At one point the Campbells even bred hunting dogs which were specifically trained to hunt down members of the McGregor clan. Throughout the 16th and 17th centuries many of them were forced into little more than banditry. This seems to have been the case with Gilderoy, though it is difficult to be absolutely certain. The information we have clearly reflects the Government's attitude that he was a criminal, and government went so far as to proscribe the McGregor name in 1603, which is a clear sign of their intent towards the Gregorach.

It seems that Patrick had been leading an active band of cateran for some time. They based themselves in the mountains to the north of Braemar and raided extensively throughout Aberdeenshire, Buchan and Moray. They are referred to in contemporary documents as 'limmers' and 'an infamous byke of insolent and lawless thieves.' Patrick had been declared 'a notorious rebel, sorner and oppressor' by the Government, so he must have known what fate awaited him when he was eventually caught. The sentence passed on him and his men including his cousin Johnne Forbes McGregor, is presented here to give a flavour of what passed for justice at the time. They were all (Register of the Privy Council of Scotland, vol. VI (1905), p. 301):

To be drawin backwards upon ane cairt or hurle, fra the tolbuth or wardhous to the mercat croce of Edinburgh, and thair to be hangit quhill thay be deid; and that the said Patrick Gilroy and Johnne Forbes sall be hangit upone ane gibbet quhill thay be deid, quhilk gibbet sall be advanced ane grit degree heicher nor the gibbet quhair upone the rest sall suffer; and thaireftir the said Patrick Gilroy and Johnne Forbes their heidis tae be striken of frome thair bodies, with thair richt handis, and the said Gilroy, his heid and richt hand to be afixt on the eist or nether bow poirt of Edinburgh, and the said Johnne Forbes, his heid and richt hand to be put upone the west poirt thereof . . .

As there weren't many cateran hanging around Edinburgh it is difficult to imagine who was supposed to be discouraged from cattle stealing by this.

Coll Ban MacDonald

—————◆—————

Before we look at the tales of the cateran tradition it will be an advantage to investigate one or two more definitively historical characters to see how they behaved in the matter of cattle-raiding. Coll Ban, as he was known to the Highlanders, on account of his fair hair and handsome appearance, was the son of Gilleasbuig, or Archibald, 1st of Barrisdale, the 5th and youngest son of Ranald, 2nd of Scotus who succeeded Lord MacDonell and Aros as Chief of Glengarry in 1680.

Born in 1698, Coll was already a living legend at the commencement of the '45 and Prince Charles Edward was not slow to offer him a colonel's commission and to his son Archibald, that of a major. Coll is believed to have been educated at Rome and is described as 'a gentleman of polished behaviour, fine address, and fine person'. He was at least 6 feet 4 inches in height and possessed of such enormous strength that his name was respected and feared throughout the Highlands. On one occasion he is said to have pursued and caught a roe deer in a corrie of Mam Barrisdale with no other assistance than that of his own limbs. On another occasion he attempted to lift a restive stirk that refused to be driven into a ferryboat, and finding his arms too short to encircle the beast, bridged the gap with his Highland bonnet. He then lifted the animal and threw it into the boat. Displaying another feat of strength he was alleged to have been able to heave up to his knees a large boulder lying on the drive in front of Invergarry Castle, which few very strong men were able to lift on to a short pin fixed into the ground beside it. It was rumoured that his courage did not match his strength, that he yielded to Cluny Macpherson in single combat and that he was wounded by the latter in a duel. The former claim is improbable, but it is on record that a duel did take place between them.

Early in his career Coll was on very good terms with his cousin, John MacDonell of Glengarry who granted him charters to many properties on the estate, including the Kytries, Culla- chies and Inverguseran. He also added to his territorial impor- tance through his two marriages: the first in 1724 to Catherine, daughter of MacKenzie of Balmuckie, by whom he had two sons, Archibald and Alasdair; and the second in 1736 to Mary, daughter of MacKenzie of Fairburn, by whom he had a third son Coll – acquiring lands in Ross and in Sutherland.

He was appointed Captain of the Watch and Guardian of the Marches on the west side of the county of Inverness by the local landowners: so much confidence had they in his ability to protect their herds from the numerous caterans and outlaws who preyed on their well-fed black cattle. For his services, Coll extracted from his clients a steady income called 'blackmail' said to be upwards of £500 per annum. From this and his numerous other sources of revenue Coll was able to build for himself a most beautiful two-storeyed mansion at Traigh in Inverie on the west coast of Knoydart. It is described as 'beautifully covered with blue slate, and having eighteen fire rooms, besides as many more without chimnies'. There can be little doubt that Coll was a large-scale cattle-lifter himself and that his clients appointed him on the basis of 'setting a thief to catch a thief'. But it must be remembered that cattle lifting had since time immemorial been regarded by the Highlanders as a manly and honourable pursuit. Burt in his 'letters' says of Coll (following quote from the Clan Donald Society of Edinburgh website – www.macdonald60.fsnet.co.uk):

He is said to have carried out the art of plunder to the highest pitch of perfection, besides exerting all the common practices, he imposed that article of commerce called blackmail, to a degree beyond what was ever known by his predecessors. He behaved with genuine humour in restoring on proper consideration the stolen cattle to his friends. He observed a strict fidelity towards his own gang, and yet was indefatigable in bringing to justice any rogues that interfered with his own. He considered himself in a very high light, as a benefactor to the public and preserver of general tranquillity.

Murray of Broughton writes in his *Memorials*:

McDonell of Barrisdale is a man whose character is almost as well known as that of Lord Lovat's . . . He has a small interest called Apin in the County of Ross, and is presently married to a Daughter of McKenzie of Fairburn, which enabled him to raise betwixt two or three hundred men in that Country who he join'd to those living on his wadsett lands in Knoydart, and then declared himself independent of his Chief. He has, for sometime past, fell upon a way to procure an yearly pension from a great many gentlemen of the Country to protect them from theift, by which he has gained a good deal of interest, which nevertheless proceeds much more from fear than love.

General Wade, who was active in driving roads through the Highands in the 1730s, wrote of the caterans' activities and that they

. . . go out in parties from 10 to 30 men, traverse large tracks of mountains till they arrive at the lowlands where they design to commit these depredations, which they choose to do in places distant from the glens they inhabit. They drive the stolen cattle in the night time, and in the day remain on the tops of the mountains or in the woods with which the Highlands abound . . . Those who are robbed of their cattle follow them on the track and often recover them from the robbers by compounding for a certain sum of money; but if the pursuers are in numbers superior to the thieves, and happen to seize any of them, they are seldom or never prosecuted. The encouragement and protection given by some of the chiefs is reciprocally rewarded by allowing them a share in the plunder, which is sometimes one half, or two-thirds of what is stolen.

The pro-Hanoverian *Edinburgh Evening Courant* for Monday 11 August 1746, reports:

There was found in Barrisdale's House a Hellish Engine for extorting Confession, and punishing such Thieves as were not in his Service (for as he took Black-Mail for preserving the Cattle of the Country round about to a great extent, he entertained many such) it is all made of Iron, and stands upright, the Criminal's Neck, Hands and Feet are put into it, by which he's in a sloping Posture, can neither sit nor stand.

But the Sobieski Stuarts in *Tales of the Century*, 1847, states the 'engine' of 'torture'

was simply a sort of 'jougs' – the Scottish iron 'stocks' – used for the same purposes as those of wood, which were to be seen in every village, and the yard of every parish church in England . . .

On one occasion, however, Coll's activities did get him into serious trouble with the authorities, and in 1736 he was tried before the High Court of Justiciary at the instance of four tenants of Glenorchy, with concourse of Duncan Forbes, His Majesty's Advocate. The charge was being

guilty and accessory, or art and part of soliciting and inticing and the fradulent suborning and eliciting diverse persons to bear false witness against their knowledge and conscience . . .

by rewards, promises, threats, and other corrupt means, to bear such false witness in a process he then told them was intended to be brought, when he imagined he had prevailed with those upon whom he practised to comply with the request in conspiring, by false witnessing, to defame and ruin the pursuers.

It was further alleged that the panel:

by subornation of witnesses, had endeavoured to found a charge against them by being art and part in several depredations committed upon James Menzies of Culdares and his tenants.

Coll's defence was along the following lines. The depredations and robberies on the properties of Breadalbane and Glenlyon had of late become more frequent and had reached such a pitch that the persons from whom the cattle had been stolen were likely to be ruined, and their country laid waste. And although occasionally some of the cattle had been recovered, this was attended with heavy charges, often more than the value of the retrieved stock. It had been concluded that such regular raids from one heritor's property by strangers could not be carried out without the concurrence of persons living in the neighbourhood, and it was obvious that the remedy for preventing such practices would be to endeavour to discover by whose assistance these depredations were committed on the property of a particular individual while his neighbours remained unmolested. Once the 'assistants and outhounders' were detected and punished, and the robbers thereby deprived of protection and encouragement, their lawless practices might at least be curtailed.

In February 1734, 'the panell', i.e., Coll, 'being in Edinburgh about his lawful affairs, had occasion' to meet Menzies of Culdares who had acquainted him with the circumstances which had led to his sufferings. In August of the same year, new depredations having been committed, Coll had been called on by Culdares to assist in recovering the latter's cattle, which were supposed to have been lodged in his neighbourhood. Coll had then called on his cousin, Glengarry, in order to recover the spoil, part of which had been found in Glengarry country, and part in Lochiel's, and had returned the whole to the owner. About the middle of October thereafter, cattle were again lifted from Culdares and his tenants, but on this occasion the thieves were pursued by Menzies' tenants through the Braes of Lochaber into the lands of Locheil and Glengarry. The pursuers then appealed to all the gentlemen in these districts, including Coll, who used his influence to locate the stolen cattle. Being informed that some of them were in Lochiel's country, he wrote to Cameron of Clunes, Lochiel's bailie – Lochiel being absent at the time – and succeeded in having the spoil returned to the rightful tenants with promises that the price of the remainder, which had been slaughtered, would be paid.

During these inquiries the culprits were discovered and acknowledged their guilt to Clunes and MacDonell of Shian; they also revealed that some of the prosecutors were accessories. This was reported to Menzies of Culdares by the tenants who returned with the cattle and at that laird's request, two of the leading caterans, Ewan Mor MacPhie and Kenneth Kennedy were brought to Culvullin in Rannoch where they testified before witnesses that certain of the prosecutors by the name of 'M' Inlester' had been accessories in the raids and that one of them had been demanding his share of the booty.

Coll's trial took place on 10 February 1736, when the jury 'by a plurality of voices', found the prisoner not guilty. This was only one of many instances where the law of Scotland proved itself inadequate when trying to deal with cattle-raiding, a situation that no doubt contributed to the government's frustration.

The Halkit Stirk

The Halkit Stirk who gave us the phrase 'The School of the Moon' was a well-known cateran of the late 17th century. It seems that he got his name because he was a foundling, an abandoned baby. He had been left outside the farmhouse of Pearsie at the foot of Glen Prosen, one of the beautiful glens running into the southern Grampians from Strathmore and the Braes of Angus. The lady of the house was awakened by the sound of a child crying, and her husband told her to go back to sleep; it was only 'the croon o the halkit stirk' – the mooing of the white-faced steer, a young calf. As is so often the case, the gudewife knew better and went out to find the infant, who duly acquired the nickname of 'the Halkit Stirk'. Others have contended that he got his name because of his powerful physique and his peculiarly white face. He was so successful as a cateran over much of Scotland that he came to the attention of the Privy Council in Edinburgh. His given name is never mentioned in official records and he is referred to either as *An Gamhainn Cirinn* in Gaelic, or 'The Halkit Stirk' in Scots.

It seems likely however, that he was a MacDonald, originally from Lochaber, that hotbed of cateran activity, and that he moved to somewhere in Strathspey. In 1660 the Laird of Grant was given special orders from the Commissioners of Estates in Edinburgh to capture the Halkit Stirk and have him sent to Edinburgh for trial. Grant was successful in apprehending the Stirk, but before sending him to Edinburgh he got in touch with the Commissioners, and sent them a letter via a kinsman, James

Grant of Achernack, telling them of his success. There was, however, a qualification. Grant informed the Commissioners that the Halkit Stirk had a great many friends amongst the MacDonalds and that before he sent him south, sureties of good behaviour should be demanded from the Chief of the MacDonalds, MacRanald himself, and other chieftains of the clan. Grant wanted them all to accept that he was only 'carrying out orders' for the government and that there would be sureties taken from all the branches of the MacDonalds in Lochaber, Glengarry, Badenoch, Rannoch, Glencoe, Glenlyon, Glengaule in Strathearn, and Strathnairn. From this it is obvious that the Halkit Stirk had many friends and supporters amongst his own clan. The fact that the MacDonalds were the largest of all the clans makes Grant's discretion understandable.

The Commissioners declared they would ensure no harm came to the Grants, and if any did, they would make reparations for any wrongs or injuries. They then directed Grant to deliver the Stirk to the Magistrates of Aberdeen who would then send him to Edinburgh for trial. Grant however seems to have had second thoughts about the cateran for he got in touch with the Lord Advocate himself and asked for a meeting. At this meeting he brought up the possibility of the Halkit Stirk being released, effectively into his own custody, with Grant putting up security, probably in the form of a bond. The story is that the Stirk's friends among his own clan had prevailed upon him to intercede on the cateran's behalf. Surprisingly, this worked, and the Halkit Stirk was set free. Tradition tells us that it wasn't long before he was back to his old activities.

It was after this episode that the Halkit Stirk was wounded in a *spulzie*, or raid, at Ri-daros close to Loch Uaine and lived with the Stewart family near Ruthven while he recuperated.

However not everyone was impressed by the Halkit Stirk. Mention is made in the Court Book of the Regality of Grant for the years between 1698 and 1703 of the punishment meted out to Margaret Bayn at the local Baron Baillie Court. She was charged with a series of offences including 'haunting with the Halkit Steir and sundry broken men and Kethren [Cateran]'. For consorting with these known criminals she was to be taken to the cross at Grantown and 'bound thereto, and her bodie made bare from the belt up, and scourged by the hangman with thratie [thirty] strypes, and ane of her ears cutt off, and she to be then banished out of Strathspey for ever'. This sounds pretty brutal but it is quite likely that Margaret considered herself to be lucky! After all, she had already been banished from Strathspey several years earlier with her father.

The Halkit Stirk eventually died in his bed, but a statement attributed to him on his deathbed perhaps gives a flavour of how the cateran saw themselves. He declared that he had never taken anything from the poor, that he had been kind to the widow and the fatherless and that he had always gone far away from his home district for spoil.

The Battle o Saughs

⇒·◊·⇐

This battle is reported in Warden's *Angus or Forfarshire* and concerns a raid on the village of Fern, nowadays a tiny hamlet on the northern rim of Strathmore. Strathmore runs north-east from Perth to Stonehaven on the coast and Fern is about ten kilometres to the north of Forfar. This was the site for a cattle-raid somewhere around the end of the 17th century that shows many aspects of what can be considered traditional behaviour. Although the precise date is uncertain, the battle took place before the last great upheavals of the Jacobite rebellions. Fern is right on the edge of the Grampian mountains, and although the people there were Scots-speaking farmers, they too still held on to many of the old ways.

Warden tells us that the raid took place not at the end of summer, but in spring. In traditional fashion the cateran who had come down through the mountains from Deeside on a Sunday night, 'lifted' a considerable number of cattle and horses on Monday morning and were already heading up Glen Lethnot at first light before the people of Fern were awake. When the raid was discovered all the men from the immediate area were summoned to the village by the tolling of the kirk bell. Only the previous year, James Mackintosh of Ledenhendrie, a farm a few kilometres north-east of Fern, had rescued some of his neighbour's cattle from cateran who had come down from the north. There could be little doubt that this too was a cateran raid, but obviously much more organised and by the amount of beasts taken there must have been considerable numbers of the

48

cateran. The idea of tackling a heavily-armed group of cateran was not to the liking of many of the village people, though they were sick and tired of having their cattle lifted. Mackintosh was furious and harangued the assembled crowd about their lack of fighting spirit. He and his close friend David Winter, of Peathaugh, an ex-soldier, were both keen swordsmen and, considering themselves of Highland descent, thought of themselves as honourable Highland gentlemen. They were also well aware of the tradition of the Cothrom na Feinne. Between the pair of them they managed to enlist the aid of about thirty men and went of in pursuit of the lifted livestock. Many of the young men with them had firearms. Reaching Shandford, just a kilometre away they were told the cateran were led by a notorious Highlander by the name of Mackenzie who had taken the name of that earlier famous Highland cateran, The Halkit Stirk. At Tillybirbnie, about five kilometres from Fern they met a shepherd who told them the cateran had passed not long after dawn and that there were about twenty of them. Ledenhendrie* hurried them along. On by Nathro they followed, moving north-west through Glen Lethnot. The cateran route was clear – they were heading up Glen Lethnot then along the Water of Saughs and up on to the plateau between Glens Clova and Esk. From here they would head north and meet the Capel Mounth road down into Glen Muick on Deeside. The Capel in later years became one of the regular drove-roads by which the Highland cattle were transported to the great cattle trysts at Crieff and Falkirk, from where many went south to England.

The Fern men pressed on up the glen and on past Hunthill. A few kilometres on by the headwaters of the Water of Saughs – the Saugh being the willow tree – they came upon the cateran who had stopped for a bite to eat.

---

* Ledenhendrie: in those days men of property were generally known by the name of the lands they farmed – useful in districts where, like among the Highland clans, many people shared a surname.

The cateran leader, seeing them approach, came forward to meet them on his own. Nearing them he asked who their leader was. At close quarters the Halkit Stirk was an awesome sight. Well over six feet tall, strongly built, and armed with sword and pistol, he looked every inch the Highland warrior. Ledenhendrie stepped forward, saying 'I am.' 'Well then,' said the cateran, smiling, 'shall we settle this man to man, with swords? And the winner shall take off with the cattle?'

Ledenhendrie was in a bit of a fix. Here were all the stolen beasts, his men outnumbered the Deeside men, and they had more firearms. However he and Winter had spent many years following the warrior's code and there was little he felt he could do. He agreed to fight the giant Highlander, man to man. This was a mistake. Well over six feet tall, Mackenzie had a vast reach and soon showed that he was a veritable master with the sword. Soon Ledenhendrie was in trouble, barely managing to fend off the Highlander's attacks. Then the cateran made a quick lunge and cut two buttons from Ledenhendrie's waistcoat. Laughing, he stood back and said he could just as easily have taken his life, so why not just admit defeat and avoid any bloodshed?

All seemed lost. Ledenhendrie had given his word to abide by the result of the fight. There was clearly no way he could defeat this giant. Then a strange thing happened. The two groups were drawn up opposite each other with the combatants in between them. They were several hundred feet high up in the foothills of the Grampian mountains. All were staring at the fighters, Ledenhendrie already tiring and the Halkit Stirk towering over him, smiling as he waited an answer. All of a sudden a hare jumped up from the heather between the two groups and dashed off up the hill. One of the Deeside men shouted, 'They've brought a witch!' and fired his long gun at the animal. He missed but the bullet flew on and killed one of the Fern men. Immediately the Fern men, not understanding the Gaelic, thought the cateran were trying to gain an advantage and opened fire. The Halkit Stirk closed on Ledenhendrie, a grim look on his face. Winter, realising the danger his friend was in ran around behind the giant Highlander and cut his hamstrings. The giant fell to his knees but continued to try and attack Ledenhendrie.

Mackintosh took a step back and the giant Highlander asked a dying request of his young opponent. Saying he had no wish to die fighting, he asked the young man to bid him farewell by shaking his hand. Ledenhendrie agreed and was moving to give the Halkit Stirk his right hand, when he was warned by a shout from one of his companions. The cateran had taken his dirk in his left hand and in the nick of time Mackintosh stepped back and, as the cateran lunged, ran him through with his sword.

Elsewhere the cateran had taken bitter punishment. With the Fern men mainly having guns they had managed to avoid much swordplay and all the cateran but one lay dead in the heather. Only one of them had escaped and he only got as far as a nearby ridge before expiring. The hillside where this battle took place was thereafter called the Shank of Donald Young, supposedly after this last of the cateran, and local tradition says that the battle was fought between the two white stones on the side of the Shank which can be clearly seen from the spot called Potty Leadnar on the hill of Meg Swerie to the west. After burying the dead the Fern men were driving the cattle back down Gen Lethnot when they were met by a party of their neighbours who had at last summoned the courage to follow them. You can imagine what must have been said. There is a report from 1853 saying that in the 1780s a flood in the Water of Saughs had exposed some of these burials.

There are several points of interest about this particular tale. It comes from a time when the old clan ways were beginning to change but were still recent enough to have an influence on the Fern men, who probably considered themselves Lowlanders, or at least as part of general Scottish society. The Highlanders even as late as this probably still held on to their ancient beliefs and way of life, seeing themselves as free spirits and answerable to no one but their chief and their kin. Both sides seemed ready enough to follow Cothrom na Feinne, agreeing before a blow was struck that the outcome would be settled one-on-one, regardless of the clear superiority in numbers and firearms of the Strathmore men. The story clearly says that one of the Deeside men fired at a hare.

Despite having been Christian for a millennium, many people in the Highlands still believed that witches had the ability to change their shape into that of other animals. Anne Ross in *The Folklore of the Scottish Highlands*, p. 70, tells us: 'Witches . . . could be met with in the form of animals, the hare being the most common shape for metamorphosis.' It was the Highland raider's suspicion of deceit on the part of his enemy that led them to thinking he was himself trying to take unfair advantage. There are several versions of this story, but all agree on the main points of the tale and all agree that the Shank and Little Hill of Donald Young at the head of Glen Lethnot were named after one of the cateran, but given that we are told only one Fern man was actually killed, it seems more likely it was his name that was given to the locality. How would the Fern men have known the cateran's name?

The leader of the Deeside men was following the ancient traditions of the Highlanders. They did not see anything morally wrong in lifting cattle, so there is nothing odd in his taking on the identity of what he saw as a famous and successful warrior. Although men still carried arms in Scotland at this time, the Lowland areas were effectively under government control, subject to national laws and doubtless regarding the Highland raiders as some kind of throwback. But at the same time we have the attitude of Ledenehendrie and Winter, who both wanted to follow the warrior's way. When it came to the actual battle though, Winter had no hesitation hamstringing his friend's opponent from behind. In his defence we might consider that once the other Highlander opened fire on the men of Fern the rules were off and it was open battle. The Halkit Stirk's last attempt to take his opponent with him is something that has been noted in the behaviour of clan warriors on several occasions. It might just be a matter of personal revenge, but equally it may hark back to the ancient belief when it was the custom for a warrior falling in battle to want to take an enemy with him to the land beyond death. This fits in also with what we know of the Norse warriors who believed they would end up in Valhalla if they were lucky, just as the Highlanders thought of going to Tir na Nog, the Land of the Ever Young. Death in battle was an honourable end, and all the better if you took some of your enemies with you.

This tale is also illustrative of one of the confusing aspects of Scottish history. The Highland Fault Line is a line that runs from Loch Lomond on the west, north-east through Strathearn and Strathmore to near the coast at Stonehaven. It is a clear geographical marker between the lowlands of the valleys of Strathearn and Strathmore and the Grampian mountains on their north. Much has been made of the Highland Line in historical terms with the Gaelic-speaking, pastoralist, clan society on one hand and the Scots-speaking, lowland agriculturalists on the other. The inference is that the Highland Line was in fact a border between two different and increasingly mutually antipathetic societies.

However, the situation is not so simple. All along the Highland Line there are glens running north into the mountains. These glens have been populated since the Bronze Age and all of them have, or have had villages at or near the entrances to such glens. These were places where people met and mingled – perhaps initially just to trade but over time the Highland Line became an area where, even if the populace was not completely bilingual, they were used to dealing with people whose first language was different from their own, and who lived under different social

arrangements. Professor Sandy Fenton described this phenom-
enon at a conference a few years ago, as being more like a
Highland sausage than a Highland Line. This is a good analogy –
there was an area where the two societies were in constant
contact over many centuries where the two cultures mingled,
people traded and marriages between the two communities took
place. It is also not accidental that the great drove roads of the
17th and 18th centuries followed the tracks that had been used
by caterans for centuries, if not millennia.

The Battle of Saughs was not the only notable cateran raid into
Angus. From the head of Glenesk there comes another story of
caterans coming down from the north, though this story is a
tragic one.

The Rose of Glenesk

Glenesk is just six kilometres north-east of the site of the Battle of Saughs. It is a long curved glen running north-westward from just outside Edzell into the mountains.

This story is set in a late period. James Cameron had fought in the British Army and had been one of the soldiers who carried the dying General Wolfe from the Heights of Abraham after that famous victory in 1759. He married a French-Canadian lass who sadly died soon after, in childbirth. At this point James decided to return to his home at the head of Glenesk with his infant daughter, Flora. He settled at Tarfside, with his daughter and his beloved small collection of books and lived a quiet industrious life. Flora grew to be a remarkable beauty and fell in love with a local lad, Ronald Maclean of Inchgrundle, on the shore of Loch Lee at the head of the glen. James was happy with the match, as indeed was Ronald, who had managed to secure the affections of a lass so bonny she was known as the Rose of Glenesk. One early summer day an old blind piper was led into the glen from the mountains by a wee lad. They came to Cameron's cottage at Burnfoot and Flora came to the door to give a few coppers to the blind old piper. This caring contribution was to have tragic results, for the blind piper was none other than a notorious cateran from Deeside, known as Donald Dubh Mor – Big Black Donald. His disguise was to allow him to spy out the land in Glenesk for he was planning a cattle-lifting expedition. However, as soon as he saw Flora his intention changed. He decided then and there that he must have this beautiful young woman for his own. Picking up the information that there was to be a Highland tournament – the predecessor of the more modern Highland Games – in nearby Glen Clova on 25 August, the cateran leader left the glen.

The day of the tournament came round and all the young, and some not so young, lads and lasses of the glen headed off over the path at Inchgrundle towards Glen Clova. All, that is, except for Flora. A neighbour was sick and, kind lass that she was, she offered to keep an eye on her. James Cameron and Ronald Maclean were with the party that set off, unaware that they were being watched. Donald Dubh and his men were hiding in the heather above Loch Lee waiting for their moment. The happy band were halfway to Clova when they heard a distant sound. It was a piper, back in Glenesk, and he was playing 'Lochaber no More', the recognised signal for a cateran raid! They ran to the top of Craigmaskeldie and down in the glen saw several steadings on fire. There seemed to be three main areas that had been attacked – Tarfside, Glenturret and Gleneffock – and the cateran chief had split up his men to make resistance more difficult to organise. Cameron and Maclean ran as fast as they could towards Burnfoot. They got there just in time to see Donald Dubh emerge from the cottage with the struggling Flora in his arms, wrapped up in a great woollen cloak. Other cateran were in attendance. Ronald immediately ran at the cateran, drawing his sword, while James was attacked by two other raiders. Donald Dubh threw Flora to the ground and drew his own blade. The two young men were evenly matched and at first neither seemed to have the advantage. Flora scrambled to her feet and throwing off the cloak saw her betrothed fighting with this wild cateran. She let out a scream. This distracted Ronald momentarily and the cateran managed to disarm him. Nothing daunted, Ronald stood his ground as another cateran ran up and joined the attack on Flora's father. Donald Dubh smiled and lunged at the defenceless Ronald. Just at that Flora threw herself between the two men and took Donald's sword straight through her heart! Donald stepped back aghast. Ronald let out a mighty roar and leapt bare-handed on the cateran chief. By now even more cateran had come up, and as Ronald knocked Donald to the ground they ran forward and the young man was stabbed through and through. The caterans turned to see that James Cameron too had been slain and went to help their chieftain to his feet. But as they pulled the body of Ronald Maclean away from Donald they discovered that the Glenesk man had bitten through his throat, and there was nothing they could do to save him. It was a sad band of cateran who went north over Mount Keen later that day, carrying the body of Donald Dubh Mor.

The Men of Rannoch

—⟫•◆•⟪—

Rannoch Moor, that bleak and strangely beautiful stretch of land between Loch Tay and Glen Coe is one of the most inhospitable areas of Scotland. It was long a place of lawlessness. It had been fought over by the Menzies, MacGregor and MacDonald clans as well the ever-ambitious Campbells. Various nearby clans at different times sought the help of the government in Edinburgh against their enemies on the moor, but the area was never really subdued till some time after Culloden. By the 18th century many of its inhabitants were in the business of blackmail. It was clearly an area that could provide a handy bolt-hole for those who wanted to escape the law, or the attention of other clans. In the period after Culloden it took on a new lease of life. This is from the *Statistical Account* of 1797, written by the local minister, the Reverend Duncan McAra.

Before the year 1745, Rannoch was in an uncivilized, barbarous state, under no check, or restraint of laws. As an evidence of this, one of the principal proprietors never could be compelled to pay his debts. Two messengers were sent from Perth, to give him a charge of horning [declaring him an outlaw]. He ordered a dozen of his retainers to bind them across two handbarrows, and carry them in this state to the bridge of Coinachan, at nine miles distance. His property in particular was a nest of thieves. They laid the whole country from Stirling to Coupar of Angus, under contribution, obliging the inhabitants to pay them, Black Meal as it is called, to save their property form being plundered. This was the centre of this kind of traffic. In the months of September and October, they gathered to the number of about three hundred, built temporary huts, drank whisky all the time, settled accounts for stolen cattle and received balances. Every man there bore arms. It would have required an army to have brought a thief from that country.

This then would appear to have been a natural place for these Jacobite rebels to hide. Even in 1747, after the Redcoats had been stationed at Georgetown, the Menzies laird of Rannoch still had trouble. He obliged his tenants to bring their cows and horses to him, each man having to state how he came by them on oath if required. They were also instructed not to give quarters for two successive nights to a known thief, to hinder cattle stealing and to assist the other tenants to recover their stolen cattle. Serjeant Mor and his cousin Donal Ban Leane Cameron were among the best known of these rebels and it was Donal that McAra refers to as having been hanged. The execution took place at Kinloch Rannoch at the eastern end of Loch Rannoch in 1752. Serjeant Mor was captured the following year at Dunan on the edge of Rannoch Moor, when he was betrayed by one he regarded as a friend.

The Shieling Booth
of Brae Rannoch

While much of the country clearly thought of Rannoch Moor as a wild and dangerous place, the men who lived there saw it differently. And so did their womenfolk. This is a song, originally in Gaelic, which speaks eloquently of the life of the cateran when at home in Rannoch, and its pleasures:

My treasure has gone
To Glengarry so fleetly
Whose locks are like gold
And who kissed me so sweetly.

Best thy venture becomes thee
Of all in the valley
A suit well befitting
With thy person to tally.

The hose well becomes thee
And shoes so tight lacing
And blue coat from London
Thy fair form embracing.

When thou goest to the fair
My gear will come surely
My girdle and comb
And my ribbons securely.

The Shieling Booth of Brae Rannoch

My gloves fitting neatly
And gold them surrounding
With rare knife and sporran
Rich laces them bounding.

Why should we be gearless
Or of cattle be callow?
We'll get cows from the Mearns
And sheep from Glen Gallow.

On the shielings of Rannoch
They calm shall be feeding;
To our cabin so joyful
The drove we'll be leading.

The birds with sweet music
And cuckoo's notes swelling
At morn shall awake us,
And stags loudly belling.

Yellow Roderick's
Successful Raid?

—═►•◆•◄═—

Given the nature of Highland society and the universal pre-dilection for cattle-raiding, even Rannoch was not immune to being raided. Early in the 18th century a major raid took place by the MacDougalls of Lorne. They had come by Ben Cruachan and through Glenstrae and by the pass of the Black Mount. In the traditional style of the cateran raiders they had made off with their prey before dawn and it was only after daylight that the Rannoch men realised that they themselves had been raided. So they gathered together as many men as could be found and set off in pursuit of the MacDougalls. The Rannoch men were mightily offended and pursued the cateran in full battle order, with their clan banners waving at the head of the troop. Some of them would have been MacGregors and it is likely there were a few Fletchers, MacArthurs and some of Clan Menzies amongst them.

They were all intent on having their revenge on the upstart tribe who had dared to raid them. The MacDougalls however, were being led by a man of many *creachs*, Roderick Buidhe, yellow-haired Roderick. As an experienced raider he knew well that he should keep a weather-eye out for pursuit and so the Rannoch men were spotted while still some distance from the Lorne party and their spoil, near the headwaters of the Allt Tolaghan on the slopes of Beinn Suidhe. Roderick watched the group below and realised that he had an advantage in numbers,

So he sent off a small group of his men with the cattle over towards Glen Strae while he and the others prepared to fight. Having the high ground gave them the advantage, and as the Rannoch warriors came up the hill the MacDougalls charged. Now the Highland charge was a fearsome tactic and was generally effective, even against other Highland warriors. The shock of the MacDougall charge on the Rannoch men broke their line and threw many of them to the ground, giving the MacDougalls an immediate advantage. It was an advantage Roderick Buidhe knew must be pressed home ruthlessly if he was to prove victorious. So the MacDougall men attacked their foes with the utmost fury. The Rannoch men were only slightly outnumbered but the MacDougall charge had them on the back foot right from the start. The battle was sharp and hard, and short. Within a few minutes the slopes of Beinn Suidhe were littered with dead and dying men. So many of their comrades had fallen that the remnant of the Rannoch contingent, realising the MacDougalls now had a significant numerical advantage, turned and ran from the battlefield. What point was there in laying down their lives in a cause already clearly lost? In their helter-skelter down the slopes of Beinn Suidhe the MacDougalls said that they even threw away their arms into a lochan, or small loch, ever since known as Lochan nan Arm.

Be that as it may, the MacDougalls were jubilant. They had won the day! So stopping only to bury the fallen, they headed off south into Glen Strae with the banners of the fallen Rannoch men streaming in the air at their head. There was much singing and boasting as they went and one or two leather flasks of *uisge beatha* went the rounds. They were a happy party. They had had a famous victory and could look forward to a good profit from the cattle they had lifted from the Rannoch men.

Up ahead of them the men with the cattle were moving much more slowly and it wasn't long till they had almost caught up with them. Roderick had chosen his men carefully and the advance guard was being led by Iain Ban, Fair John, a man almost as experienced as Roderick himself. So Iain Ban kept looking behind him. Imagine his horror as he and his companions drove the cattle down into Glen Strae when he turned to see in the distance a large group of armed men following him. At their head flew the banners of the Rannoch men. His first thoughts were for the men he believed must be lying dead on the slopes of Beinn Suidhe. His second thoughts were a black anger and a deep hatred of the men of Rannoch. He ran to the rest of his group forcing the cattle on.

'Hold it, lads,' he cried, 'it looks like our lads have lost the day. I can see the Rannoch men and their damned banners coming up the hill behind us.'

'What shall we do then, Iain,' asked one of his companions.

'Well, there is no way I will let them take the cattle that have cost so many MacDougalls their lives,' Iain answered in a bleak voice. 'Hamstring the beasts.'

And he and his companions went through that entire herd hamstringing each and every one of the poor beasts. No way were they going to allow the Rannoch men to herd the animals back home. 'Better that the animals die here than that,' Iain said when they had finished their bloody work. Then he and his friends ran off into the hills as fast as they could.

It was less than an hour later that Roderick and the rest of the party heard the noise of cattle in distress, from over a small rise. They did not know what could be happening so they ran up the rise to see. And there before them lay an entire herd of cattle, hamstrung. Many men had died, not a few of them MacDougalls, and all for this. And ever since then the scene of that horror has been called *Am Monadh builte*, the stricken moor.

Serjeant Mor

—————◆————

After the dreadful slaughter at the Battle of Culloden not all of the defeated Highlanders were prepared to lay down their arms. Some of the survivors retreated into the mountains and continued to harass those they saw as their enemies. Some of those who survived the battle and others who hadn't been there met up at Ruthven in Strathspey a few days afterwards. Here after destroying the government barracks they dispersed. Charles Edward Stuart, the leader of the rebellion, headed west eventually to escape to France despite the fortune of £20,000 on his head. Some others returned home to hope that they would escape the recriminations of the government. Others, realising that the only fate that awaited them was execution at the hands of the Hanoverian Army, decided to retreat into the hills and fight on. Some of these men had fought in the French Army and were thus doubly traitors from the British government's point of view. Their only real hope of survival was to return to that most traditional of Highland pursuits – the lifting of cattle. Now, instead of showing their prowess by raiding other clans, these trained Highland warriors would have to raid to survive. Amongst this band of desperate warriors was the man known as Serjeant Mor, the Big Sergeant, stories of whom show him to have been an honourable, even heroic figure, and though he is undoubtedly historical he could have come straight from the ancient storytelling tradition so beloved of the Gaels.

John Dark Cameron came from the rugged and beautiful area known as the Badenoch, the country running through to Loch

Linnhe from around Dalwhinnie and Newtonmore. Known as Iain Dubh (Dark or Black John) he was raised in the tradition of the Highland warrior with its obsession for honour, bravery and skill-at-arms. However by the 1730s the old ways were dying out. The money economy had altered forever the old subsistence way of life. In this period too the spread of General Wade's roads through the Highlands was increasing the pace of change. The intention of the government in far away London was clear. The Highlands and the Highlanders would have to modernise or die. Even before the last sad flourish of the old warrior society on Drumossie Moor the Highlands were being opened up. Centuries of battle had not destroyed the old tribal system but the new roads, bringing a new money economy to replace the old subsistence living, struck at the very heart of Highland society. Even without the slaughter of Culloden and the ethnic cleansing that took place afterwards the old ways were doomed.

Although, like most of his countrymen, Iain Dubh, growing up in the 1720s and '30s, loved the wild hills and gentle glens of his native land, he saw little future in staying at home. Being a Jacobite by upbringing and inclination he decided to flit to France. There he would follow the well-worn path taken by so many Highland-men before him. He was a tall, strong and handsome lad and his fighting skills were well-developed. Raised to accept hardship and hunger, with all the skills of a Highland fighting man he was a valuable recruit to the French Army. Apart from his military skills, he was a man of commanding aspect and considerable intelligence, and his obvious talents soon led to him being made a serjeant. As well as being a great fighting man he was scrupulously honest and straightforward. Like so many of the Highlanders his sense of honour was remarkable. *Cothrom na Feinne*, the fair play of the Fianna, might well have been his motto.

We do not know if Iain Dubh Cameron was among those who came over to Scotland with the hopeful Prince Charlie or whether he made his own way back to join the rebellion slightly later. However, along with many other Highlanders abroad he had no hesitation in returning to the land he loved to fight for a cause so close to his heart.

For the whole of that briefly glorious yet ultimately tragic campaign Serjeant Mor gave all he could. His loyalty, skill and strength were all at the service of his prince right up to that bloody and miserable day on Drumossie Muir, and beyond. Sickened and enraged by the vicious slaughter ordered by Butcher Billy Cumberland in the aftermath of Culloden, Iain Dubh Cameron took to the hills of Badenoch with a handful of companions; they would fight on. In truth they had little choice. Government intelligence as to the identity of those fighting for the Prince was pretty thorough, and those like Iain Dubh who had fought for the King's enemies abroad, could expect no fate but death at the hands of the Hanoverians. Throughout the Highlands the British Army, with many Scottish troops, went on an orgy of pillage. Not a few old clan feuds were used as excuses for settling old scores.

The government at Westminster passed the Disarming Acts banning the carrying of weapons, and the wearing of the kilt. Cultural activities like the playing of the pipes were discouraged for all but its own soldiery throughout Scotland. Despite the offer of thirty thousand pounds, the equivalent of millions in today's money, for the capture of Prince Charles Edward Stuart, none of his supporters was prepared to betray him. The land was devastated and soon poverty was rife. If Iain Dubh and his men were to survive they must fend for themselves. The solution was obvious – they would return to the trade they had learned at the School of the Moon.

At first the targets of bands like Serjeant Mor's tended to be Presbyterian ministers in the counties bordering the Highlands. The rough rule of thumb that Jacobites were Catholic and Protestants supported the Hanoverian cause was the excuse for many attacks. Throughout 1746 and 1747 there were many reports of such raids in Perthshire, Angus, Kincardine and

Aberdeenshire. However the ministers were neither rich or numerous enough to provide a good enough living and Sergeant Mor was forced to extend his area of activities.

Any Whig, or government supporter, was seen as fair game, but increasingly all Lowland farms were seen as viable targets. The Highlands had become so poor that there was no point in raiding there. Blackmail was re-introduced and in time-honoured fashion, according to the Gaelic code of honour, any one paying the blackmail was indemnified against losses they might suffer from other bands. An argument can be made that men like Serjeant Mor were selling an early and necessary form of insurance to the Lowland farmers, and the fact that actual contracts of blackmail survive (see Appendix) shows that the portrayal of the caterans as nothing but thieves and extortionists hardly fits the picture. Soon the Big Sergeant's activities were spread over a wide area and he was successfully avoiding capture by the government troops who blanketed the Highlands to try and capture the caterans. Hardly a glen in Scotland outside Argyll, an area controlled by the government-supporting Campbells, did not have its own garrison, and patrols regularly rode through the hills between them. However most of these troops were English and the native skills and knowledge of the cateran gave them a distinct advantage in their own homeland.

Serjeant Mor's sense of honour did not desert him in his new profession and for several years no lives were lost in cattle-lifting raids by his band. It was one thing to kill a soldier who was out to kill you but another thing entirely to kill a man who was only trying to defend his own property. Due to his reputation the sergeant was admired by many folk, Lowland as well as Highland, for many in the cities, perhaps only slightly sympathetic to the Jacobite cause before Culloden, hardened their attitudes afterwards. To many of them it must have seemed that the whole of Scotland was under army occupation. Iain Dubh seemed to be cocking a snook at the government by his very existence and on more than one occasion had been known to help the poor after a successful raid. And there were plenty poor people in the Highlands.

However, things changed one day near Braemar. While he and his men were driving off a *creach* of cattle they were attacked by some of the farmers they had just raided. In the ensuing skirmish one of the farmers, John Bruce of Inneredrie, was killed. On seeing this Cameron at once called off his men, leaving the cattle behind.

The Big Sergeant was filled with remorse. He had no compunction about killing in battle; he had made his living doing just that, but this was different. The poor man had only been trying to protect his own property. Filled with remorse, Iain Dubh went off alone to a friend's farm on the edge of Rannoch Moor. This lonely spot at Dunan was in an area steeped in stories of the wild McGregor 'Children of the Mist' two centuries before. Like Sergeant Mor they too had been outlaws, with a price on their heads. Iain Dubh often hid out here when he needed to think things through. There were few options open to him. If he surrendered he would be hung, there was no doubt about that. He could either continue as he was or try to go abroad once more to serve as a soldier. The latter course held no attraction for the big Highlander. He was home in the land he loved and here he would live and die.

So Iain Dubh Cameron carried on in the cattle-lifting business and he prospered in it. Though there was a substantial price on his head no one would betray him to the government forces. To the oppressed and poverty-stricken Highlanders Serjeant Mor was becoming a hero. A story is told of an incident in the late 1740s which amply illustrates the style and substance of the man.

He was returning to Badenoch from one of his sojourns to Dunan when he met a single rider with a packhorse who appeared to be lost. He had been heading to Inverlochy Castle, just north of Fort William from Kinlochleven, when the mist came down. He had become separated from the rest of his party and was lost in the Mamore mountains. The man was an Englishman and near to desperation; he had been wandering about for hours and was exhausted and hungry. So glad was he to see another human being, he hardly even noticed that the Highlander was in traditional dress with a sword and two pistols in his belt. After promising to help, John gave the man some bread and cheese which he had in his saddle-bag.

'Thank you, thank you,' he blustered, once John had said he would help. 'I will be forever in your debt.'

'Think nothing of it,' the tall dark man said.

'Well, you have no idea how worried I was before you came along. The whole area is crawling with thieves.'

He didn't notice the look that came over the Highlandman's face as he said this and rattled on, 'I was terrified I would run into that Serjeant Mor.' He turned and looked at his companion.

'You have heard of him, I suppose?' he asked.

'I think I know of the man,' came the dry reply.

'Well, they say he is the greatest thief in the country. He robs just about everyone that has the misfortune to cross his path. I have heard that he is not averse to robbing widows and children. I know that most of you Highland people are honest but they say this man is an absolute terror.'

Having placed his trust entirely in his companion the Englishmen went on and on about the infamous Highland cateran, repeating all of the gossip he had heard in the various garrisons and taverns that he had visited over the previous few weeks. Soon it appeared that there was not a crime in all Scotland that couldn't be laid at the door of Serjeant Mor, from robbery to rape. At last John had had enough.

'Stop, stop,' he cried, 'You are being unjust to the Serjeant Mor. If he plunders, he plunders only the cattle of the Whigs and the Sassenachs who are his natural enemies. And neither he nor his comrades ever spilt innocent blood but once, and that was when a man was cut down in a melee near Braemar.'

He stopped and fixed his companion with a hard look and went on, 'The moment that man fell I ordered the *creach* to be abandoned and we drew off without another blow being struck.'

'You, what did you have to do with it?' quavered the suddenly terrified paymaster.

The giant Gael looked down at his companion and said, 'My name is Iain Dubh Cameron, I am the Serjeant Mor. There before you now is the road to Inverlochy Castle, you cannot now mistake it. I know fine well you are the army paymaster and that your pony there is weighed down with English gold, but you and your money are safe. Tell your governor in future to be sending a more wary messenger with his gold. You can tell him also that though I am forced to live as an outlaw I am as much of a soldier as he is and I would not stoop to taking gold from a defenceless man who confided in me.'

At that the sergeant gave the other man's horse a skelp on the rump and the beast, its rider and the packhorse galloped off down the road to Inverlochy. The garrison got their wages and never again did the English paymaster have a bad word to say about John Dubh Cameron, that notorious bandit who had taken neither his money nor his life.

Later that same year the sergeant entered into a business arrangement that kept him and his band well off for quite a few years. The entire band were attending the big annual Michaelmas Cattle Tryst at Crieff. This week-long fair and market took place at the end of September and included a great amount of livestock trading. It was just about the biggest cattle fair in Scotland and beasts from here went all over the Lowlands and even down to England. Rich pickings indeed for a hardy band of caterans!

Leaving their weapons at a friendly house near the town, the caterans removed their plaids and bonnets and put on Lowland clothes. These were the standard hodden grey clothing of most of the populace, which they had acquired earlier. In ones and twos they made their way into the bustling market town, mixing with the rest of the crowds but avoiding getting too close to the soldiers who were wandering about in threes and fours. Soon Serjeant Mor was sitting in a busy howff with a glass of whisky before him. He hadn't been sitting there long when a solid, prosperous looking man approached him and asked to sit with him.

Though a bit suspicious, the sergeant agreed and the man sat down.

'Well, it's a fine day for trading, don't you think?' said the stranger as he raised his glass.

'If you say so,' said Iain.

'Oh it is, it is,' the man went on, 'and I think that we might even be able to do a bit of business between ourselves.'

'What?' demanded Cameron, his right hand going inside his jacket to grasp the butt of the pistol concealed there. At the same time his left hand slid just under his right cuff where a *sgian dubh* was handily placed.

'Oh, fear not, friend,' said the man, raising both his hands clear of the table. 'I only mean to present you with a business proposition.'

Cameron, his eyes flitting round the room, looking for an ambush, sat there like a coiled spring. He could see a couple of his men in the room but nobody else seemed to be paying any attention to their table.

'Look, my name is Pryde,' the man went on in a low voice, 'I am baith a butcher and a publican in Perth. I have just bought a good handful of cattle – at a fair price I might say – an' I simply want to ask you to escort them back wi' me to Perth. What do you say?'

'Why me?' asked John, relaxing a little, but keeping his hand on his pistol. 'You dinnae remember me, but we met briefly when you and the rest of the men came through Perth. You were in need of food for your men and I recall you paid the going rate,' Pryde said, looking Cameron straight in the eye. 'I will pay well, for baith you and your men.'

'What men?' asked John, suspicion springing again to the fore.

'I ken fine who you are sir, but I think we can dae more than just a little business together. Will you take a dram?' he asked, pulling back his chair. At that point one of the other cateran stood up. John gave him a quick sign and he sat back down.

'Well,' he said, 'you know who I am, do you?'

'I do that, Mister Cameron,' Pryde replied, leaning forward and speaking in a whisper, 'an' I think we can be of advantage to ane anither.'

'Well if I am who you think I am,' smiled the big, dark man in hodden grey, speaking just as softly as the butcher, 'you will know if you attempt any treachery here, you will die, quickly.'

Pryde just smiled and John thought that at least he was brave enough, and then he said, 'I will get us a drink sir, and be right back.'

With the eyes of three cateran watching his every move Pryde the butcher went and ordered a bottle of the finest whisky the establishment had and came back to the table.

Over a glass of whisky with the butcher the deal was struck. Cameron and his friends would accompany Pryde and his cattle back to Perth where they would be paid for their trouble. However, once they were on their way and clear of Crieff, the butcher outlined his real plan. Now that they had met he would like to put in an order for as many beasts as Serjeant Mor and his men could supply him with. John Dubh's initial reluctance to take on the job disappeared as he realised that this was a fine opportunity indeed. In the ensuing months, and years, there was many a night that the cateran brought lifted cattle to Perth. It soon became a routine. At a friend's house on the Almond river near the town they would change into their hodden grey clothes and still under cover of darkness would deliver the beasts to Pryde at the back of his butcher's premises in the Upper High Street. Then in daylight they would return to the banks of the Almond, change again and head off back to the hills, a fair bit richer each time. Soon tales were being told of how Serjeant Mor would often put his hand in his sporran and help out those who were in dire poverty – and there were many enough of them.

In Perth it was remarked that the butcher was doing very well, but for all the meat he had there was never any sign of hides and that an awful lot of his deliveries seemed to arrive in the hours of darkness. However, as his prices were fair and his meat good, no one voiced their suspicions over loudly.

The reputation of Serjeant Mor, as a thorn in the government's flesh, as an honourable man to do business with and as a friend to the poor continued to grow. He had the tacit support of many and the actual help of more than a few in his 'business activities'. Try as they might the army could not get hold of him. In the late 1740s and early 1750s there were still many Jacobites in hiding and the government troops were hunting them as well as the those who had turned to the cateran tradition. One detachment was searching for the great Cluny MacPherson who had been one of Prince Charlie's close advisers, round about the Rannoch Moor. This detachment, led by Lieutenant Hector Munro, later to become a famous general, was quartered in Dunan village in late 1753.

By this time there was a considerable price on Serjeant Mor's head, but it bothered him little. He was sure that he could trust all those who knew where he might be. After all, hadn't he been safe these past seven years, even if there had been a few close shaves and more than a couple of skirmishes with government troops? As was his custom he had arrived at his friend's farm near Dunan for a few days' peace and quiet. Soon the coggie was being passed back and forth, and after a few hours the sergeant said he was ready for bed. After so many years of living on the run John could not feel safe sleeping in a house. He generally slept outside in a cave, or on the heather, and sometimes in turf-built bothies high in the hills, but if there was a barn with fresh straw to sleep on, he wouldn't pass up the opportunity. The main stipulation was that the barn had to have at least two doors, just in case.

His friend's barn had a door at either end and John headed there to sleep, as he had done so often before. He laid his sword, pistols and dirk close to hand, rolled himself in his plaid and was asleep on the straw almost immediately. Once the cateran chief had fallen into a deep, whisky-aided sleep his 'friend' crept into the barn. After so many years of friendship, greed had taken hold of the man's heart and he had decided to betray the Big Sergeant. Craftily, the treacherous nyaff removed the weapons, hid them in his farmhouse and rode off to where he knew Lieutenant Munro and his men were billeted, just at the west end of Loch Rannoch, a couple of miles away.

On hearing that the notorious Jacobite cateran Serjeant Mor was his for the taking, Lieutenant Munro wasted no time. At once he and his men of the 34th Regiment set off. Reaching the farm the soldiers surrounded the barn. Six men were sent in to apprehend the sleeping cateran. As the soldiers tiptoed into the barn, Iain Dubh awoke. Feeling for his weapons he found nothing. The next instant the soldiers were upon him. A furious struggle began. Within seconds two of the soldiers lay hurt, one badly. On and on the giant Highlander fought. At last he broke free. He ran for the door. Bursting out into the moonlit night John found himself facing a dozen levelled muskets, their bayonets shining. He was caught. Lieutenant Munro was jubilant. He had captured the notorious Serjeant Mor. Heavily chained, the prisoner was sent to Dunkeld at daylight. The following day he was taken on to the prison in Perth. In the prison here he found his kinsman and reglar raiding companion, Angus Dubh Cameron, who had been captured elsewhere. A heavy guard was placed on the city prison to prevent any attempted rescue and the trial was held the very next day.

Iain Dubh Cameron, the Serjeant Mor, was charged with the theft of cattle, sheep and horses as well as the murder of John

Bruce of Inneredrie. He was also charged, along with Angus, with stealing two sheep from the Duke of Atholl. Angus seems to have escaped with a prison sentence, but Iain knew what his fate would be. It was inevitable. The jury 'found the panel guilty, art and part, of the murder libelled; of stealing three horses and a filly belonging to John Blair in Ballachraggan; and of being by habit and repute a common thief in the country.' Though hundreds of rebel High-landers, and some who had stayed out living the cateran life after Culloden, had been transported to the British colonies in the West Indies, there to live as virtual slaves on the sugar plantations, John knew there could only be one possible sentence. He was sentenced to be hanged on 23 November.

At this time the Scottish courts still retained the office of 'Doomster'. This official's duties were simple but awful. He was the hangman, and when sentence of death was passed he had his moment in court. It was the custom for the Doomster to approach the condemned, place a hand on his or her head, and repeat the sentence, adding, 'And this I pronounce for Doom.' This was to show that he had final responsibility for the life and death of the condemned person. Without doubt it was a solemn and ominous piece of legal theatrics.

When John's sentence was read out the judge rang a small bell. A door opened and the Doomster entered, dressed in black. Slowly he approached Serjeant Mor. Despite his chains the giant Highlander struggled to his feet and freed one arm.

'Keep the caitiff [fool] off. Let him not be touching me or I will give him such a skelp,' roared Iain Dubh.

At that the Doomster fled the court in terror. However, a couple of days later the Doomster had his day. On 23 November 1753 Serjeant Mor was hanged at the Burgh Muir in Perth. His body was left to rot on the gallows as a warning to others. Nothing more was heard of his cateran followers and it was assumed they had split up and gone their own ways.

In the meantime Serjeant Mor's betrayer found that his evil

deed brought him no good. Despite a large reward and the granting of a favourable lease on the Strowan Estate he could not prosper. The common people despised him for what he had done and would have nothing to do with him. No one would work with him or for him. The gentry who had supported the Government throughout considered him nothing but a peasant and he found himself friendless. It took only a couple of years for him to lose all he had gained for his treachery and he was forced to leave the country a virtual pauper.

Serjeant Mor had been very popular amongst the people of the Highlands. He and his men could not have kept on raiding for seven years after Culloden without some support. Even while being subjected to the barbaric repression of Butcher Billy and the Westminster government there were many in the Highlands prepared to help Serjeant Mor and the other bands. They might be doomed to eventual failure but as long as they didn't admit defeat they carried the aspirations and loyalties of much of the Gaelic-speaking population with them.

Serjeant Mor and those others, like his cousin Donald Ban Leane Cameron, who was hanged at Kinloch Rannoch earlier the same year, were said in contemporary publications to have been nothing more than cattle thieves. Donald, like Iain, met his end calmly and whether or not they had an unshakeable loyalty to the Jacobite cause, or were simply trying to hang on to the fading remnants of their own, ancient, way of life, they certainly did not see themselves as thieves, common or otherwise. The fact that they were certain to fail appears to have been less important to them than their commitment to their way of life. Their pride could not be dented by defeat, only by admitting it. They kept their honour intact and that, to the last generation of a long, long line of Celtic warriors that stretched back into pre-history, was what ultimately mattered.

Duncan Ban Leane

Like his cousin Serjeant Mor, a member of the Cameron clan, Duncan Ban Leane stayed out after Culloden. He worked closely with his cousin in the years after Culloden but was captured by an Army patrol on the edge of Rannoch Moor in 1752. In general, up to this time when rebels, or cattle thieves, as the Governemnt always called them, were caught, they were sent to Perth or Edinburgh for trial. This time however, the authorities reckoned they would set an example locally. After all, much of the raiding on the Lowlands which they were deter-mined to stamp out, was carried on by cateran who hung about Rannoch Moor throughout much of the year, certain that, whenever the army approached they could find someplace to hide in that desolate place. The capture of Duncan showed that this would not always work, and the persistence of the army was well noted by the local population. So it was decided that Duncan would be hanged in Kinloch Rannoch. The decision was made before his trial as there was no way on earth that he wasn't going to be found guilty and strung up. At his trial he complained bitterly that he was being tried as a thief. His words show clearly what many, if not all of the cateran of this period believed they were doing.

'It is hard', he declared, in chains in the court, 'to be hanged when I have never committed murder or robbed man or house, or taken anything but cattle off the grass of those with whom I am at feud.'

By his way of thinking, the supporters of the Government

were all his enemies because he had sided with Charles Edward Stuart, and by the philosophy of the School of the Moon at which he been trained, the raiding of one's enemies cattle was not only not criminal, it was an honourable exploit. However, the government saw it differently. They were determined to put an end to the Highland way of life that created such exemplary and fearless warriors as Duncan, for as long as the clan system survived they could never be sure that trained warriors would not take up arms against them. It is generally believed that from the time of Duncan's hanging things began to change around the wild Rannoch Moor and when his cousin was hung the following year the last of the Rebellion was over, though the odd cateran raid did take place over the next few decades.

A Long-kept Secret

In the early 1780s Duncan, son of Hugh Mackenzie of Ballachulish, was on his death-bed He had been taken ill with what was most likely a heart attack and was fading fast. Now in his late seventies, Duncan had had an eventful life. He had seen the old ways of the clans with their warrior traditions fade away in the face of modern society and had himself played a bit part in the '45. His family were gathered around him, knowing that the end was near. It was at this point he told his family of an incident that had happened thirty years earlier.

Throughout the 1740s and into the 1750s, the Red Army, as the British Government troops were known throughout Scotland, were busy all over the Highlands trying to stamp out the cattle-raiding that the last Jacobites had turned to after Culloden. Although much of the Army's activity was based around the dozens of small garrisons that existed throughout the Highlands, there were occasional large-scale campaigns aimed at trying to eradicate the last of the cateran.

One day word arrived in Ballachulish that a big contingent of the British Army were on their way to Rannoch to gather up all the cattle they could find there. This was where the cateran took the herds when they didn't have an immediate market for them, and there would no doubt be a lot of them grazing in the hills adjoining Rannoch Moor. When he heard this Duncan went immediately to the smiddy in the centre of Ballachulish.

Arriving there he saw the smith, Angus Robertson, busy at his forge.

'Good day, Big Angus,' he said, 'have you heard the news?'

'Och, good day to yersel, Duncan,' the smith replied, 'what news would that be?'

'Well, it seems there's a big lot of the Red Army going to be coming up to Rannoch. It seems they've been charged with rounding up all the cattle they can find there,' he went on.

'Och now, that's a bit of a problem then, is it not?' Angus replied. Given the fact that the behaviour of many of the Red Army included the habit of taking whatever they wanted, both Duncan and Angus had actually sent some of their own cattle to Rannoch under the protection of a couple of Duncan's cousins. They had passed through Ballachulish not long before with a lifted herd and Angus and Duncan had passed over their own small herds to Duncan's cousins for safekeeping. It might be fair to say that it wasn't only the soldiers they were worried about. Some of the cateran were pretty unscrupulous and would take anything they could get their hands on. Given the general uncertainty of the times it had seemed a sensible precaution.

'What do you think we should do?' asked Duncan.

'Well, have you any idea how soon they're coming?' the smith replied.

'Well, I heard they could be marching north anytime now,' Duncan said.

'In that case I think we had better just head over that way ourselves and see if we can get our beasts out of their road before they arrive, don't you think?' the smith said rubbing his chin.

'Aye, I suppose there's no muckle other choice,' Duncan muttered glumly.

The idea of a hard slog over to Rannoch and then the problems of getting past the various detachments of the Red Army around Glen Coe while driving their own cattle seemed beset with possible danger. However, there seemed to be little option if they wanted to keep their cattle. So they got themselves organised and made for Rannoch. On the way they saw four soldiers picking on a woman they had stopped from passing them by. Though dressed in little more than rags, she was a young and pretty woman, and the way the soldiers were making fun of her worried Angus. There had been incidents enough of women being molested, and worse, since Culloden, and Angus feared the situation would only deteriorate.

'I will not allow those oafs to harm that lass,' said the smith to Duncan. 'I am going to go and help her.'

'There are four of them,' says Duncan, 'I had better come with you.'

They approached the soldiers, one of whom, a tall gangly fellow with buck teeth and yellow hair sticking out from under his cap, had taken the woman by the elbow.

'Come on now, lassie, there's no harm in being friendly to a handsome bunch of soldiers,' he smirked, and his companions laughed.

'Leave her alone this minute,' came a voice.

The soldiers turned to see who was speaking. There before them were two men, one well over six feet and strongly built, the other a little smaller but powerful looking. Both were dressed in hodden grey, the homespun cloth of the times, and wore Highland bonnets.

Now these soldiers, like many of their companions, were convinced that most of the Highlanders were in fact rebels and thieves. In fact they had nothing but contempt for the natives, and the fact that the only weapons these two appeared to have were the staffs they were carrying, probably accounted for the buck-toothed soldier's response.

'Get out of here right now, you rebel swine,' he spat, 'if you know what's good for you. This is none of your business.'

'I said, leave her alone,' repeated Angus, by now within a few feet of the soldiers.

At this the soldiers went for their swords and the young woman was thrown to the ground. Duncan and Angus though had done their own share of fighting and before the yellow-haired soldier could barely get his sword from the scabbard Angus felled him with his staff. Likewise Duncan put down one of the others as he too drew his sword. As the other two stepped back, the Highlanders grabbed the fallen swords just as the remaining two soldiers came at them. The fight was short. Within not much more than a minute the two soldiers lay dead.

The two men looked at each other then Angus went to help the young woman to her feet.

'Och, thank you,' she said. 'Thank you for what you have done, but you will have brought great trouble on yourselves.' As she said this she looked down at the unconscious yellow-haired soldier. She shivered, then spat on the recumbent figure.

'You now what these scum would have done, if you hadn't stopped them?' she asked looking at Angus.

'Aye. I think we understand that well enough,' he said, also looking at the two unconscious men.

'Well then,' said Duncan, 'we had better decide what to do. If that buck-toothed swine ever comes round, he will no doubt have all three of us shot as rebels. There's no way our word will stand before his, the way things are.'

'Aye, I know,' replied the big smith, with a sad look.

Turning to the woman he said, 'Look lass, just you be on your way and forget all about this. It never happened. We'll sort things out, don't you fash.'

She took a hand of each of the men and blessed them before hurrying off. They knew what they had to do. So it was that a couple of hours afterwards the two continued their journey to Rannoch. Behind them, a short distance into the trees beside the road at Ballachulish were four fresh graves, each one containing an English soldier and his arms. Duncan and Angus managed to bring their own beasts back from Rannoch before the main contingent of the British Army arrived but for the next thirty years they kept the secret of what had happened that day. They knew they had little choice in what they had done, and though it was regrettable how two of the soldiers died, neither of them doubted for an instant that they had been right to intervene, to protect the young woman. However it had always lain on Duncan Mackenzie's conscience, and so it was that he got it off his chest just before he died.

Russell and the Cateran

Despite the widespread presence of the Red Army soldiers throughout the Highlands after Culloden, cateran raiding on the Lowlands continued for many years. One of those who suffered from the attacks was a man called Russell, the factor of the Earl of Moray's estates, who himself farmed a large stretch of land from Earlsmill near Darnaway Castle, Forres, down along the Findhorn River to the Hill of Aitnach overlooking Lochindorb. One day one of his cowherds came breathless to Earlsmill to tell him that a bunch of Highlanders had lifted the cattle grazing on the slopes of the Hill of Aitnach and were heading west with them. Realising he hadn't a moment to lose, he gathered together as many men as he could, armed them, and set off in pursuit. Because of the constant threat of cateran raids, landowners whose loyalty to the government was not in question were allowed to keep firearms. Russell realised that the cateran heading west would have to go through the Streens, a narrow gorge on the Findhorn river and the perfect place for an ambush if he could get his men there before the cateran arrived. So they set off at a good pace and, as the raiders were slowed down by the cattle they got to the spot before them.

Russell placed his men behind rocks and trees along the narrow path by the river at a spot where the glen widened a little, and sat down to wait. He didn't have to wait long, for only a short while later they heard the lowing of approaching cattle. Soon enough the herd came into view accompanied by fourteen Highlanders. Each one was armed with sword, dirk and pistols, and a few of them were carrying what appeared to be rather old-fashioned guns. Once they were all in plain view, Russell stepped forward.

'Halt,' he cried, putting his gun to his shoulder, and aiming at the lead Highlander. At that point, as planned, his men stepped from hiding, each of them aiming at a Highlander. As there were twenty-odd men in his party, he had the advantage. The leader of the Highlanders, a short, red-haired, wiry little man, shouted a command and the Highlanders, ignoring the pointed weapons, ran up and formed a line either side of him, drawing their pistols and swords as they did so. Stood there they were a fearsome sight. They seemed in no way bothered by the presence of the Moray men. They had a short discussion as Russell and the others looked on and then the leader stepped forward after placing his sword and pistol on the ground.

He came up to Russell and spoke. 'Well then, are you for peace or for battle? If you are for war, you are in great danger, but if you are for peace we can talk things over and maybe meet each other halfway.'

'I will listen to what you have to say,' said Russell.

'Well then, perhaps we can come to an agreement,' replied the wee red-haired Highlander.

'But how can I know that I can trust you?' asked Russell, aware that his original advantage was fast disappearing, his men were not battle-hardened veterans like the Highlander, and if it came to a fight he had no idea what the result might be.

'Trust,' spat the Highlander. 'A Lowlander like you asks if he can trust the word of a Highland gentleman!' He looked angry but managing to restrain himself, 'If,' and he stressed the word; 'if we can come to an agreement here today I will swear on my dirk to keep my word, how does that suit?' Now Russell had lived in Scotland all his days and knew enough about the Highlanders to realise this was the most solemn oath any one of them could give, an oath they saw as more binding than a Lowlander swearing on the Bible.

'Fine, fine,' he replied, 'what then do you propose?'

The Highlander immediately asked for a considerable sum of money to leave the herd and disappear into the hills. From his point of view the money would be handier than the cattle, which he would have to arrange to sell. His asking price was too high and the two of them stood there in front of the two bands of armed men and haggled. At last a price was agreed. It was a price that Russell was prepared to pay to avoid the possibility of him and some of his men dying to defend the cattle, and a price that, while maybe not as much as he would have got selling the cows elsewhere, was still enough for the Highlander to consider it a profitable venture for him and his men. So the two men shook hands and the Highlander spoke.

'Now, you must look over the beasts to check that none are missing,' he said, and noticing the surprise on Russell's face, gave a small laugh and went on, 'I told you we keep our word and I am giving back all that I have taken.'

Russell and his chief cowherd, a man much relieved at the way things had gone – having just become a father for the first time he was looking forward to seeing his son grow up – went to check the beasts. There was one beast missing, a small dun cow,

On being told this, the wee Highlander's face darkend and he turned to his men. 'Ewan. Come here, I need a word with you,' and at that a young man stepped forward. He was a tall handsome man with a fair open face. The two of them talked briefly in Gaelic and then the leader turned back to Russell. 'You may be easy about the beast. It will be back on your lands come the morning. You have my word.'

Again the two men shook hands and the Moray men turned the cattle and they headed off back down the river. Once they were out of sight the wee Highlander, Callum Beag, spoke again to Ewan. 'Now Ewan, you had charge of the rear. What were you thinking of to lose one of the beasts. I have given my word to the Lowlander and you must redeem my pledge. I have told Mr

Russell that the dun cow will be on his pasture by morning. My word must be kept.' There was no mistaking the determination in Callum's eyes.

'I promise I shall see that it is so,' nodded Ewan and at once, sheathing his sword, putting his pistol in his belt then, turning and bounding off like a deer through the heather, he ran off south-east up the side of the hill. Within seconds he was out of sight and the others turned and headed upstream.

Luckily, Ewan had a suspicion about where the dun cow might have gone. Earlier on as they neared the village of Dulsie not long after gathering in the herd he had noticed a man on the hillside watching them. He thought he recognised him. If he was right it was a well-known thief from Dulnain over in Speyside. This would be just the kind of trick he would get up to. He was the kind who took advantage of the troubled times to feather his own nest and the Highlander had nothing but contempt for him. Ewan knew the hills well and had a fair idea of the way he would go. By the time he caught up with the Dulnain man, night had fallen and they were both making their way by the light of the moon. The thief was having some trouble getting the cow through a narrow pass in the hills when Ewan dropped down from the overhanging rock in front of him.

'I'll have that cow you stole back now, I think,' called Ewan, standing with sword in hand and his pistol, cocked and ready to fire, pointing straight at the thief's heart.

'Oh, quite the brave Highlander aren't you, with your sword and pistol, while I have but my sword,' spat back the thief, as cunning as he was dishonest.

'Well then,' replied Ewan, 'that's easily taken care of,' and placed his pistol on a nearby rock.

At once the thief leapt at him and struck. Ewan parried the blow. Dishonest and cunning he might have been, but the Dulnain man was no coward and no mean hand with a blade either. So they fought and gradually the Dulnain man edged closer to where Ewan had laid down his pistol. This soft High-land fool might consider it a matter of honour to fight fair, but he wasn't about to be so stupid, the thief was thinking. As soon as he was near enough he made a thrust at Ewan, who backed away slightly. The thief made a grab for the pistol and in a single movement brought it to bear on Ewan and fired. Luckily it misfired, there was a flash in the pan and Ewan was on the thief laying him out with a sword blow to the temple. Pausing only to take the man's sword and throw it off among the nearby rocks, Ewan secured the twice-stolen animal and headed back towards the Hill of Aitnach. As dawn rose over the hill the dun cow was there, calmly chewing the cud among the rest of the herd.

It wasn't long after this that Russell again confronted a band of cateran. He had been over in the hills south of Buchanty on business for the Earl, when he came in sight of the Dobrach Burn which runs into the River Divie. There below him, snaking along the burn, was a straggling line of cattle being herded by a group of men in Highland dress. As the Disarming Acts were in force banning the wearing of the kilt or plaid he at once realised it was another *creach* taking place. He ran over the hills and down to a nearby farm to ask if they were the Earl's cattle. No, he was told, it seemed that the Highlanders had come thity miles or so driving a herd that they had lifted from Sir Robert Gordon of Gordonstoun. Sir Robert was a good friend of Russell's and the latter decided he could hardly let this matter pass without intervening. So he called all the men he could get together and arranged for them to be armed by some of the local landowners. In this case it meant upwards of forty men and they knew there were only about a dozen Highlanders. They then set off after the cateran. They caught up with the men and cattle within a couple of hours and as they ap-proached, the Highlandmen formed a line between them and the cattle.As he got closer he realised it was the same man he had had dealings with before, Callum Beag.

Confident in the superiority of numbers – three-to-one was good odds even against skilled warriors – he approached Callum.

'Right,' he said, 'there will be no bargaining here today. You are considerably outnumbered, and if you do not hand those cattle over immediately it will cost you all dear,'

'Mr Russell,' replied the wee Highlander, 'I would not expect such a thing of you. When last we met we both acted with honour and no harm was done. You got back your own beasts but it is not honourable for you to be stopping me taking the beasts of another; this is not how a gentleman should act.' At that he sadly shook his head, while surreptitiously counting the number of armed men that stood behind Russell.

'Well, you and I have different notions of how a gentleman should behave, and I am determined not to let you pass from here with the cattle you have taken from a good friend of mine,' Russell said sternly.

'Well then,' the Highlander replied in a dry voice, 'you are among your own here and have the great advantage of numbers, but I warn you now, you will come to regret this day.'

At that he turned, signalled to his men, and they all ran off like hares up the burn, leaving the cattle where they stood. Russell considered that he had done what any honest man would do and paid no attention to the implicit threat in the Highlander's words. He had the cattle delivered to Sir Robert Gordon and was pleased a few days later when he in turn sent him a dozen bottles of fine claret as a thank you. What he didn't know was that the intelligence network of the Highlanders was keeping an eye out for him. Callum considered that he had stuck his nose in where he had no business to, and was determined to have his revenge. Their viewpoints regarding the lifting of cattle could hardly have been more different. During the following winter Russell had to go to London to transact some business on behalf of the Earl of Moray. In those days this was a long and arduous journey and it usually took several weeks to get there and back. The journey south took place with no notable incidents but coming back up through the Drumochter Pass into Strathspey he ran into a wild storm. By the time he had got to the inn at Dalwhinnie he was wet and frozen and relieved to get inside. He had hardly begun warming himself at the fire when the landlord came over to him.

'Mr Russell, sir, I think ye had better be keeping a weather-eye oot. Last nicht twa dozen muckle armed Heelanders came by lookin for ye,' he said. 'Their leader was wee fiery, man cried Callum Beg. I tellt them ye werenae here but they went through the haill place ransackin everythin. I was feart for my life an they threatened tae burn the inn doun aroun ma ears. But then they calmed doun an asked for meat an drink an then acted like nothin had gone wrang at all. They had a feed and a good drink but then I tell you the wee fellow surprised me. He asked me for the bill and paid it in full, I tell ye I was michty relieved when they left. They headed off north.' he finished.

This was disturbing news indeed and any thought of moving homewards disappeared. Russell was no coward but he had just one man with him; they were unarmed and it was a long way to his home at Earlsmill. Following the landlord's advice he re-turned through the Drumochter Pass the next morning to Blair Atholl, waiting there till the landlord sent word to the Earl of Moray, who arranged for an escort of armed men. Several days later a troop of forty armed Moray men arrived to take him home. They travelled carefully with outriders and scouts to the front and back of the main party but no signs of trouble were evident till they came into the wilderness of the Drumochter Pass itself. High up on the hills above them they saw against the snowline the gleam of weapons and the ocasional flash of tartan. Still, thought Russell, with forty men, they won't attack. Luckily he was proved right, but the Highlanders shadowed them for miles before disappearing suddenly. Again he came to the inn at

Dalwhinnie, but even with such a substantial force he decided that discretion was the better part of valour and after a hot meal they went off in a northerly direction. He found out a few days later that this had been a wise move. That same night the Dalwhinnie inn was surrounded by a force of almost a hundred armed Highlanders – Callum Beg had called on all the cateran hiding out in the area to come to his assistance and help him have his revenge on Russell of Earlsmill. For a long time Russell kept armed guards pemanently stationed at Earlsmill and never went anywhere without a substantial bodyguard. However, he heard no more from Callum Beg and within a few years the raids of the caterans had almost entirely ceased.

The Spanish Swees

⇒◆⇐

A *swee* or *swey* is the Scots word for the metal bar used for hanging pots which used to be fitted in every cottage over the open fire. Up in Glenglass overlooking the Cromarty Firth there were a group of seven cottages whose sweys were something special. They originally came from Spain and there is a story to tell of how they got to Glenglass.

Now, back in the days of the School of the Moon things didn't always work according to the rules. When bad blood had developed between two different clans, or even between septs of the same clan, things could easily turn nasty and there were times when it wasn't just cattle that were lifted. Sometimes the lads or lasses who were tending the herds were kidnapped as well, and they could end up spending many years as little more than slaves for the raiders who had taken them. In such cases ransoms were sometimes paid, but if the people who had been raided didn't know who it was that had carried out the attack, well, things could get difficult.

One day in the hills above Glenglass young Mary Ross was looking after the cattle from her clachan in the glen below. Like many of the shieling bothies, the roughly built structures in the high pastures, the one where Mary was staying with a couple of her friends was in sight of the clachan in the valley below. However, it was one of those hot summer days when a haar or mist blew in from the sea and it had blanketed the glen. Up where Mary and the three other lasses were looking after the cattle, the weather was glorious. Mary, at eleven years of age,

93

was the youngest of them, the others being a year or two older. Looking after the cattle as they fed on the lush grass of the high meadows was work, but it wasn't hard work really. It wasn't much past Midsummer and they were enjoying their time away from their families.

All that changed in an instant.

The four girls were finishing their lunchtime meal one day, just outside the bothy when they looked up to see what they most feared. It was a bunch of cateran! Heavily armed and wild looking, the caterans were running silently towards the girls over the Highland meadow. Screaming, the girls turned and ran uphill away from the oncoming men. Mary had only got twenty yards or so when she tripped in the heather, winding herself as she hit a large stone. Before she could get her breath back, a large rough hand held her by the neck.

'Just stay still lass an nobody'll get hurt,' a voice spoke. She lay there, still, as she heard the men shout to one another.

'The rest have given us the slip,' one cried.

'Ach well, let's be away with the beasts, before they can get down to the clachan,' came a reply from over towards Mary's left.

'The haar will stop them getting back in a hurry, but let's move quickly,' the man holding Mary down called to his friends.

'Right, lass,' he said as he pulled her to her feet. 'There's not that many of us, so I think you will have to help us herd these fine beasts through the hills.'

Mary was aghast. She was being lifted by these caterans as if she was no more then a beast herself. She looked up at the man. He was a medium-sized red-haired man with a thick beard just beginning to speckle with grey. He shoved her in the direction of where his comrades were beginning to herd the cows. There were only three of them. In her fear she had thought there were a dozen or more. There was nothing she could do but do as she was told and within minutes the three cateran, Camerons who had come up from Lochaber, and the wee lass Mary, were driving the Glenglass cattle south into the hills.

They had only been going an hour or so when Mary remembered the story of Wee Hector who had escaped from just such a cateran bunch two years earlier. He had pretended to hurt his ankle and went slowly and more slowly till they at last just left him and he had run home. Just as she was thinking to try this herself, the man who had caught her came alongside her and spoke.

'Well, lass, my name is Archie; that there,' pointing to a big dark man, 'is Ragnald Dubh, and that young lad over there is Lachlan Ban.' The man being pointed at was hardly more than a boy, the fair hair on his chin just beginning to show, and Mary thought he couldn't be more than sixteen or so. The fair-haired young lad looked back at her with a fierce look, and she shivered as if it had become cold.

The next week or so were a bit of a blur to Mary in later years. The cateran drove the cattle into the hills and carried on through the short summer's night, not stopping till about six in the morning, when they holed up in a hidden corrie. That same evening they were on their way again, taking a twisting hard route through the hills. Mary knew her father and the rest of the men from Glenglass would be out looking for them but these cateran seemed to know what they were doing and there was never any sign of pursuit. At last, a few days later, they came through the hills to Marlaggan, on the shores of Loch Arkaig.

The exhausted Mary was given warm food and shown a place to sleep in the end of Ragnald Dubh's house. Like most Highland houses the humans were at one end and the family's beasts were kept at the other end when they weren't out grazing. For the next three years Mary's life was little better than that of a slave. Ragnald's wife, Beathag, worked her hard, and although she wasn't cruel she didn't show the young lass much kindness. Ragnald himself always spoke kindly to her and made sure that she wasn't too uncomfortable. However, she was a captive and even though she slowly began to fit into the life of the clachan at Loch Arkaig – things were not that different from back home – she was aware that people kept an eye on her to see she didn't run off. If she did escape and get back home the Camerons knew they might well be raided by the Rosses in consequence. Though most of the Camerons tended to ignore her, Lachlan Ban seemed to take a special pleasure in abusing her. Now the Highland attitude towards women had always tended to be a fair one and he didn't beat her, but he never missed an opportunity to insult her or shout at her. She learned to keep out of his way whenever possible. However, after a couple of years this began to change. Mary began to enter into the first flush of womanhood and as her figure filled out and she grew taller she had all the signs of turning into quite a beauty. This seemed to anger Lachlan Dubh and on a couple of occasions he had to be told to control himself by Ragnald and some of the older men. By the time she had been four years amongst the Camerons, Mary had turned into a beautiful young woman and one day she ran into Lachlan. She had been down at the loch doing some washing for Beathag and was coming back through the woods. She was enjoying the warm summer's day and a bit of quiet when she sensed something. She looked up, and there before her was Lachlan Dubh looking at her. She stopped and he walked over to her.

'Well, Mary, from the North,' he said with an ominous smile, 'you have certainly changed since we brought you here, a snivelling brat.'

He brought his hand up to her cheek and she flinched.

'Ach not good enough for you, am I?' he uttered in a low growl, 'We'll see about that.' He reached to grab her, when over her shoulder she saw a couple of the clachan women coming towards them through the woods. 'There's people coming,' she whispered as he grabbed her arm. He spun around, and at once released her, ready to walk away. He had just gone a pace or two when he turned and said. 'Well, we will have other times, Mary from the North.' Then he strode off. Mary stood there shaking with tension as the women passed, giving her a bit of a strange look.

Now forcing women might be a dishonourable act to most Highland men, but she had heard enough to know that there were always a few who thought nothing of it, if they could get away with it. And Lachlan was definitely of that sort. Living in the same community as him she had noticed how vain and arrogant he was, and how disinclined he was for anything involving hard work or application. She realised, now that he had shown his hand, that he would not be slow in coming after her. Her constant daydreaming of escape had to stop. She had to get away. Well, she thought to herself, now is as good a time as any.'

Without hesitation she turned away from the village and began to walk through the woods to the north. She carried the washing with her. If she put it down somebody would find it and they would know she had run off. Soon she was into a section of the wood that was overgrown and out of the way. She was on the lower slopes of Sgurr Mhurlagain and well out of sight of the clachan, so she could go as fast as she liked. Mary was a bright lass and had been paying attention whenever anybody talked of the country to the north. She could remember little of her journey down here, but she was sure that if she kept out of sight and cut over the mountains as far as Loch Cluanie she could go down Glen Moriston and up by Loch Ness towards home. She had no food, but there were a few plants and herbs she could identify, and she had her secret.

Dreaming of escape had been Mary's way of dealing with her position. So she had laid a plan or two. In the pocket of her simple dress there were seven tubers of the Bitter Vetch plant. This was the plant that the Highlanders harvested every autumn and hung up to dry in the rafters of the dark houses. The tiny tubers on the roots of the plant, each one no bigger than her thumbnail, were the Highlanders' last defence against starvation. Often enough over the centuries, the clansfolk were faced with bad seasons and little food. When the food ran out these tiny tubers were their salvation. Each tiny piece of the plant was enough to keep an adult going for a day. Even as far back as Roman times the Caledonian people had known of this remarkable plant, and Mary had managed to hide seven of the tiny tubers against the possibility of escape. She had taken to carrying them with her at all times. There was really no safe place to keep them in Ragnald's house. If they had been found she knew she would be even more closely watched.

However, here in the woods, as she made her way up the hill there was nobody to see her. She knew it was only a matter of time before she would be missed, but if she was lucky she might have an hour or two. She knew there were men who would be able to follow her trail through the forest, so while going as fast as she could she tried to make as little disturbance as possible. At one point she walked up through the waters of a burn for several hundred yards. Over the next two days she travelled north, keeping in cover wherever possible and hiding often. The same day as she ran off she saw a group of Camerons coming down the hill into Glen Kingsie and hid herself in a murky pool in a peat bank, with her head just above the water, and hard against the side. She wasn't seen.

Luckily for Mary the weather stayed clear. While this meant she was constantly checking behind and around her for signs of other people, she had no problems with which way to go. As she didn't know what word the Camerons could have sent ahead of her and who their friends were, the best bet she thought, was to avoid people completely. So it was that nearly a week later she found herself in Strathglass, south-west of Inverness. By now she was extremely hungry – the wee tubers had kept her going but she wanted good warm food.

That day she came into a clachan at Fasnakyle and was given food by a friendly woman there who was pleased to follow the rules of hospitality and give a stranger food. When Mary told her what had happened to her, the woman who had relations in Easter Ross, decided to help. From then onwards Mary always had somebody to call on as she moved north, and a couple of days later she had found her way back to Glen Glass.

Here she was treated as if she had come back from the dead. Her mother and father, sister and brothers were ecstatic to see her again and Mary cried for days. She was a topic of conversation for the whole area and all the young lads in the district became aware of just what a beauty she had turned into. So it wasn't that long before Mary was wooed and married. Her husband was James Ross, a young man of some standing who was well thought of. In the course of time they were blessed with three bonnie bairns and Mary was quite content. Occasionally she thought of her years of captivity but the raising of three childen and the love of a good man kept her well content in the main.

Till one September. Mary and James had moved into a house that was about a quarter mile from the nearest clachan. It was set in a wee glen, the ground of which was fertile, and here they grew their crops and raised a fine wee herd of cattle. The clachan was just out of sight round a crook in the glen, but James and Mary were happy being so far distant from the rest of the people there. In truth, they took a great deal of pleasure out of each other's company and life there was good. Till that September day. She was cooking in the house when she heard a noise at her door. She came to the door of the house and there were seven Camerons. Her husband was away further down the glen with their eldest boy, and she was alone with her two other children. At first she did not recognise any of them, but immediately her heart was in her mouth. There was no doubt these were Camerons on a cateran raid and they had decided to bide their time at her place

99

before raiding further down the glen. They demanded to be fed and as she ushered her children back into the house before her, one of the Camerons, who had been standing some way off, keeping watch, turned towards her and her heart nearly stopped. He was a man in his late twenties with a great scar running across his left cheek. No longer the handsome youth he had been, she still knew him. It was a Lachlan Ban, and here he was walking towards her door. She turned away quickly and began to busy herself cooking. Lachlan though, did not recognise her. True, she had grown even taller and filled out a bit more since she had fled Lochaber, but she was sure he would soon seem to know her. The Camerons all came into the house and sat around or sprawled on the floor as she put on a large pot of venison.

'I will need to go and get more water,' she said to the man who appeared to be in charge.

'All right, but don't think of trying to get word out. Your bairns will be staying here with us,' growled the Cameron.

So she went out to the well with a pot for water. There at the door the cateran had placed their muskets – fine, shining, new muskets. These new armaments had come to Lochaber on a boat from Spain the previous year. The Camerons had all been delighted with these state-of-the-art weapons, and had left them, fully primed and loaded, sitting at the door of the house in case of trouble. Quick as a flash Mary knew what to do. She ran to the well and filled her pot. Then she ran to the seven muskets and poured water down the barrels of each one and over the firing mechanisms, quickly wiping away the surplus water with her apron. Then she ran back to the well and was just getting back to the door of the cottage when one of the cateran came to see where she was. She brushed past him and went back to her cooking. As she added water to the pot and stirred it she could see out of the corner of her eye that Lachlan was watching her closely.

Her heart thumped in her breast. Surely he would recognise

her at any instant. What could she do? Her children were playing at the feet of these cateran. How could she get them out? Then she had it. Acting as calmly as she could she pretended to slip and knocked the contents of her big pot on to the fire. Immediately the room filled up with smoke and the Camerons ran out into the other room, some of them going outside. 'Quick,' she whispered to the two bairns who were coughing and spluttering and beginning to cry, 'I'll put you out of the window and you must run to the clachan and tell the men there are cateran here.'

The children did as they were told and climbed through the window space. They were only three and four but this sounded like fun to them. Mary stuck her head out of the window to get a breath of air as she dropped the children to the ground. At that she realised that the smoke from the fire was swirling over the house and that someone might notice the ongoings from down the glen. Just at that she heard a voice shout 'Fire! Fire at James and Mary's.'

In those days the fear of fire was instilled in everyone and it only took seconds for a group of about a dozen men to be running up the road towards Mary's home. Outside, the Camerons realised that they were about to be discovered and decided they would give themselves some time to retreat by shooting some of the locals. As the men from the village, some of them carrying buckets and pans, came round the corner they saw the Camerons.

Drawn up in a line, each cateran had his brand new musket at his shoulder and each had immediately drawn a bead on one of the Ross men. 'Fire!' shouted their leader. There was a series of clicks and nothing else. The Camerons looked at each other and at their muskets. Something had clearly gone wrong. But they had no time to figure things out before the Glenglass men were on them. Most only had their dirks with them and swung the buckets at the heads of the cateran. The Camerons hardly had time to draw their swords. They were overwhelmed by superior numbers, and despite fighting as hard as they could, within minutes the seven of them lay dead. A good handful of the Rossmen were injured but none had lost their lives. Mary's quick thinking had made sure of that. She hadn't hesitated. The fears she had felt so long ago had come surging back and as James took her in his arms she burst into tears.

After the bodies were taken off and buried the local chieftain came to Mary and said. 'Well, Mary. Your quick thinking surely saved a few lives today, and probably a good deal of our cattle, we have had a wee chat and we think you should have their muskets. They are all fine new ones and if you sell them you will make a pretty penny,' he said.

'No, thank you, but I would rather that they were not used again as guns. There has been enough killing here. I shall put all my problems behind me once we have made these gun barrels into swees, one for me and one each for the first six houses in the clachan.'

The menfolk grumbled a bit at the idea – they hated to see such good weapons go to waste – but all the women of the place thought it was a good plan. And in time the six nearest houses in the clachan, as well as Mary's, had brand new swees, swinging over the fires, holding the cooking pots. And as the women said, 'A gun might get your meat, but you need a good swee to hold your pot over the fire to cook it!'

Cam Ruadh

An Cam Ruadh – the one-eyed, red-haired man. This unlikely hero lived in the first half of the 17th century and was held in such high esteem that two different areas claimed him as a native. The people of Glenshee maintained that he lived in Glen Taitnach, near the Spittal of Glenshee while Dee-siders claimed that he lived at Alltamhait in Glen Clunie, up towards Braemar. Wherever he lived he was a mighty warrior and tradition has preserved a great deal about him, including a detailed, if some-what gruesome physical description.

His name was John Grant and he was little more than five feet tall. He had bowlegs and flat feet and was quite startlingly ugly. His broad flat face had a pug nose and beady eyes, his cheeks were red and blotchy, with the veins sticking up. Below each eye there was an unsightly lump and the whole of his unfortunate face was covered with thin, straggly, red bristles. His one good eye was a brilliant blue, but the other was an opaque horror, streaked with red and permanently open. His lips were thin and could hardly cover his big, uneven and squint teeth. On top of this grisly sight was a shock of coarse red hair that is said to have resembled a hedgehog.

His body was short, stocky and exceedingly strong. His voice, it seems, was high and squeaky. His character in most respects was as unattractive as his person. He was dreadfully stubborn and quick-tempered, and though a man of deeds rather than words he had a waspish tongue. Tradition tells us that he was as cunning as a fox and as tenacious as a bulldog.

103

Despite all these shortcomings Cam Ruadh wooed and won himself a wife while he was still quite young, and he seems to have been a good and loving husband. Skilled in all the fighting arts and peerless in strength and stamina, especially when it came to running, his great delight was in his archery skills. With his one good eye he could see a bluebottle on a grey stone at twenty yards – and hit it with an arrow. It was generally believed in his time that no one in living memory had ever shot an arrow half as far as Cam Ruadh. His strength and accuracy were such that it is said he could fell an ox or hit a midgie.

With his skills and temperament it was no wonder that he was to the fore in fending off the cateran raids that were so common-place in his lifetime. Most of the raiders he came up against were from Argyll, following the age-old tradition of raiding the eastern Highlands, just as the eastern Highlanders had long been raiding in Argyll. An example of his shrewdness and tenacity survives in the story of the white cow.

Cam, knowing that there were raiders about, had fetched a white cow from nearby and stuck it with a group of a couple of dozen black beasts, the normal colour for the Highland cattle of those days. He also hobbled the white cow to slow it down. This was done very carefully, so that no one would notice anything in the dark. Thus he laid his plans and sat down a short distance from the cattle. Sure enough, in the middle of the night the cateran came, gathered in the entire herd and set off in total silence towards the West. Now the white cow was soon at the back of the herd, just as Cam had planned. Her milky white shape was the only thing that could be seen in the deep, dark night. Cam came along behind the herd, waiting for a sound. It was the sound of stick hitting the white cow to hurry her along. As soon as he had heard it he fired an arrow just above the white cow's back. A minute or two later he passed the still warm body of the cateran he had shot. The white cow was falling farther behind the rest and another Argyll man came to the back of the herd. Again there was slight sound of a cow being hit, the twang of a bow and the dull thud of an arrow finding its mark. It didn't take the Argyll men long after the fourth of their number was shot to figure something was up and they fled off into the night leaving the cattle on the track. Cam Ruadh however reckoned the cattle could be left to their own devices and he pursued the cateran through the night, catching up with them where the Allt Chroskie joins the river Ardle, near Kindrogan, and there they met their ends. It is said that the stones of the burn were stained red with their blood, and the place has ever since been shunned after dusk.

The raiders were sometimes known as cleansers because of their habit of lifting everything in their path and leaving glens as clean as a whistle behind them. On their raids into the central area of Scotland the Argyll cateran had often felt Cam Ruadh's powers, many of them failing to return to their own lands. One time, however, Cam Ruadh became sick of fighting and especially killing. Although fighting was an honourable activity and he had a great reputation he had just had enough of killing his fellow human beings, whatever the circumstances. The previous two years had seen a great deal of raiding, times were hard all round due to a succession of bad years and in many of the raids there had been an air of desperation. One day in late spring he announced that he had taken a vow that for twenty-four hours from midday he would raise no hand or arrow against cleanser or Kern [cateran] except in self-defence. For one brought up in the tradition of the warrior Gael this was a remarkable statement and mutterings were heard that no good would come of it. They were quiet mutterings. No one would openly speak out against Cam Ruadh. That same night a large band of Cleansers crept into Glen Isla and Glenshee. They were from Argyll and had been hiding in the hills in small groups for much of the spring in that year of 1644. By dawn they had gathered a fine *spulzie* or prize, and went back the way they had come. Dawn came to the crofts and the loss was discovered. Messengers were sent between Glen Isla and Glenshee and the men armed themselves. When the men from both glens met there was some dispute as to who should lead them, and Highland pride being what it was, neither side would give way. Matters were resolved, ominously, when some of the Glenshee men set off after the caterans leaving the rest of their companions still arguing with the men from Glen Isla. Given that the raiders had to be in considerable numbers to have lifted so many beasts, this was a tragic mistake.

Those that were left could come to no better agreement than that they should follow the raiders in two distinct groups. The plan was simply to try and catch the rieving party between both forces and then surround them. It was a poor plan. A messenger was sent to MacCoinnich Mor na Dalach, Big MacKenzie the laird of Dalmore near Braemar, asking him to bring all the men in his immediate area to the fray. Cam Ruadh stood back from all discussion. He was under his vow, but when the first Glenshee men set off after the cleansers he quietly followed them at a short distance.

The Glenshee men were to pay a terrible price for their impatience. Strung out in several small groups they fell easy prey to the greater numbers of the Argyll men. The Glen Isla men headed up the hill of Meall Odhar from where they could see what was going on in the Pass of Cairnwell. This was where the raiders had turned against their pursuers and a heavy toll was being exacted on the men of Glenshee while their neighbours looked on from the heights above. Even when the smith of Glenshee with his seven strong sons attacked a twenty-strong group of the caterans head on, the Glen Isla men held back. There was no sign of Cam Ruadh. Still bound by his vow, but beside himself with frustration at being unable to help his friends, he had crawled up the hill behind the caterans. From behind a large boulder he could look down and see, all too clearly, the slaughter below.

One by one, the smith's seven sons fell fighting the Argyll men. As each one died the brave smith cried, 'Fight today, lads, grieve tomorrow.' He kept looking north for help but none came. At last he was left alone, standing over the body of his last son and surrounded by enemies. Still he fought on. He was wounded several times and he fell to his knees still flailing at his enemies with his sword. He was obviously dying and all but one of the Argyll men went off to follow the herd. This last one came quietly forward to finish off the smith. The smith had turned his head again to look north for a sight of the Braemar men. No one was coming. The sun was high in the sky as midday came round. The cateran raised his sword. There was a twanging sound and the dull thud of an arrow hitting flesh. The cleanser leapt high in the air as the arrow struck and as he fell the smith used the last of his strength to dirk him. As he died the cleanser returned the compliment and the enemies fell dead in each other's arms.

At midday his vow was passed and Cam Ruadh was set upon revenge. Immediately he moved after the group of cateran heading after the herd. They hardly knew what had hit them. Suddenly, as if from nowhere, arrow after arrow fell among them. Each one found its mark. As their companions fell around them the Cromar men were in turmoil. Where was their assailant? The rain of death continued till nearly a dozen lay dead or dying. Then a gust of wind lifted the corner of Cam Ruadh's plaid and he was spotted behind his boulder.

With their war cries ringing out the caterans ran up the hill towards the boulder. As they came near, Cam Ruadh notched his last arrow to the bow-string. He aimed and pulled. The arrow snapped. Cursing, the bow-legged archer threw his bow towards the closing caterans, turned and ran up the hill. On came the cleansers, sure now they had their man. But when it came to running there was no one to touch John Grant, an Cam Ruadh.

Bounding through heather and juniper bushes, over streams

107

and through bogs he ran. His speed was taking him away from his pursuers with every step. One of the Cromar men saw what was happening. Stopping, he knelt down and notched an arrow to his bow. He fired at the running figure. Straight and true flew the arrow. With a thud it hid Cam Ruadh in the shoulder. As one the Argyll men cheered, expecting him to drop. However the Glenshee bowman never flinched; he simply kept on running till he was out of bowshot.

The group of Argyll men chasing Cam Ruadh turned and went back to their companions. A cheer went up from the surviving Glenshee men spread throughout the pass. An echo of that cheer seemed to ring out louder! It was MacKenzie and his men from Braemar. The Glen Isla men on top of Meall Odhar started cheering too. As the noise rang out the cleansers looked to the north. There coming over the hill was MacKenzie of Dalmore and over a hundred fighting men. Realising the situation had turned against them the Argyll men fled. They left behind them the cattle, sheep and horses they had fought so hard to defend, and the bodies of the Glenshee smith, all his seven sons and several more brave fighting men, among them a number of their own from Argyll.

As the cleansers fled with a force of the men from Braemar harrying their rear, the Glen Isla men came down to join the assembled Braemar and Glenshee men. MacKenzie himself called the Glen Isla men cowards and told them to be off. In normal cases this insult would have led to blows but the Glen Isla men sheepishly went away. It was a long time indeed before the people of Glenshee would have anything to do with their neighbours in the adjoining glen.

With the cleansers driven off the Glenshee men gathered up their flocks and their dead. With help from the remaining Braemar men they set out for home in sorrow. Nearly thirty of their number had been killed and there were many widows and fatherless children in Glenshee after that. As they got back into Glenshee many of the women on the crofts called out to Cam Ruadh that he had an arrow in his back. His reply was simple: 'I know that myself already.'

Getting home the hardy archer sat on a stool and told his wife to pull the missile from his back. She pulled, and pulled but the arrow wouldn't budge. All the while her husband didn't make a sound. It was no good, they'd have to try something else. Cam Ruadh thought of a way to solve the problem. He lay on his face and had his wife stand on his back, a foot on either side of the arrow. At his word she gave a mighty heave. Out came the arrow, with a sizeable lump of her husband's flesh. All this provoked was a short grunt.

As soon as his wife had dressed the wound, Grant fetched a bow and a quiverful of arrows and placed them by the door. Then he proceeded to eat a vast meal of roast venison, for like the rest of the Highland population he had a great appetite for red meat and believed it could do him nothing but good, especially if he had been wounded and lost blood. The wound was never mentioned again and after his meal he went about his work on the farm as if nothing had happened.

But something had happened. He had lost many friends including An Gobhair Mor, the Big Smith, and his seven fine sons. Never again would Cam Ruadh be loth to bear arms against the cleansers. The fight with the Argyll men became known as the Battle of Cairnwell and the spot where the cateran dead were buried became known as Kateran's Howe. This spot is just by the road to Braemar and for many years was a stopping point for the Perth to Braemar coach. The horses would be rested and fed and the passengers would be told the tale of the Battle of Cairnwell. Their attention would be drawn to fourteen mounds, one of which was about seven feet long. These were the caterans' graves, the longest believed to be that of the cleansers' leader, a petty chieftain of the MacDiarmaid clan, a raider who had died with one of Cam Ruadh's arrows through his heart.

This MacDiarmaid chieftain himself had seven sons, none of whom had been on the raid that led to the Battle of Cairnwell. When their clansmen returned empty-handed to Cromar and they heard what had happened, they resolved to avenge their father's death.

A few weeks later spies, disguised as pedlars, were sent into Glenshee and had no trouble finding out that the man they were after was John Grant of Glen Taitnaich. The whole area was talking about his exploits at the Cairnwell. As soon as they knew their intended victim the seven MacDiarmaids set out for Glenshee. Coming down the side of Ben Earb above the Spittal of Glenshee in cold, damp weather, the Argyll lads came across a wee bachle of a man tending a herd of cattle. He was wrapped in a tattered old plaid and was standing in the drizzle muttering to himself. This was of course Cam Ruadh himself, out grazing his own beasts and those of a couple of recently widowed neighbours. He was a bizarre sight and the MacDiarmaids assumed he was a simpleton. Strangely for a man of his awareness and experience, he was unaware of the party till one of them tapped him on the shoulder. Turning, he found himself surrounded by a group of heavily-armed men, obviously brothers, quite clearly strangers, and, he realised, strangers from Argyll. They saw an ugly wee man so ill to look at that a couple of them even turned away.

'Old man,' said the eldest, 'can you tell us where we can find John Grant of Glen Taitnach?'

At this Cam Ruadh bared his teeth in a grin that made the MacDiarmaids shudder and said in his squeaky voice, 'Och, well, maybe, perhaps I can.' Realising who these men must be, he decided to let them think he was indeed simple-minded. Reaching out, he touched one of the men's bows while he repeated 'John Grant, mm, John Grant,' as if he was thinking awful hard. All the time he was excitedly stroking the bow. The eldest of the brothers, who had succeeded his father as chieftain, decided to humour this daft auld carle.

'You can have a shot of it if you tell us where we can find John Grant,' said MacDiarmaid.

'Oh yes, oh yes,' shouted Cam Ruadh, reaching for the bow. One of the other brothers, laughing, handed it to him.

When the devious Cam Ruadh placed one end of the bow on the ground and held it like a walking-stick the brothers fell about laughing. The young chieftain asked if the old fellow would like to learn how to use it. At this Cam Ruadh's head bobbed up and down and he actually drooled. Barely keeping a straight face MacDiarmaid chose a nearby tree, pointed to it, then drew, notched and fired an arrow into its trunk in one swift movement. At that Cam Ruadh began to jump about in feigned excitement, all the time making a laughing sound with his high squeaky voice.

'Now it's your turn,' the Argyll chieftain said with a smile, 'Try and hit that boulder over there, on the other side of the stream.' He pointed to the boulder abut thirty metres away from where they were standing. After a few fumbling attempts Cam Ruadh seemed to get the idea and began to let fly arrow after arrow at the rock. All missed their mark by a good bit. His companions found the display hilarious. At last Cam Ruadh had one arrow left in the quiver he had been given. Just at that moment a sparrow landed on the grey rock. He took aim and fired. The arrow hit the wee bird and he whooped in excitement and splashed through the burn to pick up the bird. He picked it up and began to dance around while the MacDairmaids were shaking their heads and laughing. They were really enjoying the show.

As he danced round and round the big, grey boulder, the canny redhead began to gather up the arrows. After every few arrows he would go back and lay them by the boulder, all the time looking at the bird in his hands and laughing squeakily. Soon he had gathered up the last of the arrows and went back to the rock. The MacDiarmaid chieftain called to him to come back over the burn. Cam Ruadh notched an arrow, knelt behind the boulder and drew his aim on the eldest brother. 'I am John Grant, known as Cam Ruadh and I think you know of my skill with the bow,' he shouted. The horrified MacDiarmaids were rooted to the spot.

'Mercy,' cried their leader 'and we'll retire without any bother.'

'Off you go then,' replied Cam Ruadh.

The MacDairmaids were brave men but they weren't fools, so they turned and ran. They knew only too well of this man's skill with bow and arrow. As they fled Cam Ruadh followed behind them giving an occasional shout to hurry them along. Once he was satisfied they were heading home he turned back towards Glenshee. 'The poor fools,' he muttered, running the sodden bow-string through his fingers. The leather thong had got soaked as he ran through the burn and was useless. He had bluffed his would-be attackers with a wet bow string. His cunning had served him well. This wasn't the last time Cam Ruadh was involved with the Cromar MacDiarmaids. Further enraged by having the tables turned on them by their father's killer their thirst for revenge was only increased. They decided to have another go at John Grant, this time in the depth of winter. Again their spies went through Glenshee and this time they found out exactly where Cam Ruadh lived. No one would expect them to attack during the bad weather and waiting till the worst of the winter weather they set off to settle their account with Cam Ruadh. However, bad as the weather was when they left their home in Argyll, by the time they were approaching Glenshee it was much, much worse. A wild blizzard was blowing by the time they got to Cam Ruadh's cottage and even these tough Highland warriors were in danger of death from exposure and exhaustion. They closed in on the cottage but it was all barred and shuttered against the storm. The door seemed impregnable and if they forced a window they would be noticed and it was unlikely that Cam Ruadh wouldn't be able to pick off most of them as they entered the house, they were so exhausted and cold. So they stood in a line along the wall of the cottage outside the door, slowly freezing, waiting for some kind of opportunity.

Meanwhile inside the cottage Cam Ruadh and his wife sat snug by a blazing peat fire. At the other end of the long black house the animals snuffled in the dark and the whole building was warm and safe from the mighty storm blowing outside. As they sat by the roaring fire the wind outside died down suddenly. Mrs Grant looked at her husband and asked, 'What would you do Cam, if the Cleansers came by tonight?'

'I would let them in by the fire and give them meat,' he replied.

'And then what would you be doing?' continued his wife.

'I would let them sleep through the worst of the storm,' he said in his high voice.

'And what would you be doing then?' asked his wife, astonished at this seeming show of moderation.

'Och, I would let them be gone when the storm passed.' said her husband.

'Be as good as your word,' cried a gruff and quivering voice from outside the door, 'for we are in a terrible state out here.'

Realising that his enemies were indeed at his door, Cam Ruadh sprang to his feet, picking up his sword and dirk. 'Surrender your arms first,' he shouted.

'Send your good wife to the door and we'll give them to her,' came the reply.

Mrs Grant went to the door and in the wild, blowing snow of the blizzard one by one the MacDiarmaids handed over their weapons. They were taken by Cam Ruadh and hidden in the rafters of the cottage. When he was satisfied he had all the arms by checking on the numbers outside he let the half-frozen MacDiarmaid brothers come in. A couple of them had to be carried in and they all went right to the blazing fire with hardly a look at their intended victim. It was obvious that their journey through the blizzard over the mountain passes had weakened them past any thought of revenge. Their only thought was to get out of the blizzard.

Cam Ruadh was as good as his word. While a sheep was brought through from the other end of the house, slaughtered, butchered and put on to cook, Mrs Grant gave her unbidden guests bannocks and cheese to keep them going. Her husband brought out a large jar or two of ale and a coggie of whisky. Within a short while the MacDiarmaids were fed and warmed and ready for sleep. They all knew that in these terrible conditions they could never have flushed their intended victim from his snug den. Had they attacked it was unlikely most of them would have ever seen Argyll again. All knew it but none spoke of it. Once they were all fed and warmed the eldest of the MacDiarmaids spoke up, 'You have saved all our lives this night, John Grant. I think we will no longer be looking for revenge. You have shown us such hospitality as our father always showed strangers and we thank you for that. Will you shake my hand on that?'

'I will indeed,' said the strange looking wee man, and put down the sword that had never left his hand since he heard the voice from outside the door. So the two enemies shook hands and all thought of revenge disappeared.

The result of all this was that Cam Ruadh and the MacDiarmaids entered into a mutual alliance in times of need. Though he was but one and they seven, the brothers knew it was a fair bargain, due to Cam Ruadh's near legendary skill with the bow, and his great guile. For two days the blizzard blew, and when at last the Argyll Cleansers left for home they knew they had a staunch and loyal friend in far Glenshee. And Cam Ruadh was well satisfied – he had made friends of his enemies.

It wasn't long before this mutual alliance was put to the test. The following summer the MacDiarmaids found themselves in open warfare with a local clan who outnumbered them substantially. A young lad was sent over the hills to summon Cam Ruadh. As soon as he got the message he fetched his weapons, said goodbye to his wife and set off at a run. The young messenger told him where to go and was soon left far behind. Over the Moulin Moors and down to Pitlochry he went, without a stop. Then he went north and turned west to take the road along by Loch Tummel and Loch Rannoch and down by the Black Mount into Argyll. Less than two days later, having covered over seventy miles of the Highlands he came to the MacDiarmaid home. Here he was met by the brothers' mother. He asked where they were. She looked askance at this ugly, bow-legged wee bachle. 'Are you here to help them then?' she asked.

'I am that indeed,' replied the wee man. Although he was fully armed with broadsword, dirk, targe and his beloved bow and arrows he hardly had the look of a mighty warrior to her eyes.

'Well, you're late, They have gone already. Anyway, it strikes me that if they'll do with you, they'll do without you,' said Mrs MacDiarmaid.

'That may very well be the way of it, but I'll go and see anyway,' came the reply.

So she pointed out the direction in which they had gone and told the strange wee man where he might find her sons. At once he ran off at a great pace and was soon out of sight. He caught up with his friends in the very nick of time. They were in flight before a much larger group of their enemies when Cam Ruadh came over a ridge above them. Running to a suitable position Cam Ruadh knelt and set about his work. Shaft after shaft flew straight and true, and soon the glen below was littered with still and writhing figures. Each arrow found its mark. The pursuit slowed and then stopped. Seeing their chance the MacDiar-maids turned and charged. Soon their enemies were fleeing from the swords of the brothers and the deadly arrows of a man they hadn't even seen.

The meeting between John Grant and his allies was a joyous one. Once again he had saved their lives and the brothers were suitably thankful. They lavished praise upon the wee man and took him home to their mother. There they introduced their friend to her and told her of how he had saved their lives with his great skill as an archer. Though grateful for his intervention on her sons' behalf Mrs MacDiarmaid was a lady of some character and remarked that she still didn't think he looked much like a warrior.

This caused great hilarity amongst her sons who proceeded to repay the hospitality they had received at Cam Ruadh's house the previous winter. They had won a notable victory with their friend's help and celebration was the order of the day. The celebrations went on for several days before the one-eyed archer set off home. His activities in Argyll only added to his fearsome reputation and fear of his future intervention helped keep the MacDiarmaids free of attack by their enemies.

Cam Ruadh's reputation and his friendship with the Mac-Diarmaids cut down the attacks by cleansers on the Glenshee area and his life became more peaceful. However, raiding went on and it is said that it was Cam Ruadh's example that led to the ploy of including a white cow in every substantial herd of cattle so that trailing caterans by night would be a lot easier, a ploy that served him and his neighbours well.

In all future situations Cam Ruadh was always to the fore, though with his reputation the need for actual battle had become much reduced. At last at a good age John Grant, An Cam Ruadh, died peacefully in his bed at home. He left behind him a fund of stories that still, more than three centuries later, can thrill and excite us. An unlikely hero he might have been but a hero nonetheless.

Spirit Castle

Given the nature of clan society it is hardly surprising that sometimes cattle-raiding could lead to wholesale battle and great tragedy. The Highlanders' sense of honour and readiness for battle could easily transform into pride, even arrogance and bloodthirstiness. Once they were aroused there is little doubt that many of the clan warriors were capable of quite extreme brutality. Back in the time of Alexander MacDondald, Lord of the Isles, in the fifteenth century, he gave Hector Buie Maclean the role of Warden of the area around Glen Urquhart. This area was regularly raided by cateran from Lochaber, whose raiding all over Scotland was partly because of a lack of good pastureland in their own area. There were those however who said it was just a matter of inclination, and a preference for battle over work of any kind. Now the most powerful of the Lochaber chiefs was Lochiel, head of the Cameron clan, and Alexander was hoping that Hector would be able to do something about controlling Lochiel. Alexander himself had suffered too often at the hands of Lochaber raiders and Hector was well aware that there was bad blood between the Lord of the Isles and Lochiel at this point.

Throughout much of the Middle Ages there was a great deal of coming and going between Scotland and Ireland. Since as long ago as the Stone Age people had been coming back and forward between the northern Irish and Scottish coasts and there were many inter-related families. One summer Lochiel had been invited over to Ireland by one of their high-chiefs and decided to do it in style. The Highland clans were always keen that their chiefs should be the equal if not the superior of all other clan chiefs, be it in dress, manners and in the number of attendant warriors they had. This was something that the whole clan appreciated and the chiefs themselves, of course, were always delighted to cut a dash. So it was that Lochiel went off to Ireland, determined to demonstrate his status to his Irish friends and taking with him most of his Cameron clansmen. This of course left the Lochaber clan lands open to attack.

Now Hector Maclean had been given his position by the Lord of the Isles because of his intelligence and cunning. For many years he had been developing a network of contacts, not just amongst his own and related clans, but amongst the tinkers, the travelling tinsmiths and other artisans and merchants who frequented the Highlands and Islands of Scotland. Thus it was that, sitting in Castle Bona, near Dores on the east bank of Loch Ness, he heard about the preparations for the Camerons' visit to Ireland before they had even left! He realised that he was being presented with a chance that might never come again.

It was only a day or two after Lochiel and his men had sailed off to Ireland in a veritable armada of birlinns, that the Macleans came marching down the Great Glen to harry Lochaber. Hector had laid his plans a good while before and could now put them into action. This was no simple cattle-raid but a wholesale harrying of the area. It was payback for years of Cameron raiding and the Macleans lifted everything they could carry from both sides of Loch Lochy. Apart from every cow, horse, sheep, pig and goat they took armaments, furniture and a great deal of the store-corn that the Lochaber people had put aside for the winter. There was of course considerable resistance from the warriors left behind but they had no chance against much superior numbers. Many of them died fighting and there were considerable casualties amongst the Macleans. Hector really did 'cleanse' the area before heading back to Castle Bona with a couple of dozen prisoners as hostage. He knew that Lochiel would seek revenge as soon as he returned and found out what had happened, so the hostages seemed a sensible precaution. Lochiel returned to find the lands around Loch Lochy devastated.

After first organising food for his people – he had a considerable amount of gold and had taken most of it to Ireland, Lochiel began to lay his plans. His sense of honour would in no way allow him to let this attack pass without fighting back. In fact it took a great deal of effort on his part to stop many of his clansmen from heading north as soon as they discovered what Hector had been up to.

'Caution, lads,' he said to his assembled men, 'caution for a while, then the day will come. And you have my word that that day will not be far off.' This last statement was met with a rousing cheer; the Lochaber men would not have to wait long for revenge.

Now Lochiel, if not as cunning as Hector, was no fool, and he too could access information from contacts throughout the area between Lochaber and Inverness. He reasoned that a head-on assault on Hector, whom he found out was at Castle Bona, would probably result in the immediate slaughter of the dozens of hostages, women and children amongst them, that Maclean had taken with him. He needed some kind of bargaining power to try and release the hostages. Soon word came that two of Hector's sons were in Glen Moriston, hunting. At once he called together a couple of dozen of the most experienced cateran in his clan and sent them off under cover of night towards the north. Their task was to capture the Maclean brothers and send word back to Lochiel. They were then to hide out with their prisoners till Lochiel and a great force of Lochaber men, from his own and other clans, could come up to them.

A couple of days later word arrived that Hector's sons had been captured and Lochiel sent round the *crann-tara*. This was the ancient summoning signal for the Highland clans. A cross of wood, with one end of the transverse bar burnt and the other dipped in goat's blood, was sent around all of the clan. All that the bearer had to tell the men of the clan he met, was where and when. They then had to gather up their armaments, with food enough for a week's or even two weeks' campaigning, and make for the rallying point. A runner would arrive in one clachan with the fiery cross and a man from there would run on with it to the next clachan, and so on, each runner then going home for his own kit before reporting to the rallying point. It was an ancient, extremely simple and spectacularly effective way of mustering the men. Within a few hours the entire complement of a clan's fighting men could be assembled. All ready and kitted out for raiding or battle and ready to be off at a moment's notice.

Within a few hours Lochiel had a force of between six and seven hundred men, more even than the four hundred plus who had come south with Hector Maclean.

The Lochaber contingent headed up the Great Glen towards Castle Bona, picking up Hector's sons and their escort on the way. Hector soon heard word of their coming and sent a messenger to tell them that if they did not retreat immediately he would kill all his hostages. Lochiel spoke to the messenger himself.

'Go you and tell Hector Buie that I have his two sons here with me. If he harms a hair on the head of any of my people, the same fate will follow for his sons. Now go.' And at that the Maclean messenger ran back to tell Hector what had happened. The Camerons and the others pressed on and soon came to Castle Bona. Hector looked out from his castle and saw that he was surrounded. He also saw that a messenger was coming to the castle. This was a cousin of Lochiel's who had come with an offer of a prisoner exchange, after which there could be a meeting to see what would happen next. Hector realised that his position was not that strong. If he gave back the prisoners he would be losing control of the situation. In truth he was surprised at Lochiel's boldness. He knew how Lochiel concerned himself with his people and thought that the threat of killing the hostages would have kept him off. His plan had not worked and Hector grew angry.

Lochiel had a large body of men. He couldn't get out to raise all his own support, which might not have been enough anyway. This was a mighty show of force by the Lochaber clans. He got angrier and angrier as he saw his plans falling to pieces. In any set battle at the moment he had no chance against the Camerons. Intelligent, cunning and capable he may have been but Hector made a fatal mistake. He let his anger get the better of him. How dare Lochiel blithely demand the release of the prisoners and then a further parley. He would show him how a true warrior faced up to things!

Calling on his closest aides he gave them their instructions. Down on the plain the Camerons could only watch as one by one their relatives were killed and thrown over the battlements. Fathers watched as their sons and were killed, sons saw their fathers die and the hearts of the Lochaber men turned to stone. The two Maclean brothers were brought forward and Lochiel ordered them to be hanged there before the castle walls with their father looking on. If he had hoped to face down Lochiel he had failed. His anger had got the better of him and Hector could only watch as his sons kicked out their last breaths at the end of a rope. Then the Lochaber men attacked the castle, It was a strong enough built castle but much of it was wood and the Camerons used fire arrows to set it alight. They cut down a great tree in the nearby woods and despite men falling under the fire they smashed the door of the castle to pieces with it. Then they streamed in to Castle Bona. After what they had been forced to witness there was no hope of mercy. Every last living being in the castle was put to the sword and in the desperate hand-to-hand fighting there were a great many men from Lochaber who fell, never to see their homes again. Hector died, as a warrior should, fighting his enemies, but his people payed a desperate price for his anger and pride.

The castle was smashed to pieces by the Camerons, many of them near mad with grief and anger. Such was the amount of blood spilt here that no one ever tried to rebuild the castle or even to live close by it. In fact such were the dark comings and goings of wraith-like figures, the strange and awful sounds that surrounded the place at night that the locals began to call it Spirit Castle. The locals maintained that the castle was haunted by both sets of murdered prisoners who were said to have joined forces in the spirit world to take revenge on all the humans who had treated them so despicably. No one would go near the place and even in the hours of daylight few would even venture close. Spirit Castle developed a reputation for real horror, and travellers were told to avoid the spot if they could. The unfortunate spirits who were tied to the place are said to have haunted it right up to the 19th century when at last even the foundations of the old castle were removed to make way for the Caledonian Canal.

Chisholms versus Macleans

Some of the raiding between clans expanded to conditions of all out war. Given the pride of the Highland warriors, their clan loyalty and their readiness to fight at a moment's notice this is hardly surprising. In the early 1660s Hector MacAlasdair of the Clan Maclean had been caught and hung by the chief of Clan Chisholm after a series of raids that had been undertaken under cover of the war between Cromwell and the Highland Jacobites. The Highlander with his loyalty to kin and clan might get involved in national political affairs, but his basic interests were shaped by his upbringing within the clan system. So it was that even civil war could be seen as an opportunity for raiding and plunder. There is an echo here of the third-century Roman writer, Dio Cassius, when he described the tribal peoples of Scotland thus: 'They are fond of plundering, consequently they choose their boldest men as rulers.' Things would not appear to have changed much between then and the 17th century!

Hector MacAlasdair left many relations behind him and his sons decided they would have their revenge. John Maol, Bald John, Allan and Donald along with about sixty others from the Badenoch fell on the Chisholm lands around Glen Urquhart in May 1663 and in the dead of night lifted forty cattle and headed back south through Glen Moriston and the Great Glen. The Chisholms, numbering more than a hundred men, chased after them as soon as the *creach* was discovered. They came over the to Great Glen's eastern side to the Corrieyarrick Pass where they managed to find twenty of the cattle.

John Maol and the others had seen their pursuers approaching and had decided not to stand and fight. They were reluctant however, to let the Chisholms have their cattle back and before they left the scene they hamstrung most of the cattle. So when the Chisholms arrived there was no option for them but to slaughter the beasts and drive home the few that had not been hamstrung by the Macleans. The Macleans might not have gained much from the raid but it had certainly been costly for the Chisholms.

In November of the same year the Macleans returned and in the dead of night set fire to four barns full of corn at Buntait. They fled under the cover darkness, leaving a scene of devastation behind them. This wasn't raiding. No attempt had been made to take the stored grain. It had been deliberately burnt as an act of revenge. Still though the Macleans weren't satisfied and wanted to wreak even further revenge upon their enemies. On 24 March 1664 they came down from the hills on Buntait again and burnt a total of twenty-two houses, leaving a few of the locals dead among the burning ruins. This had gone far beyond inter-clan cattle-raiding, and Robert Chisholm went to the Court at Edinburgh and had the raiders declared rebels, thus allowing him and his allies to pursue them with fire and sword. An excerpt of the writ given out by the court gives a flavour of just how vicious life could be at the time:

> if in pursuit of the said rebels, their assisters or accomplices, there shall happen fire-raising, mutilation, slaughter, destruction of corns or goods, or other inconveniences to follow, we will and grant, and for us and our successors discern and declare that the same shall not be imputed as crime and offence to our said commissioners, nor to the person assisting them in the execution of this our commission.

Not for the first, or the last time, the central authorities in Edinburgh were exempting one group of Highlanders from the actions that they were hunting another clan for committing. The situation was complicated by the fact that Chisholm was deeply in debt and was therefore extremely reluctant to travel outside his own clan lands in case some of his creditors served him with a writ and had him locked up as a debtor. On his own lands amongst his own clan he was safe. He applied for protection while he carried out his commission but the King's Commissioners were in no hurry to suspend the law for any clan chief. They were happy to have them fall upon each other in the time honoured tradition of divide and rule but they were hardly going to lift the law.

However, it wasn't only Chisholm who was commissioned to go after the Buntait raiders. The Government Commissioners thought their best way forward was to follow the time-honoured practice of setting a thief to catch a thief.

Now the clansmen did not consider themelves thieves but skilful cattle-raiders and the man that was set on the cateran on this occason was a man well-versed in the ways of the School of the Moon. This was Iain Donn, John Grant of Glenmoriston. However Iain Donn took his commission as an excuse to settle some old scores with the Robertsons of Inshes near Inverness and promptly attacked and burned all the barns at Culcabock. He totally ignored the Macleans. The Robertsons of Inshes themselves went to court to have a judgement against Iain Donn and the matter dragged on for four years, during which time Chisholm could only look on in frustration. The upshot of it all was that effectively the Macleans got away away with it. This is yet another example of the incapacity of the Scottish legal system to deal with the actions of Highland cattle-raiders.

Black Donald the Egyptian

Donald Farquharson lived near Braemar in the middle years of the 18th century. A tall strong man of very dark complexion, he was known as a redoubtable warrior and a crack shot. For many years he was closely associated with Farquharson of Allancuaich, a local chieftain. Donald's nickname suggests that he probably had some gipsy blood, as gipsies or travellers were often known as Egyptians. Perhaps, like the famous freebooter James Mac-Pherson, of 'MacPherson's Rant' fame, his mother had been a gipsy. However given the propensity amongst Gaelic speakers to give each other nicknames, perhaps he just looked like a gipsy. He first came to prominence on a revenge raid to Lochaber after caterans from there had murdered Farquharson of Coldrach. Now the details are unknown of how Farquharson died, but it probably had something to do with previous encounters between raiders from Lochaber and the Braemar men under Coldrach's leadership. On many an occasion he had got the better of the Lochaber men. Whatever actually happened the Braemar men were set on revenge for their chieftain's death and what better way to have their revenge than to go and raid the Lochaber men themselves.

So a force of five hundred Highland warriors, under the leadership of Farquharson of Invercauld set off to cross the country. Up the River Geldie, through Glentarf, by Loch Erroch and through Glen Roy to Loch Lochy, they came down into Glen Albyn, not under cover of darkness, but in broad daylight, pipers playing at the front and banners waving. As the pipes roared out the 'Braes o' Mar', they swept along the banks of the loch, driving all the livestock before them and ransacking every substantial house they passed. They came so swiftly and in such numbers that resistance was impossible and the Lochaber people melted away before them, retreating into the hills. Back to Strathspey they headed. A day or two later they were gathered with their booty at a spot still called Laggan a-bhagaiste, the hollow of the baggage, about a mile from the Linn of Dee, five miles to the west of Braemar. Now all the way back from Loch Lochy they had been followed by two young lads who had regularly come within earshot and called out, begging to get their father's cattle back. They repeated that they were poor and the cattle were the only thing between their family and outright starvation. The persistence of the brothers, who were MacDonalds, eventually wore down the Braemar men and they were given back the cattle they claimed were their father's. The upshot of this act was that the MacDonalds settled near Braemar and in effect joined the cateran who had raided them!

Now, on the way to Lochaber a strange event happened which made Donald the talk of the whole country roundabout. Stopping with Allancuaich at a friend's house Donald was put out by an old woman who kept staring at him. It was making him feel uncomfortable and when he complained she still continued to look at him after he stormed out. The old lady then said, 'A pretty man, a pretty man, pity he is destined to such an end.' This was too intriguing and Farquharson of Allancuich pressed her to say what she meant by this. In reply, she said that Donald would hang himself by his own garters. She further said that he might get some help if he went to mass every Sunday, but she doubted it. On hearing of the spae-wife's prophecy Donald was much troubled and for several months after the Lochaber raid he made absolutely sure that he got to mass on time every Sunday. One Sunday however the Dee was so swollen by recent heavy rains that he couldn't cross. He was stuck at Auchindryne, unable to get to the church for mass, and was extremely agitated. Like many Highlanders, he was a church-going Catholic but the old ways had never totally disappeared and he feared the power of the old woman's prophecy. The second sight, as it was known in the Highlands, was something everyone was aware of. Seeing Donald's agitation, a local cowherd, who worked for Allancuich, and fancied the idea of owning these by now famous garters said, 'Don't make such a fuss about a mass. I sell you the right and title in the benefit of it, for your garters.' So Donald gave him the garters. That very same night, when all the servants were being called to dinner, it was found that the young herd had hanged himself in Donald's garters! The spae-wife's prophecy was part right at least.

In troubled times Donald the Egyptian was involved in many skirmishes against caterans and his reputation grew. He even served some time in the Black Watch, the government raised Highland company that tried to put a stop to the ancient clan raiding in the years before 1745. The regiment was formed in 1742 by the then Prime Minister William Pitt at the suggestion of Lord Forbes of Culloden. In the 1730s the Farquharsons and McKenzies were at loggerheads and after a lot of skirmishing and brawling fighting men from both sides gathered at Corrie Bhu near Braemar. Neither side was really set on battle, but when clan pride was at stake things were always dangerous. Several go-betweens went back and forward trying to stave off hostilities. One tall dark figure was seen pacing up and down among the Farquharsons exclaiming, 'Blood, blood'. The chief of the McKenzie faction asked who the wild fellow was. The answer came, 'That is the Egyptian and he has sworn that if a ball be shot today it will be his endeavour to send the second one through your heart.' Such was Donald's reputation as a crack-shot that peace was soon made. Some years later all of Scotland was in turmoil as the Pretender arrived and the Egyptian immediately joined Charlie along with his cousin Donald

MacRobaidh Mor. Now he was as skilled a warrior as Donald Dubh but much more bloodthirsty and he actively enjoyed killing. Both of them had served some time in the Black Watch, but when it came to the test they stood with the Pretender and the pair of them refused to admit defeat after Culloden. They returned home to plague and torment the Redcoat garrison at Braemar. In the period after Culloden there were garrisons of government troops all over the Highlands and there were regular patrols looking for those rebels who had refused to surrender. In Braemar and the immediate vicinity there were over one hundred and twenty troops, some of them regularly scouring the countryside. Given that there were Highlanders on both sides, the government troops tended to have a pretty good idea of who they were looking for.

One of the sergeants in the garrison at Braemar made a point of regularly visiting Donald's old mother to tell her what he was going to do to her son when he caught up with him. It was plain that he had been one of those involved in the slaughter after the fateful battle, and that his belief was that the only good Jacobite was a dead one.

One night, feigning being at the end of her tether, she said that her son would meet the sergeant in Coire-nam-muc if he left his gun, and they would fight with swords. Now the sergeant might have been a brutal and disdainful man but he was no coward, and had a high opinion of his own skills as a swordsman. At once the Englishman put down his gun and set off. At that the Egyptian climbed down from the top of the box bed where he had been hiding and with his superior local knowledge got to the rendezvous first. The sergeant arrived and they set to. At first they seemed evenly matched; they were both big men and experienced in battle. However Donald had been brought up since childhood to handle weapons and soon began to get the better of the sergeant. The sergeant began to tire and no matter how he tried he could not get past the Highlander's guard.

Eventually, with a quick twist of his blade, Donald disarmed his opponent and laid him low with a blow from the pommel of his sword. When the sergeant regained his senses he was lying bound hand and foot.

'Now, sergeant, suppose you had me as I have you, what would you do?' inquired our hero.

'Indeed I should kill you,' replied his prisoner.

'Well, as you have been so candid I will spare your life but you shall remember the Ephiteach [Egyptian] to the latest day of your life,' replied Donald.

At this he stripped the soldier, tied his clothes to his back, and untying his legs he whipped him with birch twigs all the way to the Castle Park gate. After this outrage, efforts were doubled to arrest Donald but the Sergeant was *not* to the fore in these attempts.

One night Donald placed a torch on a pole opposite the castle, lit it and lay in wait with half a dozen loaded muskets. As he intended, the soldiers in the castle thought it was poachers and sent a party out to deal with them. As soon as they were close to the light Donald started firing. He was so quick and accurate that the soldiers thought they were in a major ambush and fled, leaving several of their number dead by the river, known long afterwards as Putan Sassenich, the Englishmen's Pool. After this, things got even hotter for Donald and one English captain known as Muckle Miller was particularly brutal dealing with the folk of Deeside in his attempts to bring Donald in. While this was going on Miller's wife – wives accompanying soldiers on active duty was common then – was getting near to childbirth and the captain, a tall strong and handsome man determined to convey her to the Lowlands to get proper medical attention, as if bairns were never born on Deeside. He rode down to towards Glenshee, with his wife following on her horse. They had just got to the the Cairnwell pass when they were stopped by Donald Dubh pointing a gun at him.

Miller demanded swords and fair play but Donald said, 'Such play as you order your men to give me and my countrymen and that is 'shoot them down, bayonet them, shoot them down.' Donald had been so sickened by the man's behaviour that he had no intention of treating him with any honour or respect and simply shot him. The Captain fell dead from his horse and Donald turned to his wife.

She looked straight at him, with not a blink of fear in her eyes.

'I will take you down to the Spittal, and the people there will help you and get you back to your own people,' he said to her. She just nodded and the pair of them set off, leaving Miller's body lying by the roadside. Now Donald had been impressed by Mrs Miller's fortitude but her next comment nearly took his breath away.

'You know I don't have to go back to the Lowlands,' she said as they rode, 'You could marry me.'

Donald look turned and looked at her in amazement. He was speechless. 'Well, after all,' she went on,' Miller killed my first husband and married me. You wouldn't regret it.'

Once he had found his voice again, Donald assured his companion that he could not take a wife, living the outlaw life as he did, but that he surely appreciated the honour of being asked. Later when he told his friends about it they all agreed that women could be much more frightening than men, no matter which part of the country they came from. It wasn't long after this that a farmer in Glenlui, near the Linn of Dee, seduced by the bounty on offer, betrayed Donald and his cousin to the Redcoats and they were dragged in chains to Invercauld Castle which the Redcoats had also garrisoned. The laird, Farquharson of Invercauld, was angry and upset at their capture. He was no out-and-out Jacobite but the behaviour of the British Army in pursuing the rebels had turned his stomach and he felt nothing but sympathy for his fellow countrymen. The army officers tended to be suspicious of all Highlanders who had not actually carried arms on behalf of the king and the quartering of a troop of soldiers in Invercauld was one way of ensuring that he gave no help to the few remaining rebels in the hills. Well, that was the plan anyway.

When the two Donalds were dragged in chains to Invercauld they were thrown into the vaults at the foot of the castle, which had served as a dungeon at various times in the past. The soldiers had decided to await the return of their captain from Aberdeen before the prisoners were executed. They were known rebels and what need was there of a trial? Farquharson decided that he had to do something to help the prisoners, and preferably without compromising his own safety. Now he, like all prominent Highlanders of the time, carried a considerable stock of whisky in his castle. This was the locally made peatreek, a fearsomely powerful drink to those who were not raised with its startling strength. Once the prisoners were secured and the soldiers sat down to eat he brought out a greybeard, or flagon of whisky and invited all present to try it. The smooth tasting liquor was greatly appreciated by the soldiers and the bottle passed round and round. It was soon empty, but Farquharson merely had another one brought, asking if the men on sentry duty would like a dram as well. This was considered a good idea by the soldiers round the table who were all well oiled by this time. They were delighted at this hospitality and it didn't take long for them to get blind drunk. Within a couple of hours all but the Captain's secretary were asleep in their chairs or at their posts. Farquharson had sent word to the prisoners to be ready to escape and once the soldiers were out of action they wasted no time in breaking down their cell door. The secretary however had suspected something was going on and on hearing the noise of the door shattering below he ran down stairs, grabbing a gun from a slumped sentry as he passed. Just at that moment the two big Highlanders appeared in the corridor still handcuffed. The secretary made a run at them with the bayonet trying to drive them back. Then he tripped, accidentally of course, over the foot of one of Farquharson's men. The two Donalds jumped over his prostrate form, ran up the stairs and off into the night, There on the hill a group of their friends, well warned in advance, were waiting to strike off their cuffs. The secretary, a brave and dutiful man, realising there was no help to be had from the soldiers lying drunk all over the castle decided to ride off to Aberdeen to summon help. He leapt on a horse and rode off into the night, but as soon as he was out of the castle Invercauld sent word to Donald Dubh and the two ex-prisoners set off in pursuit. He realised that if the man got to Aberdeen his part in the escape would be difficult to hide and he would face serious charges, perhaps even the death penalty for aiding and abetting the escape. The two Donalds would have to go and stop him. They were to light a signal fire on Craig Chliny if they caught him to let Invercauld know it was safe for him to remain at the castle. If there was no fire the chieftain would have to join the Egyptian and his friends living wild in the hills, before more soldiers arrived from Aberdeen. The secretary had the advantage of being on horseback and having a head-start but it did him no good. In those days the Deeside roads were still little more than dirt-tracks and the hunters had the advantage of a lifetime's knowledge of the area. So, even on foot, the remorseless High-landmen managed to catch up with their prey between Tullich and Culbleen. By the time they had him in sight, it was daylight and MacRobaidh Mor shot the horse from under the fleeing Englishman. The two Highlanders ran up to where the secretary lay sprawled on the ground and then, despite Donald Dubh's protestations about the man's defenceless state, his cousin finished him off with his sword as he lay on the ground. Wiping the blood off his sword with a piece of the dead man's coat he said simply, 'Dead men tell no tales.' They buried the body nearby.

An inquiry into the escape and the disappearance of the

secretary was held and several of the soldiers were disciplined, but there was no definite proof against Farquharson. After this though, Invercauld was under suspicion and an increased garrison was installed in his castle. Feeling that he must do something to help his benefactor Donald Dubh came up with a plan. The laird, it seems, always sat at the same place when dining in Invercauld Castle, and this was in front of a window. Donald sent word for the laird to move his position one night. Just as the meal was being served that night a bullet smashed through the window and went right through the back of the chair where Invercauld usually sat, taking off the thumb of the serving man and splattering the haggis he was carrying all over the wall in which the bullet buried itself. All rushed to the window in time to see a tall dark figure beyond the river who waved his gun in the air and cried, 'That is for the traitor Saxon laird of Invercauld from me, Donald Dubh, the Egyptian.' The ruse was successful and Invercauld was cleared of the suspicion of complicity with the outlaw cousins. Eventually even the ardour of Donald Dubh cooled and he even ended up dying in his bed at a good age, unlike his cousin who fell victim to a relation of one of his past victims not long after this exploit.

Big Donald

One of the cateran who regularly preyed on the people of the Braes o' Mar was a man called simply Domhnull Mor, 'Big Donald'. He was from Lochaber and might have been a Cameron. Whatever clan he belonged to he epitomised both the courage and inventiveness of the truly successful cateran. One time he had come over to Glencluny on the road from Blairgowrie to Braemar. As usual with cateran raids they rounded up the cattle before dawn and were heading west when they realised that a substantial body of the local men were on their trail. It was obvious that they were greatly outnumbered and some of Donald's followers suggested they should abandon the cattle and make straight for home. This was not an acceptable idea to Donald's way of thinking. They had gone to a lot of effort to 'lift' the cattle and he was determined to keep them. Telling his men to keep together and herd the cattle in front of them as fast as they could he said he would bring up the rear himself with their piper. As soon as they had disappeared over the hill to the west Donald put his plan into action. He sent his piper down towards Glenshee, playing as he went. So, as the Cluny men came over the hills they heard the sounds of the Pibroch of Donald Dubh to their left. The piper had been well instructed by Donald Mor. He would play for a short while on the shoulder of a hill then stop and run over the brow of the hill before repeating the exercise on another hill further south. Being on his own he could keep up a good pace, and despite stopping to play he kept well ahead of his pursuers.

Eventually he came into Glenshee, fifteen kilometres to the south. Here he was seized by the locals who, seeing a stranger, noticed that he was drenched in sweat and correctly assumed that he was being pursued. Meanwhile Donald had rejoined the rest of the men and followed the Baddoch Burn up to Loch nan Eun and then went through the hills towards Glen Tilt and off to the west. When the Glen Cluny men reached Glen Shee they were enraged to find they had been led on a wild goose chase. Furious at both the loss of their cattle and the way they had been duped by Donald Mor they shot the piper out of hand, hardly behaviour that fitted in with the idea of cothrom na Feinne. Donald Mor and the rest of the men got safely back to Lochaber, but soon word came of the fate of the piper who had fulfilled Donald's orders so well and at such a cost to himself.

Disgusted at the Cluny men's actions Donald vowed to avenge the death of his piper. He decided there and then to mount another raid in the area, this time on Glenshee. Very few of his companions could be persuaded to join him, reasoning that the area of Glenshee and Glen Cluny would be a bit like a hornet's nest, with all the people of the area looking out for raiders and all the men going about fully armed at all times. There were others however who agreed with Donald that the people in Glenshee would not be expecting another raid so soon after the first one and would probably not be on their guard.

So it was that Donald set out with a small but committed and experienced band of warriors to raid Glenshee. Sure enough, taking care to move as surreptitiously as they could through the hills, they found that the cattle of Glenshee were hardly guarded at all. So again Donald's skill at moving cattle silently in the hours before dawn came into play and they disappeared into the hills with the very best beasts that they could find. They made great speed into the hills but as the morning sun rose the mist came down. Now the mist in the Highlands can be so dense that you can hardly see your hand in front of your face, and unless you know the ground extremely well the best plan is always to stop and wait till the mist clears. So it happened that Donald and his men were forced to make camp at Corrie Shith. Sure that the mist was so thick that the Glenshee men would also have to stop, Donald gave permission for a fire to be lit so that they could all have a hot meal. But amongst the Glenshee men on their trail, along with a healthy number of their cousins from nearby Glen Isla, were some who refused to let the mist stop them. Some of the pursuers felt that going on might just lead them into a trap, but there were local men there who knew these hills extremely well and were determined to get after the cateran. There was fierce argument as they all assumed that Donald Mor had a large band with them, they had no idea at all that there were only a total of eight men ahead of them. The upshot was that a group of about the same number, headed up by a couple of experienced warriors from Glen Isla, went on through the mist. At length they saw a faint glow ahead of them in the mist. A fire! Surprised at the audacity of the Lochaber raiders they crept slowly on through the heather. Soon the mist was drifting enough for them to see there were just more than a handful of men around the fire. Still they could not be sure that there was not a larger number somewhere nearby. So rather than charge the men they decided to open fire from a distance. So those with guns knelt, took aim at the dim figures through the mist, and fired. Immediately two of the figures fell and the others disappeared into the mist. Slowly, still unsure of the numbers ahead of them, they advanced on the corrie, just as the mist began to rise. Suddenly they could clearly see that the Corrie was empty of all but the cattle and the two still figures by the fire.

When they came up to the fire they recognised Donald Mor lying there with the remains of his last meal still in his mouth. Now it was customary when possible to bury dead warriors on the battlefield where they lay and this was what was done. However, something then happened which perfectly illustrates the code of honour that existed among the Highland warriors, even if the killing of Donald Mor's piper tells of the opposite. On hearing of Donald Mor's death his relatives and friends decided they didn't want one of their chieftains lying on the hillside. So, under a flag of truce a group of Lochaber men, all of some standing in their community, came to Glenshee and asked if they could take up their hero's body and have it re-interred in the kirkyard at Glenshee. They presented such a gracious and honourable aspect to the Glenshee men that their request was granted and the Lochaber warrior Donald Mor was buried in the sacred ground of Glenshee kirkyard.

Although this was done, the man who had actually shot Donald Mor that day at Corrie Shith lived in fear of revenge for the rest of his life. The fact that the deputation from Lochaber had consisted of obvious men of standing only increased his fears, and for the rest of his life he was never seen outside without a gun in his and a sword by his side. Even by his own hearth fire he kept the gun handy and on more than one occasion almost shot a member of his family, coming in on him unexpectedly, such was his paranoia.

A Nice Surprise

In the early years of the 18th century Seumas Mackintosh was a farmer at Balchraggan near Loch Ashie to the south of Inverness. Like many others in the areas bordering the Highlands his family had moved on to relatively fertile low-lying ground, forsaking the traditional self-sufficiency of the clan way of life for more modern farming, and the attendant money economy of the Lowland areas. He was aware that there were cateran in the hills to the south of his land. He regularly saw the tracks left by them driving herds of cattle and other beasts from raids on Ross and Sutherland, but thought himself immune. They were a particularly nasty bunch as they were adept at passing the blame for their activities on to others and stirring up quarrels between neighbouring clans. In the ensuing struggles they would always make a profit for themselves. However, as he knew a few of them were from the Mackintosh clan themselves it never crossed his mind that they might do him any harm. He had been doing well, successfully farming cattle, and one year he bought himself a fine, dun-coloured stallion about seventeen hands high. It was a fine horse and he was very pleased to be able to afford such a handsome beast. Apart from its strength and size it was a very biddable horse and Seumas soon grew very fond of the beast, which he called Luath, Gaelic for fast. Nothing gave him more pleasure than going for long rides through the hills and down to the coast, well aware of the admiring glances the beast drew as they passed through the clachans and villages of the area. The cateran in the hills however had taken note of his new acquisition and it was only a matter of a month or so later that his horse was lifted in the night. He tried in vain to follow its trail without success. After a couple of miles the horse had been led into a stream and he was pretty certain that it had been walked out over rocks, leaving no discernible trail. Sure as he was that it was the wild bunch in the hills to the south, there was little he could do. He couldn't raise the whole country for the sake of one horse so he just decided to bear his losses. However, he promised himself that if he could ever help anyone against the cateran he would certainly so do. The following Christmas his wife was busy preparing food while her husband was out tending his cattle. It was a wild night and she was hoping he would come home soon out of the storm. She kept going to the door to look for him, but there was no sign. Eventually he came back just as the weather broke. They were sitting down to their meal when they heard a noise; it was the whinnying of a horse.

'Heavens wife, if he is still alive, that is the sound of our good dun horse', Seumas shouted as he jumped from his seat. They ran to the door and there in the moonlight was the dun stallion. Seumas was absolutely overjoyed that the beast had found its way back to Balchraggan. He had thought he would never see the beast again. He had even more delight when he saw that strapped to its back were two ankers of whisky and tied to its tail was a fine black pony which also had two ankers of whisky on its back. The celebration of the New Year at Balchraggan that year was imminent, and Seumas wasn't about to look a gift horse in the mouth, as the saying goes. Even if the victims of the orignal theft traced the dun stallion's tracks, he had plenty of witnesses that it had been stolen from him in the first place and, as to the whisky, well, the evidence wasn't around for long!

An Gille Dubh nam Mairt, The Dark Lad of the Cattle

━━━◆◆◆━━━

Now although the cateran were brought up within the strict code of honour that traditionally applied to all Highland warriors, human nature is a complex thing. Apart from blood feuds that arose from time to time there were also examples of downright treacherous behaviour that would almost invariably lead to further acts of violence. One winter's night back in the late 17th century in Glen Urquhart, the gudewife of Shewglie heard knocking at her door. It was a bitterly cold night, and when she went to the door she found a young woman she had never seen before who was obviously about to give birth. The poor lassie had been deserted by a travelling man she had married and was too ashamed to go back to her own people in Lochaber. She had wandered through the Highlands, not knowing what was to become of her. Once the baby was born, a healthy boy, the young lass wanted nothing more to do with him. Rather than try and stay where she was and raise the child among strangers, she wanted to return home, but without the baby.

It was a tragic story, and even though the gudewife of Shewglie thought it a dreadful thing to abandon a child she agreed that the boy could stay and be raised there in the glen. However, the road to Hell is paved with good intentions they say, and as he wasn't her own child she didn't take as good care of him as she should have, and the laddie wasn't even christened. As he got a little older he was sent to tend the cattle at Shewglie and became known as An Gille Dubh nam Mairt. It was all the name he was ever given. Children being the way they always have been, he was given a hard time in his growing up about his origins. Nobody knew who his father was and as he hadn't even been christened he couldn't really be seen as one of the Grant clan, even if they were the only people he knew. The sad fact was that he not only did not know who his father was, he did not know who his mother had been either, and when he asked the woman at Shewglie, she had nothing she could tell him, other than that his mother had said she came originally from Lochaber. Now back then clan feelings ran very strong and there is no doubt that An Gille Dubh felt himself to be an outsider amongst the Grants in Glenurquhart. So as soon as he could, he up and left Glenurquhart for Lochaber, where he thought he might at least feel a bit at home. The sad thing was that no one really missed him at all; he had never been taken into the Grant family at Shewglie, a lack of hospitality that in time would prove to have been costly.

In 1692 An Gille Dubh came back to the glen, but he was the guide for a raiding group from Lochaber. And what a guide he was: he knew where all the cattle would be, and every quiet way in and out of the glen. The only place they didn't lift the cattle was at Shewglie; the raiders just passed it by. Now this raid took place in the daytime when the local people were off getting in the peats for winter and there were only a few women and children and old people in the Glen, and they could put up no real resistance to the Lochaber men. So the raiders got clean away and headed south through Corribuy, across Glen Coilty and on south towards Lochaber.

Now behind them word was sent off to the peat moss and the men all rushed back down into the glen. Now James Grant of Shewglie, who had fought at the famous battle of Killiecrankie, was chosen to lead the pursuit. Listening to the reports of the raiders he suggested that more recruits were needed from further up the glen as the numbers they had there were no match for the Lochaber men. Now James's wife Hannah was a fierce woman. On hearing her husband's advice for caution she burst out, 'I will follow the Lochaber men, James Grant, and you can stay at home and spin the wheel.' This would have been bad enough at any time, but as Hannah was heavily pregnant, well into her eighth month, it was a terrible rebuke.

Shamed by his wife's comment, James had little option but to pursue the raiders with the men that were handy. Making much better time than the Lochaber men who were driving the Glenurquhart cattle they soon caught up with the raiding party, near the spot since known as Carn Mharb Dhaoine, the Rock of the Dead Men.

As the raiders turned to face their pursuers, who they realised were few in number, An Gille Dubh and James Grant came face to face.

'I little thought,' said James, 'that you would be the one to lift cattle in Glenurquhart.'

'And I little thought that you, of all people,' replied An Gille Dubh, 'would come after us, as we did not touch a beast of yours at Shewglie.'

Despite the fact that all the men were armed and ready for battle on both sides, an agreement was reached. The Lochaber men would return their spoils keeping only a handful of beasts to satisfy their honour. Despite his rough upbringing An Gille Dubh preferred to avoid any conflict with Grant of Shewglie: he was the closest thing to a brother he had ever had. So once the deal was done hands were shaken and the Glen Urquhart men headed back with most of their cattle. They hadn't gone more than a couple of hundred paces when a hare sprang up out of the heather at the feet of one of the Glen Urquhart men and bounded uphill towards the Lochaber men. As the hare ran up the hill Kenneth MacDonald of Meikle-na-h-Aitnich swung his musket from his shoulder and fired at the fleeing animal. He missed but that wasn't the only problem. The Lochaber men heard the shot and turned to see MacDonald with his musket at his shoulder pointing in their general direction.

'Treachery, treachery,' cried several of them as they charged down the hill, certain they had been fired at by the Glen Urquhart men.

So open fighting broke out, but with superior numbers it was only a matter of time before the Lochaber men triumphed. They took the cattle and left eight men lying dead on the hillside, and one of them was James Grant of Shewglie. In no doubt that Shewglie had planned this treachery all along, a group of the Lochaber men led by An Gille Dubh, returned to Shewglie to lift the remaining cattle.

The Lochaber men returned to the glen and rounded up the cattle at Shewglie. Just as they were leaving Hannah came to the door of her house, clutching her swollen belly and with tears streaking her face. One of the survivors from the battle on the hill had told her of James's death and she realised what she had done. She looked long and hard at An Gille Dubh.

'Remember that I long befriended you and that I am now a widow about to become the mother of a fatherless child,' she said to him.

'If you are with child, bear a foal,' the young man snapped back, full of anger and a sorrow he did not want to admit to. So the raiders took off with the cattle.

The next few years were hard for Hannah, raising her son without his father, and poorer now than she had ever been. Even with the help of others in the clan, times were hard for her, and most of all she missed her husband and never ceased regretting the fateful words she had uttered on that day. The great cairn was raised to bury James and the others on the hill where they fell and time passed. But even with the passing of time the story of An Gille Dubh's return was not forgotten in Glen Urquhart. The memory of losing so many men in one day was a sore one and the tale was given the name of the Raid of Inchdrine, Inchdrine being where the raiders had first appeared on that fateful day. And in one house in particular the story was repeated time and time again.

Young James Grant heard the story before he knew what the words meant, and as he grew towards manhood the story hardened his heart. It was around 1710 when one night there came knocking at the door of An Gille Dubh's house in Glen Roy. He lived alone and had never taken a wife. He answered the door and there was a strong-looking young man who asked for quarters for the night. In Highland tradition such a request could not be refused and it was customary that no direct questions could be asked of a guest. Whatever information he or she wished to give was sufficient. This custom stretched back into distant history and was universally followed. A further complication was that the guest was under the protection of his host, which in some circumstances led to very peculiar arrangements. It had even been known for a father to defend his son's killer because he had offered him hospitality before he knew of his son's death. Such were the requirements of the ancient code of honour that underlay Highland hospitality.

Once An Gille Dubh had fed his guest and given him a drink of whisky they sat by the hearth in his house and the talk turned to the way of the warrior. Preferences were discussed, and even though his guest was only in his late teens An Gille Dubh realised the lad had some experience and considerable knowledge of weapons and fighting. He himself had been raiding from soon after he had left Glen Urquhart and felt a touch of sympathy for this young man. As the night wore on the young man mentioned the Raid of Inchdrine, the name that had been given to the raid An Gille Dubh had taken into Glen Urquhart.

'Ach aye, I mind that well, it was one of the first raids I ever went on, you know,' said An Gille Dubh, feeling safe and warm by his own hearthside. He then went on to tell of his own central role in the event, taking some pride that the story of the raid had been heard by a lad who by his appearance might not even have been alive at the time. As he finished his tale, and took a sip of whisky, looking at his guest in expectation of some positive comment, the young man stood up before him.

'The hour of vengeance has now arrived,' he shouted, his eyes burning with a fierce light.

'Who are you?' asked An Gille Dubh, dropping his cup of whisky and half-starting from his chair.

'I am the foal which the gudewife of Shewglie was carrying on the day of the raid of Inchdrine,' shouted the younger man as he pulled the dirk from his belt and drove it straight into the heart of his companion. At once he ran from the cottage, leapt on his horse tethered by the door, and took off into the night. By morning he was back in Glen Urquhart just as the light came into the sky: the same light which fell through the open door of a house in Lochaber where lay the lifeless body of An Gille Dubh nam Mairt.

A Latter-day Diarmaid, Peter Roy McGregor

━━━━━◆━━━━━

Now Peter Roy McGregor was not said to have been handsome but he had a devastating effect on the ladies. A small and extremely hirsute, red-haired fellow, he is said to have had a mole on his temple just like the mythological heroes Diarmaid, one of the Fianna, and Angus Og who lived in the timeless land of Tir nan Og, the Land of the Young. Both of these had a mole on their foreheads and any woman seeing the mole fell immediately in love with the hero. Peter, unlike these ancient heroes however, rarely made any attempt to hide the said mole with any kind of headgear! It is rumoured that he entertained as many as half a dozen women in his bothy of a single evening and he had no particulars as to whether it was the maid or the mistress with whom he canoodled – and nor did they!

In 1667 Peter and forty followers raided Keith and laid an arbitrary tax of four pence on 'ilka reekin lum', each smoking chimney. This was a bit like the practice of blackmail but this time the caterans had no intention of providing any services whatsoever – it was really plain extortion. On his way to the raid Peter met with Meg Malloch, Meg of the hairy hand, a renowned prophetess who decided to come along with them. In a pub at Cooperhill where they stopped she prophesied that if Peter wanted to avoid the 'wuddie' or the gallows he should make a point of keeping clear of the Pier of Leith. Meg went into a moaning trance before giving her predictions and the next time she started Peter kicked her to the floor, wanting no more predictions, and she hid from him under the table. In the light of his eventual fate it seems that Meg probably had the gift of the second sight. Peter and the rest of the band sat around making plans for the following day and the good things to come. With the drink flowing there were a few jokes and it was suggested that they could hang the landlord of the inn from the 'couple bauks [rafters] o his ain barn'. It might have been only a jest, but Maggie, one of the servant girls, heard them and took them seriously. She well understood that this group of Highlanders were capable of just about anything. While they continued to carouse she went to the kitchen and made a pot of sowens – oat meal and water. She then went around the main room, and, choosing her moments, poured small amounts of the sowens down the muzzle of the various firearms they had left lying about, thus spiking them. The raiders were so concentrated on their drinking and jesting that they paid no attention to Maggie at all. This gave rise to a well-known phrase in the area: 'There's sowens in your gun', which approximates to the modern and equally explicit phrase: 'you must be firing blanks'. Maggie's actions weren't needed as there was no violence in the inn that night, and eventually Peter Roy and the rest fell asleep where they sat.

Word was sent into the town of Keith that the raiders were in the tavern and the locals gathered in the kirkyard there. Led by Gordon of Glengerrock, they came with their arms and headed off via the Auld Brig o Keith towards Cooperhill preceded by a piper. Just as they were crossing the river a shot rang out and the piper fell over the bridge into the river. His pipes continued making a horrible screaming noise till he was eventually pulled under the water. Battle was closed and hand-to-hand combat was the order of the day. Soon Glengerrock and Peter found themselves fighting each other. Glengerrock began to get the better of things and wounded Peter in his sword arm. Seeing this

Peter's close friend, The Red Laird, as he was known, rushed up and took over. At that Gordon chopped straight through his left hand, almost severing it at the wrist. The Red Laird stood back, stuck his sword in the ground, pulled off his left hand with his right and threw it against the gable end of the church, and fought on. (There was a red stone in that end of the church just under the eaves, which was always harled last, and when the church was demolished it was taken to a local house). The upshot of the battle was that that Peter and his men were forced to retreat with quite a few casualties on both sides. The Highlanders headed back into the hills.

The next morning Gordon decided to go after them and on the road his party came across a serving girl from Brandybrae who was carrying an empty bottle. When asked about it she said she was off for liquor for a wounded man who was lying in the barn at Whiteley, though she hadn't seen him herself. At once the Keith men headed to the barn to be met by the lady of Whiteley farm.

'Good day tae ye, gudewife,' said Gordon from the back of his horse.' I believe ye hae a wounded man in yer barn. It is likely he's ane o the cateran we're chasin.'

'Och, I dinnae know who would tell ye that. There's nae man in my barn, I'll swear on yer dirk if you like,' replied the woman, bold as brass. Now swearing on a dirk was just about the most serious thing any Highlander could do; it was thought as good, if not better, than swearing on the Bible, but Gordon was well aware of who he was up against and his reputation as a ladies' man.

'Na, na, I dinnae think we'll need ye tae dae that,' said Gordon, and motioned his men to go into the barn. In they went and sure enough, there on the straw, covered in blankets with a plate of roasted chicken and a bottle of water by his side, was the wee red-haired man, Peter Roy McGregor himself. The farm-wife had certainly been looking after him. He was dragged

out and tied to the back of a horse, and off the party went, back
to Keith, leaving a rather sad woman behind them.

Peter was to be charged with sorning, wilful fire-raising and
robbery but the local judges realised that his popularity amongst
the ladies of the district, none of whom were in the least jealous
of his favours, would do their best to have him freed . So they
decided to send him to Edinburgh for trial. However, the word
of his capture soon spread through the Strathspey district and
round about, and a collection was soon made amongst the
female population of the area and he was bailed out for 100
crowns, a substantial sum at the time. As the saying goes the
money came from high and low, Peter being popular with ladies
of all kinds of standing in the community. However, once he had
been freed Peter soon returned to his old ways, as regards both
the ladies and raiding. He doesn't really seem to have been cut
out for the raiding life and might have been well advised to have
concentrated all his efforts on the fairer sex.

Again he was caught while raiding, and was again taken to
Edinburgh but this time he was quickly and quietly tried. To the
douce magistrates in Edinburgh he was less like a charmer of
feminine hearts than a particularly repulsive specimen of a
Highland barbarian. A description of the time says he was, 'a
man of robust make, but diminutive stature. The red hair, which
grew thick all over his body, indicated his strength, while it added
to his ugliness, and got him the name of Roy [red]. His stern
features bespoke ferocity: his keen red eyes, and nose like the
eagle's beak, heightened the terrors of his countenance, and
both at his examination and execution he bore an uncommon
severity of torture with a patience and fortitude which excited
astonishment.' One of the judges, Lord Pitmeddie, later told a
friend, 'He bore the torture o the boot wi great constancy an'
was undauntit at his execution, een tho the executioner made a
botch o it, by cutting off his hand.' This is reported in Pitcairn's
Criminal Trials of Scotland 1604–7. After this dreadful experi-

ence, the executioner was sacked forthwith, and Peter was taken out and hung in secret. His body was then removed and hung up between Edinburgh and Leith. To the judges in Edinburgh he was just a thief, and while some of his activities certainly seem criminal, at heart he probably saw himself as a Highland warrior and probably thought the people of Lowland Moray fair game for traditional raiding! Such thinking was totally alien to the judges in Edinburgh. Back in Strathspey there was a long period of mourning amongst women of all classes who missed the wee red-haired man.

Achluachrach's Bridal

James MacDonnell of Achluachrach in Brae Lochaber had at last found himself a lass he wanted to marry. It had taken him a while, he was thirty years old but he had fallen heavily for Kirsty MacDonnell, a niece of a distant cousin of his. Now he realised that the life of a married man was bound to be more taxing than the single life, so in order to set up himself and his bride-to-be in the style he wanted her to be accustomed to, he decided to lead a raid to Morayshire and bring home a good number of cattle. However, when he told Kirsty about his plans, her reaction was not as he had intended.

'Och no, James. Please don't be going on this raid, I beg you. I have had a bad sense of what will befall you if you do go. We can manage quite well without the proceeds of a *creach*, so please just stay here and we'll get married,' she told him one evening.

The look in his lass's eyes told James she was quite serious, and as quite a few in her family had the gift of the second sight such premonitions had to be taken seriously. However plans had already been laid and he had organised a substantial number of his friends to accompany him to Moray. Despite Kirsty's warning he felt that his sense of honour would not allow him to back out of a raid that he himself had organised.

So the following day he and his companions set off, leaving a distraught Kirsty behind, sure she would never see her intended again in this life. It was autumn, the best time for raiding, and over the next couple of nights the Lochaber men made their way through the Monadhliath mountains and over into Morayshire.

They came down to the lands around Kilravock, not far from the fateful ground of Drumossie Moor, better known as Culloden. With great skill, they rounded up a fine herd of cattle and retreated into the hills while the local people were still in their beds. When the sun came up there was consternation in Kilravock. Virtually every beast in the area had been lifted and word was sent to the Castle to fetch the laird. This was Rose of Kilravock, himself a noted warrior, and he wasted no time in gathering a band of armed men to set off after the raiders. Prominent amongst the band setting out was Iain Beg MacAndrew of Dalnahaitnich, Wee Iain. He certainly deserved his nickname as he was barely the size of a twelve-year-old boy. His diminutive stature in no way limited his ability as a fighting man, for he was famed throughout Moray as one of the finest archers that had ever lived.

Now in all raids it was necessary for the raiders to put as many miles as possible between their victims and themselves before pursuit was started. Men driving a herd of cattle would always be slower than the men chasing them. Travelling down through Strathearn, MacDonnell and his men made good time, and by the time they reached a place called Brochlach as night was coming on, they reckoned that they were relatively safe. They found a bothy in the hills there and went inside for a good night's sleep, leaving one of their number as a lookout.

The Moray men however were closer than they thought, and though it was a moonless night they kept on the trail by the faint light of the stars. Just as the sky began to lighten before dawn they were at Brochlach and one of them, sent ahead to scout out the land, returned to tell them he had seen their cattle round a bothy with a sentry standing a few yards off on a small rise. Queitly they crept through the heather, and just as dawn rose they leapt up and charged down the hillside to the bothy. The sentinel shouted a warning, fired a couple of arrows at the charging Moray men, and, realising that he and his companions were outnumbered about three to one, took off into the forest behind him. Such was their surprise that only James MacDonnell and one of his men were out of the bothy before the Moray men were on them. No time for parley here.

'Leave the cattle and scatter lads,' shouted MacDonnell, and ran off towards the forest, sword in hand, closely followed by one of his friends. The others were just beginning to spill out of the bothy when the sound of a bowstring releasing an arrow was heard. And then another. Two arrows and James MacDonnell and his closest companion lay dead in the heather.

'Fine shooting, Iain Beg,' one of the Moray men shouted. And in the half-light of the dawn it certainly had been. The rest of them fell on the Lochaber men near the bothy. The fight was short and brutal, and within a few minutes all of the Lochaber men lay dead. Well not quite all. The sentinel had run into the forest to save his life, but he was no coward. He had hidden just inside the trees to see if he could help his companions but the affair had been too quick for him to do anything. But he had heard the name of the man who had shot down the cateran leader, Iain Beg. He would remember that name he thought, as he made his way stealthily through the forest. The Moray men were too busy rounding up their cattle and congratulating each other on their victory to think of coming after him.

Two days later Kirsty got the news she had been dreading. Her husband-to-be lay cold and dead on a hillside in Moray. Once he had explained how the Moray men had surprised them the sentinel was given no dishonour, and when he told the friends at Achluachrach that he had the name, of the man who had killed him, they decided that they would have to have vengeance. Iain Beg, Little Iain – they knew his name and they knew he lived near Kilravock. That should be enough for them to find out who he was and kill him. However, they did not know just how wee Iain actually was.

Somehow over the winter the Lochaber men found out just

where Iain Beg lived, and that he was a MacAndrew. Perhaps some travelling piper or pedlar had told them, but what is certain is that their intelligence was excellent. One afternoon the following spring, when Iain Beg was sitting beside his own hearth, the door of his house burst open, and half a dozen wild cateran from Lochaber poured into the room.

Now in many of the tales of the cateran, women play a subsidiary row but that day Iain Beg MacAndrew's wife showed the guile and spirit that all Scotsmen know is a big part of our womenfolk. Realising immediately who these rough intruders were, and that her husband had no chance against them in the current situation, she did what women always do better than men: she used her wits.

'Seumas,' she shouted, cuffing Iain across the head, 'go out to the far field an fetch your father.'

Iain needed no second bidding, and the Lochaber men, thinking he was just a boy, let him out of the door. Now Iain had realised that there was a chance of Lochaber caterans coming after him and had had the presence of mind to leave a bow and a quiverful of arrows wrapped in a cow hide in the crook between two branches of a fir tree that stood ten yards from his door. He ran to the tree, shinned up it, unpacked his weapon and shouted to the men inside: 'Here comes Iain Begg now.'

The Lochaber men ran out of the door, swords in hand ready to cut down their prey. What met them was a hail of arrows. Iain's great talent lay not only in his aim but in his speed. Arrow after arrow rained down from the fir tree and each one found its mark. The last cateran turned to get back into the house but Iain's wife had shut and barred the door the second the last intruder crossed her threshold. He was pinned to the door with an arrow through his heart. All six of the Lochaber men lay dead at Iain Beg's door, but people would always say as they told of his prowess, 'His skill with the bow would have done him no good if it wasn't for his wife's quick thinking.'

Daft Davie

Glen Isla, which runs north from Strathmore into the Grampians north of Alyth, was for many years plagued by cateran raids from Lochaber. At one point things had got so bad that it became the custom for the cattle to be brought into a fold every night and a sentry set to guard them through the hours of darkness. Many of what were once thought to be simple fortified structures in Perthshire dating back to the first millennium or earlier are now understood to be cattle folds, underlying the antiquity of the cattle raiding in the Highlands! At the period under consideration the farmer at Dalvanie, by the name of Robertson, was getting on in years but he had three sons. The first two, Charlie and Willie, were fine, strong reliable chiels, but the third son had been born with less than the full complement of brains and couldn't be relied on for much at all. He was known simply as Daft Davie, though he was harmless and a likeable enough lad. Now Charlie and Willie were quite happy at first to take turn-about, watching the cattle at night. However, even after a week or so they were tired out; it was hard enough work tending the cattle during the day without having to try and stay alert every second night. So after a while their father decided to give them both a chance of a good night's sleep and watch over the cattle himself. Neither of the two older lads was happy with this at first; they realised their father was bit long in the tooth to take on the caterans if they turned up, but at last he managed to convince them it would be a good idea if they both had a night in their own beds.

The following morning about six o'clock Willie and Charlie got up. There was no sign of their father about the farmhouse so they proceeded to the cattle fold, thinking he had maybe fallen asleep. The fold wasn't far from the house, less than a hundred yards, but as soon as they crossed the door of the house they knew something was wrong. At once they sprinted to the fold. There was nothing there. Not a hide nor a hair of the cattle could be seen, and worse than that, there was absolutely no sign of their father. The cateran must have taken him along as a hostage!

Without hesitation they ran back to the house to arm themselves with sword and gun, and as Willie went off to rouse the neighbours Charlie went after the cattle. Davie, who was awake by this time, soon realised that his father had been spirited away and decided to follow Charlie. A short while later Willie came back with about a dozen armed men and they set off after his brothers. They caught up with them near Broughanreid on the western slopes of Mount Blair, and Willie noticed that somehow Davie had got hold of a gun, but concerned as he was with his father, he decided to ignore the fact. The cateran had taken the cattle south to Blacklunans, then past Dalrulzion and Craigton, and over the hill towards Strathardle. There on the slopes of Craig Eirionnaich they caught up with the raiders, resting the cattle by the still waters of Loch Mharich. The Lochaber men of course had posted a lookout and saw the Glen Isla men coming. At a shout from their lookout they scattered and took up positions behind boulders and rocks. The Robertsons and their friends came slowly down the hill, guns at the ready, when suddenly, from behind a great boulder came the cateran chief. He stepped into full view with the boys' father held before him, a dirk across his throat.

'Well then, lads, do ye think yer cattle are worth yer father's life then?' He asked with a wicked glint in his eyes.

Willie and Charlie looked at each other. There was no point in rushing him, he would kill their father without hesitation, of that

157

they were sure. Behind them their neighbours were silent. It seemed clear that discussion would be necessary. And it was just as clear that whatever the outcome it would cost them dear. The cateran chief had them at his mercy, with the dirk to Robertson's throat he had command of the situation.

No one had noticed that Davie was nowhere to be seen. He was a very strong and fit man and had been going ahead of the group and off to the side and generally straying about, constantly checking his gun and pointing it at imaginary raiders. Concetrating on following the cateran, his brothers had left him to his own devices; he could follow on as he wished. He now came up from behind.

On seeing what was happening he came up to the front of the group beside his brothers.

'What for are ye no shootin him?' he asked.

'Davie, for Heaven's sake, we could jist as easy hit faither as the man wi the dirk,' hissed Charlie, angry at his brother.

'Ach, he's jist a done auld body lads, whit's the problem,' Daft Davie replied, and in the blink of an eye he raised his gun and fired at the figures before them

Both men at once fell to the ground and the Glen Isla men ran forward to them. There lay the cateran leader, dead, shot straight through the temple, and old Robertson lying across him with a look of consternation on his face. He didn't know whether to cuddle or kick his youngest son! As Charlie and Willie lifted their father off the body of the Lochaber man Davie ran whooping down the hill towards the Loch. There the cateran, having seen their leader fall, were streaming away westward over the hill, leaving the cattle behind them. So the Glen Isla men returned home triumphantly with cattle and the hostage, safe, but whether Davie had been brave or stupid, he had surely saved the day, a situation for which his father was grateful for the rest of his life.

Donald Mor Cameron

A cateran from Lochaber called Donald Mor Cameron came over the hills to Glen Clova in Angus in the years after Culloden. Although he had only a couple of companions he was intent on lifting the cattle of the folk who farmed around Bachnagairn near the head of the River South Esk, not far from Lochnagar. The three of them worked quietly and efficiently and when the sun came up they marched off west, across the top of Glen Prosen and over through the head of Glen Isla. From there they headed up Glen Brichty and down through Glen Beag and into Glenshee. They crossed Glenshee and went up into the hills round the back of Ben Gulbain where they decided to have a rest. They had put a fair distance between themselves and Bachnagairn and thought they would be safe from pursuit for a while.

Back at the head of Glen Clova the raid had been discovered just after sun-up, and a band of men was hastily brought together. By this point most people living in the Highlands had been forced to give up any weapons they had, but the Ogilvy brothers, John and Andrew, who farmed at Holl, in Glen Clova, both arrived with guns. There was a brief discussion and the men, around twenty-four in number, headed up towards the White Mounth on the trail of the stolen cattle. It was about noon when the people in Glen Beag, busy harvesting their fields of oats, saw the band of Glen Clova men come down from the hills and head towards Ben Gulbain.

Their luck was in. Donald Mor, thinking he was well away from the scene of his lifting, hadn't even bothered to keep a lookout. He and his two companions were sitting eating bread and cheese when the Bachnagairn men came round the edge of the hill and saw them. Now, given the hard times that Scotland had suffered over the previous ten years with the '45 and the subsequent troubles throughout the Highlands, the old ideas of fair play were far from the mind of John Ogilvy. He simply saw three thieves who had stolen his and his neighbours' cattle and had forced them to a hard day following them through the hills. He didn't hesitate, but knelt down, lifted his rifle to his shoulder, drew aim on Donald Mor and fired. The first Donald Mor knew of their arrival was a bullet bursting through the back of his jaw and out through his mouth, splattering bread and cheese and shattered teeth all over his chest. He fell to his knees, and even though he had sustained such a serious wound he turned round, drawing a pistol from his belt and looking for whoever had shot him. There he saw John Ogilvy, no more than thirty yards away. John cried out, 'For God's sake, Andra, finish him aff.'

But Andra had already rushed forward. He hadn't had time to prime his gun, which he had been careful not to carry loaded. Just as the cateran brought his pistol to bear on John, Andra reached him. Holding his gun by the muzzle he brought the heavy butt down on Donald Mor's head, with such force that the doghead, the firing mechanism, penetrated his skull! Along with Andra a handful of others had rushed forwards and were attacking the other two cateran with swords. For a few minutes they held off their attackers. Then one of them fell from a thrust to the heart and the other one threw his sword and dirk at the men attacking him, allowing him just enough time to turn and run off up the hill. The Clova men stood and watched him go; they had their cattle back, and that was the most important thing.

The rest of the Clova men had hurried forward to where Andra stood over the dead Donald Mor. John came running up to join his companions. 'Thanks, brither,' he said, holding out his hand. There, over the body of the dead cateran, the two brothers solemnly shook hands before rounding up the cattle and conveying them home over the hills to Bachnagairn. They left the bodies of Donald Mor and his companion where they lay on the hillside. Later the innkeeper at the nearby Spittal of Glenshee came and took them off the hill on a couple of horses and gave them a Christian burial at the Spittal.

The story of what happened that day was handed down through the Ogilvy family and it was said that ever after that day John Ogilvy always went about armed. Even in his own house he would always sit facing the door with an armed weapon close to hand, such was the fear of cateran retaliation even in the second half of the 18th century. However, after that no Camerons ever came over the hills to Glen Clova, either to exact revenge for the killing of Donald Mor or to lift the local cattle. This was one of the last cateran raids ever to take place in Angus, and surely the very last by men from Lochaber.

An interesting sidelight on the business of cattle-lifting comes from the fact that for many years after this Donald Mor's waistcoat was kept in Glenshee. It was noteworthy for the fact that it was adorned with large silver buttons. Some say that given the nature of the cateran business, their leader would wear such a garment in case any of them should die in some place far from home and kin, in which case the silver would pay for a decent Christian burial. Others might think that it was a handy way to keep a decent sum to hand for a whole variety of unexpected situations, and there are many instances of houses in the Highlands where the story is told that some gentleman was hidden from the Redcoats after Culloden and paid his rescuers with the silver buttons from his waistcoat. The story was told in Glen Clova at Brocklas, currently lying uninhabited and desolate. Whatever the reason, Donald Mor Cameron got his Christian burial and lies forever at the Spittal of Glenshee far from the land of his fathers in Lochaber.

The Thin-legged Man

⇒•◈•⇐

One time back in the 16th century the people of Tulloch in Strathspey were in need of a new millstone. The old one had, after centuries of use, become so worn and pitted that it was a major effort to grind any amount of corn at all. To get such a major piece of equipment they would have to go all the way to Forres on the Moray coast. The method of transporting the millstone was to put a strong pole through the central hole and roll it along the road. As it was forty miles from Tulloch to Forres this task would obviously require a good number of men. So it was that virtually all the able-bodied men of the village went off to Forres to bring back the millstone. The only man left of fighting age was the man known as Fear-nan-casan-caol, the thin-legged man, who, despite his nickname was famed throughout the whole of Stathspey for his speed and endurance as a runner. Like most of the village people he was a member of the Grant clan. Only an hour or two after the men had left for Forres a bunch of Camerons from Lochaber descended on the lands round Tulloch and set to lifting as many cattle as they could get. Now Fear-nan-casan-caol was a competent enough warrior and was particularly good with the bow, but on his own there was no way he could do anything against the Camerons. As soon as he saw them coming he knew what he had to do.

He set off at a strong pace on the road to the coast and caught up with his neighbours about eight kilometres down the road. Informing them of what was happening and telling them to get back as quickly as they could, he immediately turned round in

162

the direction of Tullock once more. Within minutes he was well ahead of the rest of them and soon was out of sight on his way back to confront the raiders. He got back to the village to be told by the womenfolk that the raiders had gone off with the cattle towards the south, and without waiting for his companions he set off after the cateran.

A while later the rest of the Grant men arrived back and were sent off after him. They could clearly follow the track of the cattle to the south. A few hours later they came to Loch Einich, and to their great surprise, there were their cattle. Of Fear-nan-casan-caol or the Camerons there wasn't a sign. This was puzzling. Where could they have gone? They looked around for a while but there was no sign at all of anyone in the immediate area so they rounded up the cattle and headed back to Tulloch. The mood was one of joy, tempered with concern. Sure they had managed to get their cattle back without a fight, but whatever had happened to their friend? The next few days people kept expecting him to turn up, but as the days passed his wife began to think that he must be dead. Soon all accepted that something must have gone wrong on the hill, but there were still those who held out hope that he would turn up eventually.

Then one day the story came out. One of the women, who hailed initially from Lochaber, had gone to visit her relatives there and heard that the Camerons had in fact killed Fear nan-casan-caol. He had caught up with them at Loch Eanaich and bravely tried to hold them up by firing arrows at them from hiding. He had managed to seriously wound a couple of them before he was captured. He had been outnumbered twelve to one so he had never really had a chance. After he was killed the Camerons decided to bury him, as they realised that other Grants would be following on behind him. They had just finished burying him and replacing the turf when their lookout called that the Grants were coming. As they numbered about forty men the Camerons scattered and crawled through the heather and into the nearby trees, then off to the west without giving battle. This was why the scene had appeared so deserted to the Tulloch men. It had been said that the Camerons had buried Grant near a tree growing over a large boulder on the north side of Loch Eanaich. So it was that a sad group of Grant men climbed back up into the hills to look for their dead companion. They had little trouble in locating his body and then brought it back for a proper burial in the Tulloch kirkyard. But this was not the last they were to hear of the Camerons.

A short while later the occupant of Dalnapit near Tulloch was getting married. In those far-off days weddings were every bit as popular as they are today, and people flocked from all over the district to take part in the festivities. Unknown to the partygoers however, the Camerons were back in the area, hiding out in the hills and spying out the land. They had been greatly annoyed to lose their loot because of the thin-legged man, and had decided to have another go at lifting the Grant cattle. It was a fine September's day, and as people streamed into Dalnapit that Saturday the cunning Camerons came down from the hills and began rounding up the cattle they had been forced to give up the last time.

The wedding was in full swing when a group of young lads arrived to say that the Camerons were back. They had been off fishing in the Spey and when they returned to the village they found the cattle had all been herded off. At once a party of men was organised to pursue the cattle. They were to be led by Allan Grant of Auchernach, a man of considerable skill and experience in dealing with raiders, and also at lifting cattle himself. Arming themselves and taking enough food to last a couple of days, the Grants set off at a steady trot after the herd. They caught up with the Camerons at the Slochd of Bachdarn and came down on them from above in traditional fashion. The Camerons stood their ground for a while, but were driven off, carrying their leader. This was Iain Dubh Cameron, a man known to have a fearsome temper and a thirst for blood. He had been lucky. An arrow from Auchernach's bow had split his nose badly, and ever after he was known as Iain Dubh Biorach, 'Dark Ian of the sharp nose'. His disfigurement was there for all to see and in his heart he vowed vengeance of Allan Grant.

Now in those far-off days, although most folk lived in tightly-knit communities, people did marry across clan boundaries as we have seen, and it was actually a cousin of Iain Dubh Biorach who had married one of the Tulloch men. She was the one who had brought back the news of where Fear-nan-casan-caol was buried, but the next time she visited her Lochaber relatives she unwittngly carried some news of use to Iain Dubh. Auchenruach had gone to mill his corn after the harvest and had argued with the priest from Finlarig, in Strathspey, about who should go first to get their corn ground. The priest of course thought that he should have precedence because of his profession, but Allan Grant was having none of it, and they had words. In fact they had a blazing row, and over the next couple of weeks Allan Grant let everybody in the district know just what he thought of the Finlarig priest, a young man, relatively new to the district. According to Allan he was a jumped-up whippersnapper with no respect for his elders in the community. What would have been no more than a nine-day wonder was changed by the intervention of the revenge-set Cameron. He slipped over into Strath-spey one night, and coming to Finlarig he let himself quietly into the priest's house and slit his throat while the poor man was sleeping.

In the morning there was consternation. People were used to death, the men were all warriors and were well-attuned to the risks that came with their permanently carrying arms. But killing a priest! That was a truly evil deed and one that shamed the entire community. In those days the Church had considerable power and Allan Grant was arrested by order of the Bishop of Moray and sent off to Elgin jail to be tried for murder. He was tortured to try and make him confess, but he protested his innocence. He was a well-thought-of and important member of his community, so the Bishop thought it better just to have him locked up in a dungeon while further investigation was undertaken. The problem was that the crime had taken place in the middle of the night and there had been no witnesses. Allan's refusal to admit to the crime made it near impossible to prove one way or the other. It was a terrible crime and somebody had to pay, but the people of Tulloch sided with Allan and the Bishop realised that he couldn't just hang him for murder. So matters lay, with Allan Grant locked up in the dungeon, and the Bishop unable to find out any more about the murder. Then Allan had a stroke of luck. Iain Dubh Cameron came raiding again, this time into Morayshire, and while his fellows were lifting cattle he took the chance to go robbing people's houses. He was discovered in the act and killed the man of the house he was in. However, he failed to make his getaway, and the man's wife raised the alarm. Neighbours came running and the cateran was overpowered. Iain Dubh had a reputation as a ruthless thief, and was sent off to Inverness to be hung. While incarcerated in the jail at Inverness awaiting execution he had a stroke of conscience and confessed to the murder of the Finlarig priest. It seems he could not bear the thought of facing judgement without confessing this dastardly crime. His fear was greater than his wish for revenge on Allan Grant. So Auchenruach was released from prison and compensated for his trouble by the Bishop.

The Loch of the Farrow Cow

Rathad nam Mearlach, the Thieves' Road, is the name of an old route that passes through Strathspey. It got its name from the regular usage by caterans, generally from Lochaber who used to come through Glen Spean, by Rothiemurchus, along the south side of Loch Morlich and eastwards through the pass of Lochan Uaine. From there they would follow the line of the River Nethy down into the rich, fertile Laigh of Moray, where there were always well-fattened cattle to be lifted. Though it is not part of local tradition, we can be pretty sure that some at least of the Strathspey men followed the road in the other direction through Badenoch and into Lochaber, on raids of their own.

At one point this traditional route road goes past Loch an Eilean, the Loch of the Island, with its famous castle, and then just to the south, Loch Gamhna, the loch of the farrow cow, about ten miles north-east of Kingussie. A farrow cow is one that has ceased to have calves and the name came about after a raid on Moray by a group of Camerons and Mackintoshes who had come over from Lochaber.

They had been quite successful in rounding up a couple of dozen cows, some with calves, a few steers and the farrow cow. Having come all the way up the Nethy river and round by Loch Morlich with no sign of pursuit, they decided to stop and rest the cattle, and themselves, at the wee loch. They were mainly experienced men, and being well used to the cateran life they posted watchmen on prominent points to keep an eye out for pursuit. It was precisely this experience that was to be their undoing. Over the previous three or four seasons the Lochaber men had been repeatedly harrying the people of Moray and they had had enough. So unknown to the men sitting eating by the loch that day, they were being pursued by a substantial number of men, over fifty in number. The Moray men were determined this time that the raiders would not get clean away. Now the Camerons and Mackintoshes hadn't long stopped when a shout from one of the sentries alerted them to approaching danger. He shouted that there was a large body of men coming down from the north, clearly following the cattle trail and far too many to fight. The Lochaber men were outnumbered by about three to one, and these were not good odds. Their leader, Hamish Dubh, or Dark James, was man of some intelligence, or so he thought anyway.

'Right, lads. Here's the plan,' he said, as the cateran gathered around him. 'Tie stones to the cattle's horns and we'll drive them into the loch here. They'll sink and we can say we have seen no one else with beasts, which is of course perfectly true,' he finished with a smile, pleased at the ruse, if a bit disappointed at having to give up his prey.

The rest of the men did as he told them and large stones were tied to the beasts' horns, after which they were driven into the loch. There was just enough time for the Lochaber men to move away from the spot where the cattle had been driven into the water, and sit on a some handy boulders a couple of hundred yards from the edge of the loch, when the Moray men arrived on the scene. They were armed to the teeth and it was clear by their demeanour that they were ready for anything.

As they approached the Lochaber men, who remained sitting, Hamish Dubh stood up and called out a friendly greeting. He was met with silence as the Moray men quickly surrounded him and his men.

'I wished you a good day,' he repeated, still smiling and looking at the man who appeared to be in charge of the group.

This was a man named Grant who had lost cattle to the cateran on many occasions and was in a foul temper. He looked around, ignoring Hamish. There were no cattle to be seen. The Moray men were beginning to look quizzically at each other. They had been certain this was the cateran band they were after, but there was no sign of the cattle. And all the time Hamish Dubh was smiling at them. His companions hadn't even bothered to grab their weapons. That was hardly the behaviour of a bunch of raiders. The thought began to cross Grant's mind that perhaps they were mistaken and that this wasn't the band they had been following. He looked once more at Hamish, who smiled back and opened his arms out to emphasise the fact that he wasn't armed. Then Grant nodded and was just about to step forward and speak to Hamish when he heard a sound. It came from the loch behind him and he whirled round just in time to see the head of the farrow cow bobbing on the waters of the loch.

At once the Lochaber men grabbed for their weapons as the Moray men fell on them with a roar. Able and fit warriors they might have been, but with such odds against them their fate was sealed. The Moray men, realising that their cattle had been drowned and that they had come all this way for nothing, were in no mood for mercy. Within minutes the Lochaber men were all dead, there on the grass beside the loch where they had been peacefully grazing the Moray men's cattle just a short time before. The Moray men headed back, carrying their injured with just one beast, the farrow cow, for their trouble, and that is how the loch got its name

Cattle 1: Cateran 0

In many areas of Scotland the raiding that took place between the clans became something more. Consistent raiding could, and did, lead to ongoing blood feuds, where one act of revenge simply led to another. The Clann Gunn, living in the lands around Strathnaver and Strath Helladale in the far north had often been raided over the years by Mackays who lived in Sutherland to the west of Caithness. Raiding the more southern parts of Scotland meant long mountain journeys and the mountainous countryside of the north tended to keep them apart. Still each clan was not traditionally in the habit of raiding their closest neighbours, a practice really best avoided. There is sense in which such raids, taking place over centuries, and usually in the autumn after the harvest was in, almost had something of ritual about them. When the long moonlit nights of autumn came on it was traditional to go and raid for cattle, and who better to raid than your traditional enemies? This is difficult for us to appreciate fully today, but in those far-off times the Highlanders defined themselves by their kin and the lands they occupied, in complex and sophisticated ways which we perhaps lack the means to understand. The raiding of the warriors was a fundamental part of their lives, and they followed the traditions of their ancestors. So if your grandfather and his brothers and cousins, your father and uncles and their cousins had raided a certain clan, well, it would be a good idea for you, your brothers and cousins to raid them too. Although by the late Middle Ages clan society was changing at an ever-faster rate, there were still some things that preserved the link with the past, and the far past.

So it happened one time that a cateran group of Mackays came down on Kilchonan led by Seumas Chattaich, 'Big Jimmy of the Battles', and made off with a good *creach*. The Gunns rallied, and there was a pitched battle. The Mackays drove the Gunns off, but suffered over a dozen dead before heading back through Beallach nan Creach, towards the west. This pass, named for its regular use for raiding between the clans, sits between Ben Griam Mor and Ben Griam Beg, overlooking Auchtertoul Forest in Strath Halladale. The Gunns knew this was the way that Seumas Chatthaich would make for home with the cattle. They sent out word to their clansmen quickly and soon assembled a new force of both Gunns and Sutherlands, their close relations.

They set out after the cateran and caught up with them just after they had driven the cattle through the pass. They were just coming to Loch Drum-a' Chliabhain when the Gunns came into sight. Down the hill they charged and fell on the Mackays. Earlier in the day the Mackays had had the superior numbers and had made it tell. Now their foes outnumbered them and the tide of the battle began to turn against them. Just as things began to turn a further group of warriors appeared from behind the Mackays. These were a group of the clan who had settled in Strahnaver just over the hills from Strath Halladale. By all the codes of honour and kin, they could not but come to the help of their kinsmen, even if it led to future trouble with their neighbours in the next glen. The arrival of the Abrach Mackays, as they were called, turned the battle yet again and the Gunns were soon driven off. It was a great victory but a costly one, and both sides had suffered a couple of dozen casualties. Still that was the way of battle and the Mackays could rejoice in the fact that they still had the Gunn's cattle.

The combined force of Mackays drove the cattle down into

Strathnaver. There was only one cattle-fold on the Mackay lands there that was big enough. It was an ancient stone-walled structure but had fallen into disuse and had no gate. The walls at either end of the entrance had crumbled and there was no way of putting up a temporary gate before nightfall. The cattle needed only to be kept overnight, for Seumas would be off to the west in the morning so the chief of the Abrach Mackays made a generous offer. He would stay up all night and make sure that none of the cattle came out through the gate. This was a real token of kinship, for hadn't he and his men already saved the day for their cousins from the west? He said though that he wasn't going to spend the next day herding cattle through the moun-tians to the west so could give us a little sleep. His offer was gratefully accepted, and after tending to the wounded all went to sleep, with a fair number of them having a few mouthfuls of whisky. There would be time for a full celebration when the original party got their plunder home.

With the fighting that had gone on, not enough attention had been paid to the cattle themselves. In amongst them was young bull, just growing into his prime, who was as good as wild. It was in the middle of the night that the bull decided that he wanted out of the enclosure that was keeping all the cows bunched up. He pushed his way through the cows and came to the gate. There stood the chief of the Abrach Mackays, leaning on his sword and looking at the stars. Hearing a sound, he turned, only to see the bull charging straight for him. He didn't stand a chance. The bull caught him on his horns, threw him up in the air and he fell to the ground with a thump. The blow winded him, and as he gasped for breath the bull was on him. Unable to get to his feet in time he was gored to death as he lay there in the gate of the cattle-fold. The bull gored and tossed his body till it was like a limp rag, then with one final heave moved the body to one side. It then gave a soft bellow and headed off. Out from the fold followed all the Strath Halladale cattle, younger bulls, cows and calves all behind the young bull. Back he went up the slopes of Ben Griam Mor and into Beallach nan Creach. There in the small hours of the morning they headed back over into Strath Halladale. You can imagine the pleasure that was felt when the people there arose to see all the cattle that had disappeared to the west the day before, calmly munching on the sweet grass by the shores of Loch an Ruathair. And for long enough the Gunns enjoyed telling the tale of how Seumas Chattaich and the Mackays were outwitted by a bull.

One Beast Too Many

Iain Odhar MacDhui or 'Fair-haired John Davidson' lived at Baul on the Strath Rory River in Ross-shire in the 1740s. One of those men who was extremely proud of his ancestry, John took great delight in his skills as a cattle-lifter. However, by his time the old customs were changing and the old ways of the Highland clans were on their last legs. The old habits of the cateran trade as dictated by Cothrom na Feinne had passed out of use and the lifting of cattle was no longer the honourable practice it once had been. One day John was off raiding with two of his friends, Lachlan and Alisdair Cameron, members of a clan whose cattle-raiding had long been famous. They were not acting on behalf of either of their clans but totally for themselves. Now Alisdair was known as Allie Scholar because of an event that had happened when he was a bit younger. He was a man, like many of his time, who had never learned to read or write but had been found one day in church with a copy of the Bible in his hands which he was looking at sternly. The fact that the Bible was upside down had given the game away and he was known ever after as the Scholar!

Now the three of them one day were heading back home by Corriefearn overlooking the Dornoch Firth, and Allie had his dogs with him – four highly-trained hunting beasts of which he was very fond. They were passing above Mid Fearn when they spotted a small herd of cattle and decided to lift just one of the beasts and take it back over the hills to Strath Rory. Now this was a bit close to home, but as they saw no one about, and were only after a beast to feed themselves, they were pretty sure they could get away undiscovered. So they took a fine healthy beast from the herd and went off over the hill. They had been spotted however by a young lad by the name of Hector, who was tending the cattle for Captain Ross of Mid Fearn, his uncle. He had been lying in the heather gazing idly at the clouds floating above and sucking on a piece of grass when the cateran arrived, and had flattened himself into the heather so he was unseen. He realised that if he tried to hinder the three armed men it could easily turn out badly. He was a conscientious lad though, and decided to follow the men to see where they were going with the beast. So keeping low down in the heather he followed them up the Easter Fearn Burn between Beinn Tharsuinn and Cnon Muigh-Bhidraidh and down the Strath Rory river. On they went to Baul and the rough built house of John Davidson, with Hector constantly on their trail. He saw them take the beast into the building and crept down closer. By this time the mist was beginning to drift down from the ben and he decided to take matters into his own hands.

Boldly he marched up to the building, a rough looking structure of wood, stone and turf, hammered on the frame of the door and stepped in, calling out, 'Hello, anyone at home?'

He found himself in a big room with a roaring fire to his right and a door into another room off to his left. There in front of him stood the three men who had just killed the beast, which lay on the floor between them. Fair John stepped forward, his bloodstained dirk in hand. Holding it towards the lad he asked in a gruff voice, 'And just who are you, laddie?' The others too had their hands on their dirks as all three of the men stared at the young lad.

'Och, my name is Hector and I am on my way to my uncle's place in Sutherland. I have come up the road from Dingwall and the weather is on the turn, and I noticed the smoke from your fire. I just stopped to see if I could shelter for a bit,' he said with a big open smile, 'and maybe get a wee bite to eat.' Saying this he was looking closely at the freshly-killed beast.

'Och, right,' said John, quite taken in, 'just you wait a bit lad, and you can have all you want to eat.'

The three men expertly began to skin the beast and butcher it. A few pieces of the raw meat were thrown at Hector, who stuck them in his sporran and in the folds of the plaid he was wearing. Allie took some of the meat to the fire, stuck it on spits and placed them over the blazing peat fire. Soon there was a fine smell of roasting beef and Hector felt his stomach begin to rumble. True enough, he was hungry. He had left his bread and cheese way back with Captain Ross's herd and had gone nearly all day without food. Hector heard the sound of Allie's dogs who were clearly in the other room and beginning to smell the meat themselves. Just as Allie handed a partially-cooked lump of meat to Hector, a young lass of seven or eight came through from ben the house with the dogs on leashes. As she pulled them towards the door, shouting at them to keep quiet, she passed Hector and muttered to him. 'Ach, you can eat the meat, but you'll never have the time to digest it.' This was said with a truly frightening sneer on such a young face and Hector felt his heart skip a beat. John and Lachlan had finished skinning the beast and the latter picked up a bucket and handed it to Hector. 'Here, lad,' he said, 'take this to the well and fill it. Wee Jeanie outside will show you where the well is.'

Hector stepped outside to see that the scruffy wee lassie had tied the dogs' leashes to a sturdy bush a few yards from the door.

'They say you've to show me the well,' he said to the girl.

'Huh, all right, I'll show you,' she replied with a nasty laugh.

Now Hector realised that even if the lassie was only trying to frighten him, it might be a good idea to get away from the place and back to tell Captain Ross what had happened before night fell. The lassie took him to a well about thirty yards from the tumbledown house. It was one of those traditional wells with a circular stone wall built round it and a length of rope lying at its side to tie the bucket to. They approached and Hector looked over the wall into the well. It wasn't that deep, about ten feet, and he could clearly see that the water wasn't more than a foot or so deep at the bottom. He made his mind up instantly. Quickly he turned round, dropped the bucket, and in one move lifted the young lass up and over the wall and dropped her into the well. He was so quick she had no time to say a word and down she dropped into the water. Hector turned and ran off up the hill and into the mist. Behind him the dogs started barking, drowning out the noise the lassie had started to create inside the well. Hector could just make out what she was shouting and it was shocking language for a member of the fairer sex to be using, never mind one who was eight years old, if that. Out from the house came the three cateran, disturbed by the baying of the hounds.

'Wheesht, ye black scoundrels,' roared Allie, and the dogs went quiet, but for only a moment before starting to bay again.

'Where's Jeannie?' shouted John. 'Split up and look around lads, she's probably playing some daft game with that young lad.'

As they could see the well they went round the back of the house and into the wood there, shouting for Jeannie. Hector by now of course was hidden in the mist as he climbed the hill. After a few minutes the three men came back to the house and Allie went over to the well. He looked inside and there was Jeannie standing in the water with a black, grim look on her face.

'That laddie is a damned spy,' she roared, 'get after him.'

Allie dropped the rope to the young lass and pulled her up out of the well as his companions joined him.

'I tell you that laddie is a spy. He threw me into the well and ran off. I'll bet he's gone to fetch others,' she screeched.

'Ach, don't you fash, my lass,' said John, a grim look on his face, echoing that of his daughter. 'Allie, let loose your hounds and they'll run him down. That's what they've been shouting about, probably.'

So the hounds were loosed and the four of them bounded off through the heather up the hill to the north. They had Hector's trail in an instant. The three men ran back to the house for swords and pistols and took off after the dogs, leaving the wee lass to go back into the house and tend to the cooking meat.

Up ahead Hector recognised that the sound made by the hounds had changed. He realised they were on his trail. He knew if he could find his way up Cnoc an-t-Sobhail and on down towards the Aultnamain Inn he could get home even in the mist. He was well versed in finding his way about these hills in all weathers, but he had the small problem of a group of hounds hunting him down. And he could hear them getting closer. He kept going, and just as he could hear the hounds were within about fifty yards of him he turned. There through the mist came the four dogs. Reaching into his plaid he brought out a piece of the beef and threw it just in front of the lead hound. The hound snatched at it and so did the second one. Within a couple of seconds all four hounds were snarling and snapping at each other as they fought to get the meat. Their appetites too had been kindled by the smell of the roasting meat. As they fought Hector ran further up the hill. Within a few minutes though the dogs had eaten the meat and were on his trail again. Four more times he had to turn and throw meat to the pursuing hounds and each time it slowed them down so he could continue on his way.

After the fifth time the dogs had all had some beef, and as Hector had wisely decided to run through a couple of burns for short distances, they lost his trail. Behind them the three cateran followed by the sound of their baying. They came up the slopes of the Cnoc and Allie whistled on his dogs. They came bounding back to him.

'This mist is getting thicker,' grunted Davidson, 'I doubt the young lad can find his way in it. He might have slipped the dogs but he's just a laddie. Let's go back.'

Sure that the young lad had lost his way in the mist the three of them headed back down to Baul. Truth to tell, by now they were extremely hungry and were looking forward to a good feed. But Hector had not lost his way. By the time darkness came on, making things even harder, he had already passed the Autna-main Inn and was on the well-marked road to Mid Fearn. Even in darkness and mist he could easily follow the track. As soon as he got to Mid Fearn, even after covering all the ground he had, he ran to his uncle's house. He was given hot food and drink as his uncle gathered up a few nearby men. Then Hector having rested for an hour and more, they all went off to retrace his footsteps. Soon enough they were at Baul, and Captain Ross asked his nephew to take part in a daring plan.

John and Lachlan were sitting by the fire at Baul, Allie Scholar having gone off with his dogs to take Jeannie to her mother, who was at another house further down the glen, when the door opened. The two men turned to see who it was. There was Hector!

'Ho, Ho!' John, lifting up his Lochaber axe. 'You've got lost in the mist and ended up here again have you? Well, you will not now escape your fate my little spy he said,' as he stood up, raising the axe. He never had a chance to do anything else as Captain Ross stepped through the door and shot him with a pistol through the heart. Behind him came another three men and despite a brief struggle Lachlan soon lay beside Iain on the floor, just as dead. After this the Rosses returned home, glad to have put an end to two men who, if they had started out as caterans like so many others, had ended up as nothing more than thieves.

Allie Scholar, in no way learning from his companions' fate, carried on stealing anything he could lay his hands on for a few more years. He believed that his time was nearly up one year when he returned to a quiet pass in the hills above Loch Fannich in Wester Ross. The year before he had lifted a herd of five cattle up by Loch Broom and had made a great detour through by

Loch a Bhraoin and Loch Fannich. He had brought the young lass herding them along and high above Loch Fannich he had tied her to the branch of a tree by her lovely, long, golden hair. He had thought that it would only be a matter of hours before somebody came by to release her. But passing by towards the west a year later he found her skeleton, still tied to the fateful branch! After this Allie had less and less stomach for his skullduggery and it was only a few months after this that he came down with the measles and was forced to lie up with a fellow thief in Tain. Somehow word got out and he was arrested. Just before being hung at Rosehill by the Redcoats who were now in control of the Highlands, he told about the sad fate of the golden-haired lass he had abducted from Loch Broom, and at long last her parents eventually found out what had happened and were able to give her a Christian burial. Allie Scholar, his brother Lachlan and Iain Odhar had maybe followed some of the ways of the School of the Moon, but by the end, probably in their hearts, they knew they were little, if any, better than common thieves.

The Raid of Moyness

⟫◆⟪

The troubles between the Camerons and the Grants went on for
a considerable length of time. One surviving letter from the 17th
century gives an insight into just how the raiding of cattle was
seen amongst the Highlanders. It came about as a result of a raid
on Moyness in the Laigh of Moray, the fertile lands to the east of
Culloden, by a group of Cameron caterans. They had been
pursued into the hills by a group under Sir James Grant of Lurg.
When they caught up with the offenders Grant sent one of his
companions, a man called Meikle Lawson, to demand the cattle
back without bloodshed. The Camerons refused him point blank
and as he turned to return to his own party he was shot in the
back with an arrow. This was a truly heinous crime and a general
battle commenced in which the Camerons were driven from the
field at the cost of eight dead and dozen wounded. The Grants
were particulary fortunate in one of their number being a
particulary fine archer, one of the Grants of Kylachie. Grant
of Lurg was angered by this event, even more so than by the
normal cattle-raiding that took place. Shooting a man in the back
was a cowardly thing to do, and he wrote to the Cameron
chieftain whose kinsmen had carried out the raid to make his
feelings plain. This is the reply to him from Allan Cameron of
Lochiel.

Right Honourable and Loving Cousin, May my hearty com-
mendations be remembered to your worship. I have received
your letter concerning the unfortunate affair that has involved

our houses, the like of which has never been encountered in any man's day. But, Praise be to God, I and my friends are innocent of any intention to harm your worship, because when we went to Morayland, where all men take their prey, we had no idea that Moyness was a Grant possession. Had we really known this, we should not have disturbed it any more than we would think of interfering with your worship's other possessions in Strathspey. As it is I have suffered loss among my friends – eight of who are already dead, with a further twelve or thirteen under cure and no man knowing whether they will live or die – that I am sure your worship will take into consideration and realize that it is I, not you, who has suffered the greatest loss in this affair. Refraining from troubling you further at this time, and knowing your worship will not be offended by my thus proclaiming the innocence of my friends,

So I rest yours,

Allan Cameron of Lochyll.

Apart from showing the chief's assumption of his right to raid in Morayland, this is a fascinating piece of attempted deception. He wouldn't have lifted Grant's cattle if he had known they were his; anyway, he had suffered worse – so that's all right then!

A further complication arose from the raid of Moyness. A young chieftain of the Grants, who lived at Ballindalloch, had withdrawn from following the Camerons after the Raid of Moyness and stood accused of cowardice. This charge was brought by the shadowy group, the Clan Elders. Every clan had such a group, but they normally didn't do much except when chiefs were seen to be acting against the interests of the clan as a whole. At that point it was their duty to put the chief right, for the interests of the entire community were more important than any individual member of it, even the chief. In several notable cases this meant removing the chief from the clan lands, and there were instances of them imprisoning and even killing chiefs who stepped too far out of line. So the Clan Elders of the Grants met in Strathspey to discuss what should be done about young Ballindalloch. His punishment was a strange combination of ancient clan law and Christian penitence. Every Sunday for a year he had to attend the church service at Inverallan and listen to his kinsman, the noted archer from Kylachie as he stood up in the front of the congregation and said, 'I am the man who acquitted himself valiantly at Moyness.' After this Ballindalloch had to get to his feet and say in plain view of the whole congregation,' I am the man who acted the coward's part on that occasion.' His position as a chieftain, far from excusing him, made matters worse, and it was long year for young Ballindalloch.

Seumas an Tuim

Seumas an Tuim (James of the Hill) was a Grant who was given his name because he spent so much time out in the mountains raiding other people's cattle. He was active in the 17th century and caused so much trouble in Moray, the Mearns and even as far away as Strathearn that he came to the attention of the authorities in Edinburgh. Now James was a local chieftain, and like all Grants was nominally under the leadership of the Laird of Grant. Now although all Grants saw the Laird as their clan chief, several of the smaller branches of the clan were effectively autonomous. It was only when there was a reason for the whole clan to come together that Seumas would really put himself under the Laird's command. Most of the time he was his own master, and as he brought a great deal of wealth into the clan the chief was happy to let him do pretty much as he liked. This was not unusual in the Highland clans where local chieftains like Seumas commanded the respect and devotion of their own nearest kin. Even when he was directly contacted by the government in Edinburgh the Laird of Grant was loath to try and rein Seumas in. Apart from the amount of wealth Seumas brought he was also a formidable warrior and the Grant chief had called on his prowess often enough in the past.

The government in Edinburgh, composed of Lowland lairds and aristocrats never really understood the relationship between clansmen and seemed to think that as the head of the clan the Laird had what amounted to feudal rights over his clansmen. To the Lowlanders in Edinburgh the Highlanders were to a great extent foreigners, and it was always government policy to try and control these wild clansmen by any means possible. Try as they might, however, they could not induce the Laird of Grant to hand over his kinsman . . . After all, Seumas was a member of his clan, a close relation, and was following the traditional warrior pursuit of raiding other clans' cattle. They too had their own warriors and should have been able to fend for themselves. The fact, however, is that James was also lifting cattle from Lowland estates where the ancient clan traditions had never had any sway, and whose owners looked to the government for protection. In the Highlands, of course, most men looked to their own right hand for protection and if they needed more their kinsmen were there to be called on.

So James continued the cateran way of life up until a fateful day when he went on a *creach* to Badenoch just to the south of Strathspey. This was probably raiding a little close to home and he was involved in a battle with some Clan Chattan men who killed four of James's band before capturing him. They well knew who he was, and it didn't take long for them to send him to Edinburgh. At last the authorities had captured this notorious raider and he was locked up in Edinburgh castle to await trial. As with most Highlanders James knew that trial in the capital was pretty certain to end up one way – with him having his neck stretched. Unaware of the warrior's code of honour and the kinship ties that defined Highland society, the Lowland judges would show him no sympathy whatsoever. James was in a tight situation and he knew it.

However, he was an astute man as well as a brave and skilful one. He was also a man of some means: his raiding had brought him wealth, and like all prisoners in those far-off days he was responsible for looking after his own food. This had to be sent into the prison in Edinburgh Castle and was the responsibility of his wife, who had come to Edinburgh on hearing of her husband's capture. In amongst the provisions she sent into the castle for him were a couple of casks of butter, churned by her own hand. The night the churns of butter arrived, Seumas waited till dark, then stuck his hands deep into the first churn. There, neatly coiled amongst the butter was a long, strong rope and a couple of short dirks. The other barrel held another rope and a pistol wrapped in leather. Waiting to be sure that most of the soldiers in the garrison were sound asleep, James forced the lock on his cell door and made his way to the battlements. The garrison of course were of the opinion that no one could escape from Edinburgh Castle with its perpendicular rock faces and its great gates which were always manned. James was delighted to prove them wrong.

Tying one end of a rope round the battlements he tied the other rope to its far end and threw them both over the wall. Then gingerly feeling his way with his feet down the Castle Rock, he came down the rope to where his wife and a couple of hand-picked men were waiting. It took only a few minutes to get to where they had horses waiting. One of the City Guard had been bribed and the gate at the West Port was quietly opened to let the small group through. Off they rode in the night back to Strath-spey. This daring escape infuriated the government and a large price was put on James's head. Now that he was an outlaw many of those he had raided in the past now had the perfect oppor-tunity to get on his trail and he had no choice but to take to the hills, from which he got his name. However, despite the attention of the government – a price of five thousand merks was put on James' head by the Privy Council after his daring escape – they never managed to capture him again. It was said in the north that for every ten men hired to find James, at least five of them were tipping him off. Such was the tight-knit nature of Highland society that the writ of the government was meaningless. James spent the rest of his days amongst his own folk of Clan Grant. Amongst his own people he would be relatively safe, for if anyone did betray him it was likely that they would be immediately forced out of their own community, the only life they knew. So despite the Government's attempts to stop him James carried on with his cateran ways.

It wasn't that long after James's escape that a rumour began to circulate in Strathspey. This said that James had been killed in a quarrel with another cateran. This story was in time carried to Edinburgh, where it reached the ears of the government, but the truth seems to be that James put the story out himself and that he eventually died, peacefully, in his bed in 1639.

Cave of Raitts

———◆———

While cattle-raiding seems to have been a central function of the Highland tribal warriors from at least the Iron Age, there were those who definitely saw it as a business opportunity. One such opportunity arose in the clever re-use of an ancient monument near Kingussie. This was the Cave of Raitts, a souterrain or underground structure, lined throughout with boulders and covered with great flat stone slabs. Nobody today knows exactly what these structures were for, but hundreds of them have been found all over those parts of Scotland that were occupied by the Picts. One of the theories about them is that they were primarily used for grain storage. The local tradition at Raitts was that it had been built in one night by a group of giants and giantesses and it was also believed that the roofing slabs had originally come from a nearby standing-stone circle, a type of monument that is at least five thousand years old. Whatever the antiquity of the structure it was put to use by a group of caterans.

They were McNivens, a sept of the Clan Mackintosh who lived in the hills to the south of Inverness. One of them had the bright idea of building a cottage directly over the underground cavity. Once it was built two old ladies of the clan were installed in the place and the story was circulated that this was an act of charity on the part of McNiven. Nothing could have been further from the truth. It was part of a daring plan to carry out a whole series of raids on the MacPhersons who lived in the area. Knowing there was steady market for fresh meat and hides in Inverness, McNiven reckoned that if he could install himself and a group of his clansmen in the cave, unknown to the MacPhersons, they would be able to come out at night, lift cattle and head off over the hills towards Inverness. On the way they would meet with another group of McNivens on their own land who would carry on with the cattle to Inverness while the original group would head back to the Cave of Raitts under cover of nightfall and be safe in their hiding-place before the alarm was raised the following morning. The plan worked a treat. Night after night the MacPhersons were losing cattle and their chief was under a great deal of pressure to stop the raiding. The raiders were careful not to take large amounts of cattle at a time, which would have slowed them down but were regularly running off with up to ten or twenty beasts. This soon began to have a serious economic effect and the MacPhersons were becoming ever more concerned. At last they hatched a plan themselves to find out what was happening. It was clear that whoever was doing the raiding had some base of operations in the area. The hills around had been scoured to see if there were any cateran based in the summer shielings or other locations on the high ground, but no trace had been found. A young nephew of the chief who had been raised with relatives to the south was chosen to return as a spy. Disguised as a beggar his job was eventually to inspect every house in the area of Kingussie and Aviemore to try and discover if anything suspicious was going on. It was some job!

After a couple of weeks of this, during which there had been another series of raids, Hamish came to the house at Raitts. He had already passed this way and had been sent packing by the two old ladies who lived there, who clearly did not like strangers. This made him a little suspicious, and when he came back the second time, just after night had fallen, and knocked at their door, he complained of severe pains in his side, and pleaded to be able to sleep overnight by their fire. Now the two elderly McNiven ladies were tough customers, but like everyone else in the Highlands they had been brought up to extend hospitality, and as the young beggar seemed genuinely ill, they consented to let him in and even to let him sleep by their fire. One of the old women went to a large cupboard and opened it, asking if he wanted some food. Noticing that the cupboard was full of bannocks, cheese and different kinds of meat, he thanked them and said because of his pains all he wanted to do was go to sleep. In truth he was hungry but was playing his part of being ill. However, he awoke in the grey hour just before dawn, with an absolutely ravenous hunger on him. Lighting a fir taper from the smouldering fire he walked over to the cupboard in which he had seen the food. He opened it gently, making no noise. It was empty.

There was no cheese, no bannocks or other bread and no meat. As he stood there he heard the soft murmur of voices. Blowing out his taper, he listened hard. They were men's voices and they seemed to be coming from below his feet. He lay on the ground to listen, but the voices grew fainter. So he stood up again and the voices were stronger. Relighting the taper he looked closely at the cupboard. It was set into a strong wooden frame and he suddenly realised that it was a door, a door that led to some sort of cave. Just at that he heard the women stirring through the room and, quickly blowing out his taper and hiding it beneath his rags, he lay down again before the fire.

As the women came in they lit a lamp. He pretended to waken up. They offered him some porridge, and again feigning great pain he thanked them and left the house just as dawn was streaking the sky. Down the path in front of the house he staggered, clutching his side, but as soon as he was out of sight behind some trees he straightened up and began to run. In minutes he was at the house of a fellow MacPherson, and while he was given something to eat word was sent to his uncle to come immediately with as many men as he could.

A couple of hours later the two ladies at Raitts had some more visitors. This time there was no knock on the door. The MacPhersons burst in and the two women were hauled outside. Hamish then went in with his uncle and showed him the cupboard. They pulled and pulled at the cupboard but it had obviously been jammed from the far side. Then they simply piled dry heather in the cupboard and set it alight and went out of the house. Within minutes the whole wooden structure was alight and flames began spreading to the roof. Coughing and spluttering noises could be heard above the crackle of the flames. Suddenly as the fire blazed away the whole cupboard swung open and up rushed half a dozen McNivens, tears streaming from their eyes and their plaids held over their mouths. In the house itself the smoke wasn't quite as thick, but the whole building was now alight. As one man they took their swords in their hands and rushed out calling their battle cry 'Loch Moy'. The MacPhersons were waiting for them in considerable numbers and within minutes the McNivens lay dead as the cottage over the Cave of Raitts sent a great plume of smoke into the sky over Strathspey,

In order to unmask the McNiven plot young Hamish Mac-Pherson had taken gross advantage of the hospitality of the two old McNiven women. Just as there were rules governing the giving of hospitality there were rules governing its acceptance. Once you were under someone's roof and they had given, or offered you food, you were duty bound to fight on their behalf. Effectively for as long as you were under their roof you were seen as one of their family, with all the obligations that entailed. By this ancient tradition Hamish was guilty of betraying the McNiven hospitality, but this was of no consequence to the MacPhersons who were simply glad to put an end to the raiding. However, there is a local tradition that to this day the descendants of Hamish MacPherson suffer from chronic, untreatable pains in their sides – as a punishment for his breach of the rules of hospitality!

The Piper's Pool

Now the sense of honour and the pride in skill at arms that were so integral to the Highland warrior's view of the world, and himself, could at times develop into a quite breath-taking arrogance. There are some stories that remind us why some sayings, like pride comes before a fall, are so obvious as to have become clichés. Now there used to be a very fine arrowmaker, or stalcar, who lived at Ardeonaig, on the southern bank of Loch Tay, called Donald McKendrick. He was nicknamed the Archer, because of his almost uncanny skill with the arrows he made. He was the father of six sons, and through his training they were all nearly as good as himself with the bow. Like most men of his time he had been in fights with raiders and had carried out a fair deal of raiding himself in his younger days. Nowadays he preferred to let his sons go off in search of booty and maybe a bit of glory. However, he was always ready to defend himself and his neighbours if the necessity arose.

Well, one September day such necessity did arise. An old widow woman. Beathag Robertson, who lived at an isolated wee farmhouse above Ardeonaig on the slopes of Meall Daimh, had a group of visitors. They were caterans who had come over from Argyll and there were a round dozen of them. When they came down from the hill to Beathag's farmhouse they grabbed the calf they saw there and butchered it. They didn't realise that this was the only beast the poor widow had, and they might not have cared much if they had, for not all those who took to the cateran life were as honourable as they should have been. Anyway, they ordered her to get to cooking the beast while they sat around and laid their plans for raiding round the shores of Loch Tay. Their plan at that point was to stay at the widow's croft till half way through the night, then go and lift cattle, taking off with them at first light, or just before. However, they hadn't reckoned with Beathag, a woman full of the wisdom of her years. She knew what men were like, particularly where raiding was concerned. From her perspective such activity seemed to turn grown men back into adolescent lads, full of boasting and posturing.

Once Beathag had cooked enough meat for them they set to with a will. They had just started eating when the old lady spoke, 'Well I hope you enjoy your food. But may you not eat another morsel till you have seen Donald McKendrick.'

'This will doubtless be some great fighter nearby,' sneered the Argyll men's leader, Archibald MacDiarmaid, a sturdy brown-haired man with a hooked nose. 'Well, don't you fash, mother, there's none you have here who could stand up to us.'

This was met with a chorus of assent from his fellows, just as Beathag had thought there would be.

'Well you think so,' said Beathag, 'but I know different.'

'Oh, quite the hero is Donald then?' another of the cateran laughed.

'Aye, that he is, and his six sons are all near as good men as their father.'

'Well we shall have to see about that, then,' replied the leader.

Just at that one of Beathag's grandchildren, a seven-year old lassie came into the house. Seeing the Argyll men she made as if to run, but was quickly grabbed.

'Well, well,' said Archibald, 'just what we need. Now, lassie, I want you to go and tell Donald McKendrick that he will be getting vistors tomorrow morning at six o'clock, and to have a breakfast ready and waiting for us. If you tell anyone else, or if he sends word anywhere we will kill your grandmother; do you understand?'

The terrified lass could only nod. By this time one of the

cateran had found an old plaid of Beathag's husband, and putting it on instead of his own he went off to keep an eye on the girl. In those days each clan didn't have its own specific tartan, but there were general area-styles of tartan and a man wearing an Argyll tartan along the shores of Loch Tay would have stood out like a sore thumb. The Argyll men were pretty sure that they would keep control of the situation, as they couldn't see themselves being bested by seven men. And they were sure that McKendrick and his sons would not endanger the old woman's life to avoid a fight the following day.

Within the hour their comrade had returned with Beathag's granddaughter, Jessie.

'Well, lass,' asked Archibald with a smile, 'and what did this McKendrick have to say?'

'He asked me to tell you, you are welcome for breakfast,' replied wee Jessie, 'but that you might not like what you get.'

At this the cateran burst out laughing. Here was a man, like themselves, who would appear to fear nothing and was ready to fight them, they thought. Archibald MacDiarmaid had not asked the lassie to mention Cothrom na Feinne; he wasn't that bothered about honour, but assumed that the Loch Tay men would be looking to fight one on one. Well, they might think that, he thought to himself with a grim smile, but we are here for cattle, not honour. One of the Argyll men was Archie's cousin, Duncan MacDiarmaid, and he was a noted piper. He was a bit restless, as he had not had the chance to play his pipes for several days. It would have brought too much attention to them. Even on cattle raids he always carried his pipes and many had been the time when they had returned to their home glen driving a good *creach* of cattle with Duncan paying a stirring tune. Archie figured out what was bothering the younger man. 'Ach, dinnae fash Duncan. Tomorrow we'll see to this McKendrick lot, get the cattle we've spotted and be off into the hills. You'll have plenty chance to play your pipes then,' he said.

'All right then,' sighed Duncan, ' but I would surely like to play a sprig or two just now.'

'Ach, we would all like that,' broke in one of the others,' but I think the people by the loch would be surprised to hear Granny here playing the pipes.'

They all laughed at this and Duncan agreed it would not be a sensible thing to do to draw attention to their whereabouts.

Down at the shore, in Donald McKendrick's house, not far from Mains Castle, Donald was sitting with his sons round the big table in his substantial stone house.

'Well, lads,' he said, 'I think we had better be careful with this lot. They are holding an old woman hostage, which is not what you might call honourable behaviour.'

'Are you saying we should not fight them, father?' asked Hugh, his third oldest son, a lad just turned twenty-two and known for having a bit of a temper.

'Just take it easy, Hugh,' said the eldest of the brothers, young Donald, who was twenty-seven and married with a family of his own, 'Father is just pointing out that these Argyll cleansers might not be honourable men.'

'And there are a dozen of them,' put in Dougal, the youngest of them all at eighteen, but already thought of as having an old man's head on his young shoulders.

'So what?' snapped back Hugh. 'Any McKendrick is worth two of them any day.'

'Wheesht, Hugh,' his father said sternly, 'You are always too eager for battle. If we do go one-to-one against them it is likely some of us will die and we have no way of knowing whether they would accept fair fighting anyway. I think we should think hard about this.'

'And I think maybe we should be up and about early father,' suggested Dougal.

Now honour was one thing, and survival another. The Argyll men outnumbered them two to one and had already threatened to kill a defenceless old woman. It was this that finally made up Donald McKendrick's mind as to what should be done, and he thought it wise to listen to his youngest son as well.

So it was that the following morning, a full hour before they had said they would arrive, the MacDiarmaids were making their way down through the woods towards Donald's house near the shore. Archibald never knew what hit him. As he fell to the ground with an arrow through his throat five of his companions also fell, each of them dead or dying. The others, realising their plan had been thwarted, turned and ran from their unseen assailants. It was only a matter of minutes till all but one had been shot dead in his tracks. The last one was Duncan, the piper. He had got off a fair distance and was just passing a lochside pool when the arrow found his heart. It was only later, when his body was pulled out from the pool that the McKendricks found his pipes. From that day onwards they called it the Piper's Pool but poor Duncan never did get to play his pipes leading home a successful *creach* after that.

The Duntroon Piper

The Castle of Duntroon overlooking Loch Crinan was reckoned to be virtually impregnable. It had been held by the Campbell clan for centuries and was on the site of an even more ancient settlement. It looked out over the Sound of Jura to the northern half of that island. Jura, like most of mainland Argyll, was held by Campbells, though over the years there had been more than a little trouble between the Campbells of Duntroon and their distant cousins on Jura. Things however had been quiet for a while and a Jura piper, Duncan Campbell, had even come over from the island and settled in the area. He was a fine piper and was accepted into the clan community at Duntroon – after all, he was a Campbell. However Duncan was a part of a long-laid plan.

Many years before, there had been a battle between the Duntroon and Jura men and the mainlanders had proved victorious. The island men were believers in the old adage that revenge is a dish best eaten cold, and had appeared to accept the reverse while in fact planning far ahead. So Duncan had in fact been sent amongst the Duntroon Campbells to bide his time till the situation was ripe for revenge. A few years after he had become accepted at Duntroon he began to hear about a great raid that was being planned. The son of the local chief, Alistair Mor Campbell was ready to go cattle-raiding. Normally young Alistair would have gone off with a small band of seasoned warriors to prove himself on a cattle-raid, but his father was in the mood to hit back at the MacLarens over in Breadalbane. A couple of seasons earlier the MacLarens had raided them and he wanted to go and exact his revenge on the MacLarens around Killin on Loch Tay.

While planning the raid, one thing led to another and soon it became apparent that nearly all of the warriors of the clan were a bit restless and ready to go on a raid. Such a large body of men, almost a hundred, would be able to lift a great many cattle and other stock, so the idea was very attractive to Alistair Mor. He had no worries about leaving Duntroon Castle in the hands of a few young lads, the old men and the women. Wasn't Duntroon Castle impregnable once the gates were locked, sitting on its high, smooth rock? Anyway, Loch Tay wasn't too far off, and they would be back in a few days. So it came about that virtually every able-bodied man around Duntroon turned up one after-noon in early September with his weapons and enough food to last a week, ready to go off on the cateran trail. Most of their travelling would be done in the night and the excitement was high.

Duncan the piper realised that the time had come to put the long-laid plan of the Jura men into action. However, he had a problem. All the other able-bodied men were going on the road and he would be expected to go along. It was a great tradition amongst the cateran to come back from a successful raid with their pipers playing a victory tune in the van and great banners blowing in the wind. This return was one of the highpoints of the whole affair and the role of the pipers was a central one.

Luckily the planning of the Jura men had been thorough and he had been instructed in the use of a certain plant by one of the old wise women before he left. He had carefully found and dried some of the plant which he took, boiled in water, a few days before the raiding party was to set off. He knew what would happen but was unprepared for just how effective the plant would be. Now, although Duncan had been at Duntroon for a few years by now, he had not taken a wife and lived alone in a wee house at the far end of the clachan in the shadow of Duntroon. Here he found himself in great distress as the effects of the plant hit him. He began to sweat violently at first, then on came a blinding headache followed by bouts of violent vomiting and diarrhoea. His neighbours next door heard him in his distress and sent for one of their own wise women to have a look at him. Old Maggie came and examined him and then gave him a potion of her own to settle him and sent word to Alistair Mor that Duncan would be in no fit state to travel for a few days. By the day of the raid he was feeling a lot better, though there would be no way he could have faced the rigours of a raid to Loch Tay.

So the Duntroon Campbells set off in the gloaming on their raid without the Jura piper. By the time they were only a few miles off however, Duncan was up and out of his bed. He had some broth that the old woman had left for him, and once he had eaten he felt not too bad. Night had not long fallen when he walked out from his house with his pipes and up to a wee hillock overlooking the loch. Here, having taken note that the wind was blowing offshore towards Jura, he proceeded to march up and down playing a pibroch. The old men and the women of the place realised they had never heard it before and thought it a fine stirring piece of music. What did surprise them was that Duncan played it again and again. They were impressed by how much he had recovered. Duncan though, was finding it hard to keep going. He had lost a lot of his strength but had to play till he saw a signal. At last a torch flared over in the dark. It was followed by another, then another. Three lights burned over there on the Jura shore. His message had got through. Duncan played till the end of the piece then stopped and sat down. He was tired to the bone, but for the plan to work he still had one job to do.

He left the knoll and walked up to the castle. There at the castle gate was Old Lachlan Ban, a man of over seventy who could still walk for hours on the hill and do a full day's work. His eyesight, however, was failing him and he knew well that his raiding days were behind him.

'Good evening, Lachlan,' said Duncan as he approached, 'it's Duncan Piper. How are you doing this fine night?'

'Och, it is yourself then Duncan, is it?' replied the old white-bearded warrior,' you seem to be a bit better now. I heard you playing a bit earlier. That was a fine tune but not one I have heard before.'

'Och, it's one I learned as a lad and had forgotten. "The Dun Cow of the Black Chief" it is called, I think. I thought I should come and keep you company in the castle seeing as all the lads are off.'

' Och, good thinking, we've only a few laddies and us old fellas here. You are more than welcome. Sit and let's have a wee talk.'

So the piper sat with the old man and they talked for a while till Lachlan decided it was time to shut the great wooden door of the castle. With the pair of them it was easy enough and they retired to their beds. Duncan however had no intention of sleeping. After an hour or so he sneaked back down from where he had been lying pretending to sleep, and, after making sure no one was about he lifted the heavy bar from the door and pushed it very slightly ajar. Then as soundlessly as he had come down, he went back to his bed.

Out in the Sound of Jura the islandmen were approaching. There were more than a dozen birlinns each being rowed by six men, instead of the more normal twelve. Their oars were muffled and not a word was said as they headed for Duntroon. There was only starlight to go by but they knew well where they were going – this had been long planned. Silently they came into the shore with their oars shipped, and without a word pulled the wooden boats up on to the sands. Then, swords in hand, but expecting no resistance, they made their way up to Duntroon.

The castle door seemed closed, but as they came up to it they realised it was slightly ajar. Quick as a flash they ran into the castle and spread throughout its rooms. The first the few warriors left knew of their presence was when they were awoken up with swords at their throat. Resistance was impossible and within minutes every man capable of wielding a sword against the reivers was firmly tied up, including Duncan, who was given a bit of extra attention by being punched and slapped a few times by his cousins. 'Ach well, I hope you like it better over here now, Duncan Piper,' spat Big Donald, the leader of the attack, 'you'll not be living the good life once we have gone. Enjoy yourself amongst this lot, why don't you?' At this he gave Duncan a kick and the piper looked at him as if he had murder in his soul. The Jura men all laughed, then went about the business they had come for.

They had brought as many boats as they could find, borrowing a few from Islay relations, as they had a lot of booty to carry off. The cattle, horse and sheep were laid down, their feet tied and carried into the birlinns. Even with the numbers they had it took three round trips for them to carry off all the beasts. But they took more than that. Hardly a scrap of food or corn was left in the lands around the castle by the time they had finished. They had cleansed the place of just about everything not tied down.

When the men of Duntroon came home two days later they were all set to be welcomed as heroes. With the cattle they had lifted on their *spreach* they reckoned that there were good times ahead. They were met by their wives and children in tears. Their raid had been successful but not nearly as successful as that of the Jura men. So much food and stock had been stolen that it was obvious lean times were ahead. Several of the young men wanted Alistair Mor to organise an immediate raid on the Jura men.

'No, that we cannot do. They will be well prepared for us if we go off at them now. We will have to bide our time.' He looked around the warriors standing with him below the castle. 'It might take us some time but we will have our revenge . . . For now, let us repair what we can and tighten our belts a while.'

The chieftain realised that the success of the Jura men could only have come about by treachery. The fact that they had come with extra boats showed they had a clear plan. Their plan had been just about perfect. Alistair knew someone had to have helped them. Over the next few days he spoke to as many of the old men, women and children as he could, including Duncan. All said they knew nothing of the Jura men's arrival till they stormed up from the beach.

No one could explain how the castle door had been left ajar. Old Lachlan said he was sure that he had closed it and asked Duncan to support him. Duncan was happy to do so, sure that the behaviour of the Jura men towards him – he was carrying a lot of bruises on his face and body – would clear him of all suspicion.

Alistair Mor seemed satisfied after speaking to him, but over the next week he continued to ask quietly about what had happened. Each night he went through what had happened. At last the facts began to make some sense to him. Duncan had been out playing an unknown pibroch that night and he had been inside the castle. Still he wouldn't condemn a man till he was absolutely sure of his guilt. He went to see Old Maggie and asked her, 'Maggie, would it be possible that a man could bring a sickness on himself like that Duncan Piper had before we left?' At once Maggie grasped what Alistair meant. She looked at him long and hard.

'I think that maybe it would be. There are plants I could give you that would make you that ill. It didn't cross my mind at all, when I went to see him,' she finished, looking askance at the chieftain.

'Och, why would you have been suspicious? It is only now I can see what he seems to have been about,' Alistair said in a deadly tone of voice. 'Still, I cannot be totally sure. Say nothing to anyone of what we have discussed here, please mother.'

Maggie nodded and Alistair went off for a walk to think things through.

He was now pretty certain what had happened. Then one of the women came and told him that her son had seen three torches flaring on Jura earlier in the night of the raid. Immediately he had the lad brought to him at the castle and sat him down.

'Now, Iain Ban, tell me what you saw.' The chieftain said, piercing the lad, about nine years old, with a cold stare.

Now Iain was like all other lads and wanted to be a great warrior when he grew up, and his idea of a great warrior was, of course, his chieftain Alistair Mor. And here was Alistair Mor asking him for help. The wee lad's heart was near bursting with pride as he told him of the three torches he had seen that night,

'And what time would that be, would you know?' asked Alistair.

'Och, that's easy enough. It was just when Duncan Piper was up on the wee hill playing. He played a long time and it was awfully fine,' the wee lad said looking up in awe at his chieftain.

'Thank you, Iain Ban, you have done the clan a great service this day, and it will not go unnoticed.' As he spoke the Chieftain rose to his feet, and nodding at the small group of warriors in the room he motioned them to accompany him. He knew who and now he knew how!

Up at the end of the clachan Duncan was just coming out of his own door when he saw the Alistair and the others approach. He knew immediately he had been found out and dashed into the house for his sword. But the men with Alistair were as quick as he and he was overpowered before he could strike a blow.

That same day the entire community assembled before Duntroon Castle to hear the fate of this treacherous piper. His treachery was unforgiveable. He had hoped that things would quieten down and that maybe the same trick could be played twice, after which he would have happily returned to Jura as a hero. Now though his fate would be different.

His end was described in a poem by Sir Ian Malcolm in his *Highland Lore and Legend*:

> Sever me now those cunning hands
> and let them burn behind the fire
> make fast his limbs in iron bands
> and robe him in his last attire
> shroud in a sack form head to heel
> the traitor vile who fouls the ground
> rivet him in a monster creel
> and fling him far into the sound

This was how the Duntroon Campbells took care of the treacherous piper. The time would come soon enough when they could settle this score with the thieving raiders from Jura.

The Finlarig Christening

Back in the 17th century amongst the Highland people

> None thought it wrang to caw a prey
> Their auld forebears practised it aw their days
> An neer the worse for that did set their clathes.

Raiding was an integral part of clan life and to all intents and purposes all the adult men of a community were its warriors, both as defenders against raiding and as raiders themselves. Different clans living alongside each other would often ally themselves against raiders from other areas, which sometimes gave rise to occasions where relatives found themselves on opposite sides of the fight.

It was around 1610 that a great gathering took place at Finlarig Castle at the western end of Loch Tay. The local chief, Sir Robert Campbell, had become a father and word had been sent round all the neighbouring countryside that there was to be a celebration for his son's christening. So friends came in from far and near to join in the celebration. Sir Robert was known to be generous and well-off, so apart from the feast in the Great Hall there would be food and drink at the castle for anyone who turned up. Now although Scotland by this time had long been a Christian country there were a few truly ancient habits surviving from pagan times that continued to be observed. As ever, in kin-based societies the old men and women of the community were held in great respect, particularly those who were believed to have knowledge of the 'old ways', often combining practical knowledge like healing and weather lore with an awareness of ancient rituals.

These members of the community kept up ancient traditions and at the baptism of Sir Robert's son there was quite a gathering of old wise women and wise men. It seems that the ritual saining [sanctifying] of the bairn took place in the castle before he was christened, or even baptised, by the priest. The process was relatively simple. The child was put into a wicker basket with bread and cheese, the whole was covered by a new linen cloth tucked in tightly, and then was swung three times over the fire in the great hall of the castle. As this was done the old sages chanted an ancient spell: 'Let the flame consume thee now or never,' three separate times. This seems to have been linked to the same beliefs that underpinned great Fire Festivals of Beltane (1 May) and Samhain (1 November) that lasted well into the 19th century in Scotland. Such a non-Christian ritual is hardly surprising four hundred years ago in an area where to this day some of the oldest traditions in these islands are being kept up. The bairn had been sained and then baptised and the party was in full swing in the great hall. There were vast amounts of food and drink and the pipers were just getting ready to play for people dancing, when a messenger arrived. A group of hardened cateran, MacDonalds of Keppoch from far to the north-west had swept through several nearby glens and lifted a vast number of cattle. Just as the messenger arrived, another came running into the hall to say that the raiders were at that moment driving their *creach* over the nearby hill of Stroneclachan. They obviously knew that there was a gathering at Finlarig and reckoned that Campbell would be too busy with his celebrations to bother about them. They didn't know Campbell as well as they thought.

As soon as he heard of the raid Sir Robert called for men to go after the raiders. Many of the men in the christening party, upwards of fifty of them, gathered up their weapons and ran off to pursue the raiders. They included James Menzies, an experienced soldier, John Campbell, captain of the Finlarig garrison, John Campbell of Craichens, Balquhidder, Captain Hew Campbell and Duncan McArthur, brother to McArthur of Inschstrynie, who were nephews of Sir Robert. By the time the Campbell party caught up with the raiders at Coire nam Bonnach however, perhaps they weren't really in much of a condition to fight. Most of them had had a good few drinks in the castle and though, like all Highlanders, they were fit and active, the run up the hill had tired them a bit. Then there was the small problem of the fact that they found themselves considerably outnumbered by the Keppoch men. This raid had obviously been long in the planning and they met not half a dozen raiders, but well over sixty MacDonalds and MacGregors, all of them seasoned caterans. After a short hard fight the Loch Tay men were forced to retreat down the hill, leaving a good number of their men dead behind them in the heather. Ever since that day the stream near where they fell has had the name An t-Allt Fuileach, 'the Bloody Burn'.

As soon as they got back to the castle Sir Robert wasted no time. The fiery cross, *crann-tara*, was sent through all the local glens. The numbers at Finlarig had been limited for the christening as it was really more of a personal than a clan event, so there were many more warriors in the glens around Finlarig who were now called on to hunt the MacDonalds down. Within a couple of hours nearly two hundred heavily armed warriors had arrived at the castle, each one with enough oats and salt in his sporran to last several days on the hill. That and their arms was all they had to carry. Their breacans or plaids were both clothes and shelter for them. It was being able to move with no baggage of any kind that made the Highland warrior such an efficient fighter. At a word from Campbell they set off at a steady run. Soon they passed the spot where twenty of their own lay dead. There would be time enough to bury them later: now they were intent both on revenge and on getting back their stolen cattle. On and on they ran, without a break; a thirsty man would simply scoop up water from a burn as he passed, and a few hours later they were on the braes of Glenorchy, the lands of Robert's brother, Sir Colin Campbell, chief of the Campbells in the area. They eventually caught up with the cateran just at Coire Charmaig in Glenlochay which runs west from the end of Loch Tay. The cateran were slowed down by the work of herding their lifted cattle. In the battle which ensued most of the cateran were killed, including Angus, son of Alasdair nan Cleas of Keppoch. A lament for him was composed by the the famous poet Iain Lom, Bard of Lochaber, who was present at the battle himself. It is striking that the bard made the lament for the son of his chief when Iain Lom's own father was killed that day in Glenlochy. There were significant casualties on both sides, but the Mac-Donalds and the MacGregors suffered a crushing defeat and the Campbells and their friends returned to Finlarig with the cattle. Raiders from Lochaber and Glencoe were not seen near Loch Tay for many years after this.

Colin's Cattle

⟫•◈•⟪

There is a very famous Gaelic song called *Crodh Chailen*, 'Colin's Cattle', which was used both as a lullaby for children and as a tune to soothe fractious cows during milking. The song is said to have been composed in Glenlyon in the 1640s. The country had been torn apart with religious warfare for the previous few years and the Royalist troops of Sir James Graham, the Marquess of Montrose, contained a great many clansmen from the Glencoe and Keppoch areas. In 1644 he sent them back to their homes after the Battle of Tippermuir with clear instructions not to attack other clans on the way. However, one group of them when they reached the fertile lands of Glenlyon could not resist the attraction of the fine, fat cattle belonging to young Colin Campbell of Glenlyon. They swept away all the cattle, along with quite a few beasts belonging to his uncle, John, known as 'the Tutor'.

Now when the MacDonalds came upon Colin's cattle, they were being tended in a quiet glen full of rich lush grass by the 'banarach mhor' [the chief dairymaid], whose name has not come down to us. To help with driving the cattle, and probably with milking too, the cateran dragged the milkmaid off with them on their journey westward. Unnoticed by the cateran she had a companion, the little dairymaid, 'an banarach bheag', whose name was NicRee (men called themselves Mac, 'son of', and women Nic, 'daughter of') whose job was to tend to the calves; she had seen them coming and had quickly driven her charges into an old stone rath, or fort, at Cambuslay. Here she watched as the rest of the cattle were rounded off and driven away with her companion along with them. Now Highland men were always very proud of their courage and their skill with arms but it has long been known that Highland women are just as courageous as their menfolk, if not even more so. The banarach bheag decided that she would follow the raiders and look for an opportunity to warn the local people what was happening. Now those involved in the *creachs* and spulzies of the cateran were men who knew the hills. They had all been raised in the same warrior traditions and one thing they were always on the lookout for was anyone following them. They made their way through the hills out of sight but the little milkmaid was a match for their lookouts and kept on their trail. She was following them at a distance and not long before reaching the head of Glenlyon they turned the shoulder of a hill and were out of sight. She looked around and at that point a man came out of a wee glen about half a mile behind her.

He was leading a garron, one of the sturdy, native Highland ponies, on the back of which was a stag. Immediately she ran down the hill towards him. She didn't dare shout in case the Glencoe men up the glen should hear her. She was within a couple of hundred metres of the man when he saw this young lassie haring through the heather towards him.

He stopped, and she ran up to him. She bowed her head with her hands on her thighs as she caught her breath, and she looked up to see a kindly face looking down at her.

'Well, lass, and what is it making you race about the hills like a hare,' the man asked with a smile.

'Well,' she says, 'I am trailing a bunch of cateran who have lifted the young chief's cattle and was wondering if you could get word to him where they are,' she panted.

'I could do that sure enough,' he said, 'but why don't you get off and raise the men and I'll trail these damned cleansers?' The smile had gone from the man's face and he looked grim.

'I think you will be faster than me,' said the banarach bheag, 'but I can keep trailing them for a while yet.'

The man looked thoughtful, made up his mind and turned on his heels to run off down Glenlyon, leaving his garron and the freshly-killed stag there in the heather. The sooner he came back with others the sooner they could get back the cattle, and teach these Glencoe raiders a thing or two. The little milkmaid turned and hurried west after the cateran. Soon she had them in sight as they kept turning west and down into Glen Meuran. Their plan was clearly to skirt the eastern edge of Beinn a' Chreachain and drop down on to Rannoch Moor, then on to Glencoe. The little milkmaid saw the men and cattle turn into Glen Meuran from a safe distance, and once they had gone she ran after them. She was just turning into the glen, hugging the side of the hill in the heather, when a gust of wind blew the edge of her dress up. One of the cateran had been posted just over the edge of ground and he saw something move. Without hesitation, he lifted his gun and fired. He had a good aim and the poor wee mikmaid fell dead in the heather. The cateran came running to see who he had shot and was none too pleased to see it was a young girl. Still she had clearly been spying so it was her own fault he thought. He went back to join his fellows and tell them they had been followed.

Meantime the man the wee milkmaid had met raced off down the glen and encountered a bunch of men at Pubil. They had come up the glen looking for the cateran but had lost the trail. It was the matter of a moment for him to let them know where their enemy was, and they set off at a brisk trot through the heather.

When they found the body of the little milkmaid, no one said a word, but they knew now there would be little mercy for the cateran when they caught up with them. A little while later an banarach mhor was sitting on a rock overlooking Rannoch Moor where the cateran had briefly stopped when she heard something. She turned and looked up the way she had just been driving the cattle. There, running silently down the hillside, were a couple of dozen local men, swords and pistols in their hands. The cateran had dropped their guard after hearing of the death of the little milkmaid and the Glenlyon men were on them almost before they knew it. The fight was short and deadly. Within a few minutes several of the Glencoe men were dead on the hillside and the rest ran off down the hill, pursued by Glenlyon men. Some escaped, but not many.

When the milkmaid heard what had happened to her companion she burst into tears, and could hardly stop crying all the way back home. To keep herself from worrying about her situation she had been making up a new song as she went along with the Glencoe cateran, and a couple of days later *Crodh Chalein* was sung in Glenlyon for the first time, in honour of an banarach bheag who had given up her life in Glen Meuran in pursuit of the cateran.

A Sense of Humour

⋙⋅◆⋅⋘

In the late 1490s a group of Maclarens from Balquhidder came down to the Braes of Lochaber and lifted a herd of cattle from around Lochtrieg in the shadow of the Mamore mountains. The cattle they had lifted belonged to Donald MacAngus MacArthur. Now the MacArthurs had been the dominant family in Argyll until 1427, when Iain MacArthur was captured and executed by order of James I, and his people scattered. So ended the power of the clan who claimed descent from the son of the legendary King Arthur Smervie Mor, and the Campbells took their place in the west. However, Donald MacAngus still had some power, and he gathered up a force to pursue the Maclarens. With him Donald had Macdonalds and MacGillivantics from Lochtrieg and they caught up with the raiders on Rannoch Moor near the Bridge of Orchy. Seeing a much larger force pursuing them the Maclarens decided that discretion was definitely the better part of valour and headed off as quickly as they could, leaving the cattle behind. This was a pleasant surprise for Donald and his party who had been prepared for a fight, and they made ready to return home. However, they had to cross the lands of Fletcher of Achallader, who was at that time allied to Dugald Stewart of Appin, a man who was not popular with the MacDougalls and Campbells who lived in the area alongside some of Donald Mor's MacArthur kinsmen. As Donald headed back north with the cattle he ran into a large force of Fletchers and Stewarts being led by Dugald Stewart. They had decided to relieve Donald and his men of their herd and had considerably

213

more men. However, the arrival of such a large body of men had been noticed locally, and a lot of the MacArthurs, MacDougalls and Campbells were lurking around waiting to see what would happen.

So, when Dugald Stewart attacked Donald's party the locals all entered the fray on the side of MacArthur. Unlike many of the skirmishes that occurred in the course of cattle-lifting this turned into a full-scale battle, known as the Battle of Leachdar, and it was fought close to the Bridge of Orchy on the slopes of Ben Dorain. As was the custom, Donald and Dugald Stewart fought hand-to-hand, and each of them died an honourable death at the others' hands. Now Dugald was a tall man, while Donald was a short stocky character and one of Donald's party, Donald MacGillivantic, had thought the match between them unfair, Stewart having the advantage of both height and reach. Nevertheless, the two combatants were evenly matched and ended up killing each other. Now it is a fact that men inured to battle can develop some odd habits, and an even stranger sense of humour,

With the bodies of the two chieftains lying there, MacGillivantic, a short fellow himself and known as Domhnull Ruadh Beag, 'wee red-haired Donald', decided to cut off Dugald Stewart's head, commenting as he did so, 'Well, they'll not be able to say Dugald was taller than Donald after this.' The battle itself was inconclusive, but Donald and some of his immediate kinsmen, reflecting on the battle a day or so later, realised that his actions would surely provoke some form of revenge from the Stewarts. So they decided to go and live amongst the MacArthurs up at Glen Roy to the north-west of Loch Treig, where they were made welcome, having shown their courage at the Battle of Leachdar.

Gillesbuig Uarasach

⇒◆⇐

The name Gillesbuig Uarasach means 'Gillespie the Proud' and is a pretty fair description of a man who was a noted warrior of his time. His name was Archibald or Gillespie Mackenzie, and he lived close to Braemar in the early 18th century. A small man, but very strong and vigorous, he was a great exponent of all weapons then in use in the Highlands – claymore, short sword, dirk, pistols, guns, etc. He was also a very resourceful and clever man, but an implacable enemy. Gillespie was also very proud and in fact a bit full of himself. He always acted the gentleman, and considered any kind of labour such as farming or cattle-tending as beneath him. After one particular episode in his early life involving cateran raiders, he never went out of his house without a gun, broadsword, dirk, targe, a pair of pistols and a sgian dubh in each stocking, as well as one in each sleeve of his shirt. The reason for this arose from a series of run-ins with men from Glenshee.

The first time he ran into them, he and a group of Mackenzies were gathering firewood in the north end of Glenshee when they met a larger group of Glenshee men who were going up into the moors to collect peat. Being greater in numbers the Glenshee men began to mock the Braemar lads with traditional jokes and rhymes that they had learned as children, but they hadn't reckoned with Gillespie. Totally unconcerned about the super-ior numbers, Gillespie ran forward amongst the Glenshee men's horses, a dirk in one hand and a sgian dubh in the other, slitting the girths holding the peat baskets on their backs. All the baskets fell to the ground, at which point he gave them a real mouthful. 'Now after this say nothing of the Gairnside and Braemar men, even though you may see that they are fewer in number than you, for if ever I again hear what I have heard today I'll cut up every one of you as I have today cut your horses' girths.'

The Glenshee men were a bit shocked but also very impressed by the bravery of the wee man, and word of his bravery and readiness for combat soon spread. It wasn't long after this when he ran into another group of locals at Blackwaterford while he was returning to Braemar through Glenshee. They were all on horseback, and as the Glenshee men passed him in the middle of the ford one of them whacked his horse with a stick. Gillespie's horse reared up and he fell off, but immediately sprang back in the saddle and whipped round and stuck the Glenshee man in the leg with his dirk. The seven or eight Glenshee men swarmed round him and laid into him with heavy sticks. All Gillespie had was his dirk and his *sgian dubh* and he managed to score quite a few hits on his opponents before he was battered to the ground. The first man he had felled with a blow of his dirk to the chest had been his initial assailant. Soon however, he was unconscious, and the Glenshee men left him, and the man he had stabbed through the chest with his dirk, lying on the ground for dead. They intended coming back for their fallen comrade but were in a hurry to be off.

A while later another local man passed, and on looking closely at the prone bodies found they were both alive, if in a bad way. So he took the pair of them to his nearby house and put Gillespie in the but and the Glenshee man in the ben of the house. Four days later, both injured men were capable of taking light food, soup etc., and the man went off to the fields with his wife. His wife came back at midday to cook food and she saw Gillespie, bare naked, crawling on all fours, seared with scars, black and blue with bruises, his body and limbs swollen all over, grimacing with pain, but with his dirk between his teeth, heading for the

Glenshee man's bed. He was put back into his bed and tied down. A week or so later, as soon as he was fit, he was sent back to Braemar, but from this time onwards Gillespie never went anywhere unless he was fully armed.

Now even into the 18th century the traditional raiding went on and one night a few years after this, a group of eight Lochaber men came down into Glen Connie and Glen Dee. They made off with a fair number of cattle and the chase was to be led by Farquharson of Invercauld. He set off with thirty men, including Gillespie, and they caught up with the raiders in Glentilt, where they had stopped to rest in a shieling. Realising they were caught, their leader, a great handsome giant of a man, offered single combat to settle the day. This was accepted, and the Lochaber cateran were surprised to see that his opponent was the small, if powerful Gillespie. The chosen weapon was the sword, and the giant, with his reach and strength, thought he was on to a sure thing. However, he had not reckoned with Gillespie's speed which, combined with his stamina and strength, made him a formidable opponent. Within minutes the wee man had run the Lochaber man through and the rest of the Lochaber men were let go after being forced to swear on their dirks that they would never raid in the area again.

This only served to increase Gillespie's reputation further, and when the local blacksmith, an Gobahin Crom, the hunch-backed smith, was killed by a man called Anton in a quarrel over drink, the local chief, MacKenzie of Dalmore, called on Gillespie to get the culprit, dead or alive. Anton had of course fled after the quarrel, realising the danger he was in. Now Mackenzie let it be known that Gillespie would have no problems in getting the man, and in fact boasted of it in company, which got on the nerves of the other local clan, the Farquharsons, who had wanted one of their own to pursue the murderer. Meanwhile Gillespie was off on the trail of the culprit, whom he knew only by description, and caught up with him. Meeting resistance, he killed him. He decided to take his head back to Mackenzie as proof that he had fulfilled his commission. We can only imagine the horror Mackenzie felt when he saw that the head was in fact that of the Earl of Airlie's son who had been hunting in the woods when Gillespie caught up with him. Luckily for Gillespie and Mackenzie no one else had seen Gillespie arrive – it was the middle of the night – so they secretly buried the head and resolved to say nothing of it. It had been an honest enough mistake anyway, Gillespie thought. Again unseen, Gillespie resumed his pursuit of Anton. After a year, when Gillespie had not returned, the Farquharsons were having a great time reminding Mackenzie of his boast. Now this was unbearable for Mackenzie, and he decided to go off after Gillespie and see if he could find any word of him. He was just at the Cairnwell pass, south of Braemar, when he saw a tattered figure approaching. It was Gillespie himself.

'I thought you were dead by now,' says Mackenzie

'Ach no, no,' replied Gillespie, unslinging the bag from his back and pulling out Anton's head, 'I was just fulfilling my commission. He ran me a merry dance but I had the best of it at the end.'

They then buried the murderer's head in Gleney at a spot called ever since Tom-Antian. This of course shut the Farquharsons up, and Gillespie's reputation soared. It wasn't long after this that the cateran raiding in the area began to increase.

In fact there were so many raids that Gillespie was put in charge of a dozen men who were permanently charged with fending off or hunting down raiding parties from other clans. One day after a raid they came upon the raiders at a place called Bothan Leathan just as they were having breakfast. In customary fashion a parley took place and it was agreed that the cateran (there were almost a dozen of them), would keep half the cattle to avoid a fight and return the rest. As their leader reached out to shake hands with Gillespie he turned to his men and shouted, 'I have the best of them by his sword hand now. Lay on lads and show what we can do.'

Gillespie whipped the *sgian dubh* from his right sleeve with his left hand and shouted, 'Och, I have the best of the Lochabermen on the point of my knife,' and stabbed him through the heart. The upshot of the battle was that two of the Lochaber men escaped; the rest were killed and the cattle were returned with only a few wounds among Gillespie's men. However, from that time on Gillespie refused to shake anyone by the hand, which only added to his reputation as a man to be steered clear of.

Another time he was on his own on the high hill-tops when he saw a bunch of raiders driving a decent-sized herd of cattle between Allanmore and Allancluaich. He approached them carefully without being seen, then laid aside all of his weapons apart from a dirk which he concealed in a fold of his plaid. He then went out into the open and approached the men with a cheerful look of simplicity, greeting them as he came near. The cateran asked him if he knew Gillespie Uarasach, but pretending to be a stranger, and a bit slow, he said he didn't. Believing him to be a stranger (clan tartans weren't yet invented), they asked if he would like to help them herd the cattle. Gillespie was delighted to agree and was soon bringing up the rear alongside a speckled cow with five of the raiders.

The rest of the Lochaber men, thinking they were well beyond pursuit had gone on ahead. Suddenly Gillespie whipped out his dirk, stuck it into the speckled cow and turned to his companions saying, 'I am Gillespie Uarasach, now catch me if you can,' and sped off through the heather. The wounded cow slowed the small group down even more, but they were reluctant to leave it. That night they camped near Derry Lodge. They raised a shelter of branches and after covering it over with a few of their plaids laid themselves down to sleep with a couple of them out on the hill guarding the cattle and watching for pursuit.

Meanwhile Gillespie had gone back and gathered up a dozen

men, including Dalmore himself, the chief of the local Mackenzies, and headed at all speed up Glenlui. They came on the encampment in the misty hour of dawn but the sentries saw them coming and gave the alarm. At that, Gillespie and his men charged down the hill. In the shelter the cateran grabbed their weapons and broke out through a hole cut through the branches. All but one of them escaped through the hole before Gillespie burst into the crude structure. The last of the cateran was still there trying to untangle himself from the branches which had collapsed over the hole hacked through them. There was no hesitation in the warrior's heart and he killed the Lochaber man with a single blow of his dirk, forcing his way through the hole to see the rest of the cateran running off through the heather. As he stood looking at them go, wondering whether to pursue them or not, he heard Dalmore call out behind him, 'The devil take you, Gillepsie, you and your dirk.' Gillespie turned back to see the chief pulling the body of the Lochaber man from the wreck of the shelter. A man? No, he was no man, but a laddie, not even twelve years old. In the heat of the pursuit, his bloodlust running, Gillespie had not even noticed that he had killed a mere boy.

Up on the hill the Lochaber men heard Dalmore's shout and knew who had killed their young kinsman. He had been so excited to come on a raid as he was an only child with a widowed mother and had hoped to make her life better by profiting from the raid. The upshot of it all was that the Lochaber men let the story be told and Gillespie, who did possess a sense of honour, was obliged to give the widow a pension for the rest of her life. His reward for his actions that day was the speckled cow which, once its wound was healed, turned out to be a fine beast indeed.

Gillespie's Revenge

———◈———

Over the next few years there were several more raids on the area and in virtually every case Gillepsie either killed or saw off the raiders. His reputation grew and he was considered a real champion in the area. He ended up by securing the hand of one of the fairest lassies of the area in marriage and moved from his wee cottage in Gleney to a more substantial place near Dalnabord. For a while things were quiet on the raiding front and Gillespie settled into domestic life with his bonny young wife, spending a great deal of time hunting, as he still saw any kind of farming or cattle tending beneath his station. He left that sort of thing to his new wife. In his role of defending the Mackenzies against the raiders Gillespie had become relatively well off and was very proud of a grey mare he had been given by Dalmore. He thought he cut a fine figure riding it and was often seen on her back when he could as easily have walked. But then again he was 'Gillepsie the Proud'.

It was late autumn one year when a bunch of cateran, again from Lochaber, settled themselves in a recently vacated group of summer shielings in the hills above Braemar. The local people had returned to their homes in the glens and straths below and the cateran had plenty of time to spy out the country.

With Gillespie off somewhere else hunting, the opportunity for a successful raid was greatly increased and the leader of the raiders, known simply as Ceatharnach Dubh, 'the Dark or Black Cateran', realised that Dalmore's cattle were ripe for being lifted. So one autumn morning he lifted all of the chief's cattle. Seumas

Mor na Pluice, 'Big James of the Puffy Cheeks', as the chief was known, was furious. Gillespie was still off in the hill hunting, so after sending word to him to get back quickly, Seumas went off after the caterans himself. With him were half a dozen local men and his own two sons.

The trail of the caterans wasn't hard to follow and soon they had come upon them back up at the shieling bothies of Alltan-Odhar. Now at this time things between the Mackenzies and the Farquharsons were pretty tense, and Dalmore was expecting there would soon be trouble with his neighbours. So he was extremely reluctant to fight with the cateran and risk losing men he would need soon enough elsewhere. He decided that discretion was the better part of valour in the situation and that he would approach Ceatharnach Dubh with an offer of money for return of the cattle. Seumas was an experienced warrior himself, and before going down to the shieling he told his sons and the rest of the small band that if things were going badly and he wanted them to take on the cateran he would raise his right hand to his brow.

He went down to the cateran holding his hands high to show he had no weapon in them and proceeded to talk to the cateran leader. In such a situation it was only to be expected that the Lochaber man would want to bargain and get as much money as he could for returning the cattle. Likewise, Seumas would want to keep the cost as low as possible. So the two of them began bargaining and the men on the hillside above them watched closely. The bargaining became quite heated and both men were stamping about, pulling looks at each other, clenching their fists and shaking their heads. It was like watching a couple of horse-dealers at a market, each one trying to get the better of the other. The discussion became more heated when in exasperation Seumas forgot himself and lifted his right hand to whip off his bonnet and cast it on the ground. On the hill the Mackenzies saw their chief's hand go to his brow. A shot rang out and one of the Lochaber men, standing at the door of one of the shielings with a gun in his hand, fell dead. Ceathernach Dubh turned and ran toward the fallen man. Seumas Mor turned to wave to his men to stop firing. The Lochaber cateran reached the fallen sentry, grabbed his gun, raised it and shot Seumus Mackenzie as he stood there signalling to his men. The Mackenzies charged down the hill and a short brutal fight ensued. The cateran, with superior numbers, had the best of it, and within a short while the chief's two sons lay dead on the heather near their father's body, along with a few more of the Mackenzies. The rest were forced to retreat and the raiders took off with the cattle, leaving the bodies of a couple of their own men lying in the open air.

Only a short while afterwards Gillespie arrived with a much bigger force of Mackenzies and at once he sped off after the raiders while a great cairn was raised where the chief had fallen. Gillepsie managed to pick off one or two of the rear guard of the Lochaber cateran, but then came back. It was a sad and sorry procession that bore the bodies of their chief and his two sons back to Dalmore that night. Gillespie returned home in silence to be told by his wife that the cateran had taken all his cattle and the grey mare of which he was so proud.

Gillepsie looked at his fair young wife and said in a soft voice, 'Well, I could almost have forgiven them that, but today they have killed my chief and his two sons at the shielings on Alltan-Odhar. I swear on the blood of the Mackenzies that I will not sleep twice in the same bed, nor drink twice form the same well, till I have avenged their deaths and received the full value of my grey mare.'

His wife, looking at the implacable features of her man, knew there was no point in trying to convince him to stay home. His mind was clearly made up, and, as everyone knew, once his mind was made up, there would be no change of mind for 'Gillespie the Proud'. She did try to persuade him though, but her smiles and caresses had no more effect than her tears and recriminations. Gillespie was inflexible, he would avenge Dalmore and his sons. The following morning he dressed himself in the tattered rags of a beggar, with several dirks, sgian dubhs and a pair of pistols hidden amongst the rags. Then taking a wallet of food he kissed his wife goodbye, saying, 'I will be home when I have avenged Dalmore.' And so he left without even waiting for the sad funeral of Seumas Mor na Pluice and his sons.

For three years no one around Braemar saw Gillespie, his young wife becoming convinced that her champion husband had met his death somewhere on the Braes of Lochaber. He wandered all over the Lochaber area from end to end and back again, surviving as a beggar. His main problem was that he hadn't a clear idea of what An Cearnathach Dubh looked like. Survivors of the original fight at Alltan-Odhar had given him a rough description but it could have fitted hundreds of Highland warriors of the time. So he went all over Lochaber, from fair to fair, turning up at weddings, baptisms and funerals and all kinds of meetings where people gathered. At last he heard that a meeting was to be held at a local inn to discuss a forthcoming raiding expedition, and to share out a large sum of money that had been raised by blackmail in the south.

The tavern where the meeting was to take place was a somewhat primitive establishment. It was a long, low but wide building with a flat roof that was covered over with grass and other plants. The walls were made of stone, with three holes in each of the long sides for windows. As often as not windows like these were filled with heather to provide some protection from the wind. Inside it was hardly less rugged. A long low table stretched two thirds of the length of the room. It consisted of large flat slabs laid on boulders and along side it were similarly constructed stone seats, some of them covered with moss and heather. Behind the seats ran a space along each wall which was wide enough for two men to pass, and in the corners of the room formed by an interior wall were piles of heather which provided rough bedding. The publican of the place had his quarters behind the dividing wall, which had a gap with a wicker door through which the host would dispense both food and drink, the quality of which far surpassed the rude surroundings. Along each wall there were branches of juniper rammed between the stones where the customers could hang their weapons while they ate and drank. In all there was room for upwards of thirty men around the big stone table.

Gillespie turned up at the inn on the afternoon before the evening scheduled for the big meeting, and by dint of a few pieces of silver and a lot of flattery he got on the right side of the innkeeper. Despite his great pride, Gillespie had always had the gift of the gab, and his past three years had made him adept at drawing information from people without arousing suspicion.

He ordered half a dozen flagons of beer and asked the landlord to join him in a drink. As there was no else around at the time the innkeeper was happy to join him. After most of the ale was drunk Gillespie began to put his plan into action.

'Now, I have to be off to the far end of the country tomorrow,' said Gillespie, 'so is it all right if I just lie down in the corner here and sleep till the morning.'

'Well,' replied, his companion, 'generally there would be no problem but you know I have a large company coming in tonight . . .'

'Ach, I'll be no bother to anyone. I'll be sleeping in the heather there in the corner and I doubt if anyone will even notice me.'

'Aye, but I don't know,' the innkeeper said, stroking his chin, 'Some of the lads might object.'

'Ach, they'll not even know I am here. I want to go to sleep as early as I can and I'll be dead to the world before they even get here. In fact I think another flagon of beer would help me go off to sleep. Of course I'll pay the going rate, and will you have another yourself?' said the smiling Gillespie. At that the inn-keeper agreed he could sleep in the corner and they finished off the beer. When the cateran arrived just after dark no one paid any attention to the bundle of rags lying on the heather in the corner and as the innkeeper handed round ale and whisky he saw no need to mention his guest. The men settled in around the table, most of them hanging swords, dirks and pistols on the rude wooden hooks in the wall, and making themselves comfortable, realising that this could be quite a long night. At last a tall, powerful-looking dark-haired man with the bearing of a leader of men arrived, and went to the head of the table. Before taking off his weapons he placed a large leather purse on the table. By this time night had fallen and the room was lit by flickering torches as the drink began to flow. Before dividing up the contents of the large purse, which was money raised through blackmail, the leader and the rest of them decided to have a few drinks.

This led to a song or two, then, as things often happened, tales began to be told. And what tales! Mainly they were of just how brave the storyteller had been in some raid or fight, and they were full of miraculous dexterity, brilliant invention, dogged perseverance and various semi-miraculous feats of arms. The more outrageous the story the greater the laughter amongst the men as the drink continued to flow. One after another all told a tale. At last it was the turn of the tall, dark man at the head of the table to speak himself. Gillespie had not moved a muscle for hours as he lay there listening intently.

The dark man stood up and called for silence.

'Many fine deeds I have heard here tonight and I have to say that I have done remarkable things myself.' This statement was met with a few cheers and a great many nods and grunts of agreement. There in the flickering light he went on. 'Of all the deeds I have done I would like to say that about the greatest was the lifting of the grey mare of the fearsome Gillespie Uarasach and getting away with it. And that same day I fired one of the best shots of my life when I took the life of Seumas Mor na Pluice, chieftain of the Mackenzies of Braemar.'

It was none other than Ceatharnach Dubh himself!

At that a figure leapt on to the table before him, a figure dressed in rags but with a pistol in his right hand. The company sat in shocked silence at this apparition, as Gillepsie shouted, 'Well, here is an even better shot, Ceatharnach Dubh,' and let fire at point blank range.

Even as the blood spurted from his chest and he fell back, the chieftain shrieked 'Gillespie Uarasach', with his very last breath. Still no one moved; they couldn't believe their eyes. Seizing his moment Gillespie grabbed the nearest torch and flung it in the fire, grabbed the purse on the table and ran the length of the table to fling himself through the light wicker door. Pandemonium reigned behind him, as men clambered over each other in the gloom, searching for their weapons on the wall. 'After him, after him,' came the cry, as Gillespie threw the purse on the roof of the tavern, then quickly pulled himself up and lay flat, as quiet as he could be.

Out through the door rushed the Lochaber men, brandishing weapons, many of them with torches in their left hands. At once they split up into groups and began to comb the area. This was their own land. They knew it well, and over the next few hours there was not a ditch or a space between rocks, a bush or a clump of trees that was not searched. All through the night they searched, till returning to the tavern about an hour before dawn. Knowing of the fearsome reputation of their prey, the Lochaber men wanted to make sure that none had fallen by the hand of the fierce and fearless Gillespie while searching, so they all accounted for themselves to be sure that all had returned. They were standing at the door of the tavern as they did so and Gillespie, sure now that there was no one out in the night waiting to ambush him, quietly slid from the roof of the inn and walked home over the hills just as the assembled men began to sing a coronach for their murdered leader.

All that night and the next day he went on without stopping, and the following day too. Then he returned at last to Dalmore, having revenged the death of his chief and having incidentally recompensed himself very well for the loss of his grey mare. Before going home to see the wife from whom he had been apart for three long years, Gillespie went to Dalmore. There the new chieftain, the brother of Seumas Mor na Pluice, was delighted to see the return of the best warrior the Mackenzies had, and to hear that his brother's death had at last been avenged. If Gillespie had been a hero and a champion before he was now a living legend around Braemar. He did have some trouble at home, as his wife had despaired of his return and had been paid attention by the local cooper or barrel-maker, but he was soon seen off by our hero, with little if any blood being shed.

From then on Gillespie's life did quieten down, his fearsome reputation ensuring that no raiders would try and lift cattle around Dalmore. There were other incidents involving his martial skills on behalf of his clan and chief in his later life, though never again did he have to face whole groups of wild cateran on the hill. When at last he approached his end his friends and relations gathered round him in his bed. Realising that his time was nigh he uttered a deep sigh.

'What is it?' asked his faithful wife, who had put up with so much.

'Ach, regret, regret', came the reply in hushed tones.

'Well, unburden yourself and state your repentance,' one of his cousins, a very religious character, urged him. A priest had been sent for but no one expected Gillespie to live till he came.

'Aye, aye,' muttered another, 'let it all out now man, confess and repent before you meet your maker.'

'Pull me up, woman,' Gillespie whispered to his wife.

With the help of one of his cousins she hoisted the dying man into a sitting position. Shakingly his hand reached out down the bed and came up clutching his trusty dirk, the dirk that had never left his side in over forty years.

Then with a look of great sorrow he spoke falteringly, 'My friends, my dear wife, apart from all those that I have loosed of their lives with sword and gun nineteen . . . nineteen I say have I dispatched with this very dirk –'

There was a sharp intake of breath around the room.

'And do you now feel a true and hearty sorrow and repentance?' asked his cousin.

'Aye, that I do,' said Gillespie, his voice suddenly stronger, 'I feel the deepest sorrow and repentance that I did not stab one more to make the twenty with my dirk,' and waving his dirk above his head he fell back, even as his friends and family shrank from the dreaded weapon. He spoke no more. A priest arrived a little later and by morning the greatest ever warrior of the Mackenzies had gone on his final journey.

A Cateran's Penitence

For centuries the Cameron clan were noted for their cattle-lifting skills, and one of their chieftains was given the name Ailean nan Creach, 'Allan of the aids', such was his talent for the business. This meant that his clansmen were pretty well-off in terms of cattle, and as cattle were how people judged wealth, they considered themselves prosperous indeed and were always happy to follow Allan on a raid. However, Allan hit a slump, a bad patch, and his raids were either unsuccessful, costly in terms of bloodshed, or he was lifting so few cattle that they were hardly worth the effort. Now traces of the Old Religion, the paganism that thrived before Christianity came to Scotland, can still be found in certain parts of the Highlands, but back in Allan's time, the 14th century, there were many more survivals of ancient pagan practice. People might have become Christian on the surface, but many of the old ways were considered to be effective, so it was not unusual for people to continue ancient customs that were quite contrary to Christian practice and belief.

Now Allan was concerned that his luck had changed and he decided to consult Gorm Shuil, a local wise woman whose name referred to her piercing blue eyes. Now under the influence of the Christian church such women have generally been portrayed as witches. This is unfair, as many of them were undoubtedly no more than women who, in the course of a long life had developed a great deal of healing knowledge and an awareness of human psychology, though in many cases it seems clear they had inherited what was effectively the knowledge of ancient lore handed down for centuries. The importance of the role of such women has been obscured by the dreadful practices of the witch-hunters of the 16th and 17th centuries, who were, of course, all men. One of the skills of such women was that of divination, foretelling the future. Many of them were even said to have been able to change themselves into hares or other animals, and such shape-shifting, allied to the ability to foretell coming events, suggests they were much like the shamans who still exist in various parts of the world today.

Anyway, Gorm Shuil said that Allan's run of bad luck was such that he should resort to Taghairm, a particularly brutal form of divination. Taghairm involved raising a spirit who would be able to answer questions beyond the wit of humans to fathom. It was a drastic course to take. The practice involved roasting a cat, or even several cats, over a fire. The piteous squealing of the cats was such a horrific noise that it was believed to summon forth spirits of a particulary nasty bent, but who would nonetheless respond to human questioning. The spirit would come in the shape of a cat, but if the roasting carried on long enough it was believed that in time the Devil himself would turn up, something most people would rather avoid. It was a practice that seems thankfully to have been rarely used. Allan, a man of undoubted bravery, decided that he would follow Gorm Shuil's advice.

Standing before the corn kiln at Torcastle he slowly had a live cat turned on a spit over a blazing fire. The smell of singeing hair and burning flesh was revolting, as were the dreadful squeals coming from the poor animal. Soon a crowd of cats of both sexes began turning up round the fire. They were no ordinary cats, for each one had the power of speech. And each one said the same thing: 'That is no way to treat a cat.' Still they did not interfere directly with the process. Then a great one-eyed tom cat, the size of large dog and with glowing red eyes, came into the fire and asked: 'What do you want, human, that you torture one of our brothers so horribly?'

'I want to know what to do. My luck has changed. I have for many years been successful at cattle-lifting and this year have had nothing but bad luck. What should I do?' he asked the terrifying beast. He showed not a flicker of fear, as he looked into the dreadful eyes of the spirit animal.

'What I would do first if I were you,' the cat rumbled in a deep and echoing voce, 'is release that poor cat before some other body turns up here that you will not be happy to see.'

Allan signalled to release the cat.

'But what of my question?' he insisted.

As the cat was removed from over the fire, the spirit looked around the assembled crowd of cats and back at Allan.

'Well,' it said in its eerie voice, 'you have had a good long run but I think it is time for you to take another road. To make up for all your past acts you should found seven churches.'

With this amazing recommendation the cat turned and disappeared. Allan looked around. Apart from the piteous mewing beast lying a few feet from the fire there was not a cat to be seen. He was astounded that one of the ancient spirits should recommend such a course of action. He might have expected this from a priest, but from a spirit! Still, the beast had spoken and Allan decided to follow its advice. The poor cat was nursed for a while but gave up the ghost and died a couple of days later.

Allan went on to do as he was told and founded the churches of Cill Choirill in Keppoch and others at Kilchoan, Kildonan, Laggan, Loch Leven, Morven and Arisaig. There are those who will tell you that this story only arose because such a grand cateran could not have forsaken the School of the Moon out of some sense of Christian piety and that supernatural powers just had to be involved.

Callum Beg

Down the years when cattle-raiding was rife there were those who tended to work alone at lifting. This was hardly the same as the *creachs* carried out by groups of clansmen, and in most cases it was certainly more like what we today would consider plain theft rather than any traditional inter-tribal practice. In the latter years of the 17th century there was a man who was a crofter in the Streens, in the hills along the river Findhorn, who developed quite a reputation. He was known as Callum Beg or 'Wee Callum', and had for a while worked for Sir Hugh Campbell at his castle at Cawdor, a few miles from Nairn on the Moray coast. One day Callum was tending a fine herd of cattle on the home-farm of Cawdor when a band of cateran swooped down from the hills to lift the cattle. Not only did they lift the cattle but, they took Callum along with them to help with the herding. Soon they were up on the moors and Callum was deep in thought as he drove the cattle ahead of him with Highlanders watching his every move. He had no idea what fate awaited him when they got to wherever the cateran had come from. He was pretty sure they were from Badenoch and even if they let him go he would have a fair trudge ahead of him to get back to Moray. As he went along he began to think of plans to get out of his situation. Desperation is the mother of invention right enough, and soon he came up with a plan. The cateran, all armed with swords, dirks and pistols had not bothered to search Callum for weapons. Just like every other one of the Highlanders Callum carried the *sgian dubh* or black knife. It might not have been as fierce a weapon or as useful

233

as the dirks the cateran were all carrying, but it certainly had its uses.

As they drove south through the hills every few hundred yards Callum cut off a small piece of his own plaid and dropped it on the ground. His hope was that some sharp-eyed member of the party that would be sent out after the cattle would follow the trail. The cateran were taking a winding path through the hills to try to avoid being followed, and wherever possible they would drive the cattle through burns and across rock to minimise the trail. They had no idea their efforts were to prove useless. That night Callum spent on the hills, under the stars, along with the cateran, with a rope tied to his bound arms, which was in turn tied round the leg of a fully-armed cateran sleeping near him: escape was impossible. They were up at the first light of dawn and after a quick cold meal of oats and water they set off south again.

Later that day, just as they reached the slopes of Clapa Mor, the mountain at the headwaters of the Findhorn, the raiding-party caught up with them. There was a short sharp fight as the Moray men rushed on the Badenoch cateran in fairly heavy numbers, driving them off and securing the cattle. They had had no trouble at all in following Callum's trail and Sir Hugh himself was more than happy to get Callum a new plaid to replace the one that had served them all so well. From this time on many locals considered him a bit of a hero.

It was after this that Callum began to farm the croft in the Streens with his wife. It was thought of as a good croft and Sir Hugh had given it to him to farm as a reward. However, crofting is hard work if you want to have more than the bare necessities, and Callum began to think of easier ways of making a living. Now he was a small but stocky man of enormous strength and remarkable endurance. He soon realised that the wit that helped him trick the Badenoch cateran might serve him well in other areas. In short he resolved to go into the cattle-lifting business himself. For many years he was careful not to take any beasts from people in the area around his home, but outwith that area he was a very clever lifter indeed. He would often secrete small numbers of cattle in small, hidden corries high up in the hills, and was never short of meat. In fact he began to get a reputation amongst those of his neighbours who were less well-off than himself, for he was generous with his acquisitions. Soon nobody in the Streens would speak of him without giving him the compliment 'that honest man Callum Beg'. The local people knew fine well what he was up to, but they were part of the old clan system themselves and admired the way that he went about his business. Even if many of them were by then simple crofters they still wore the old garb and followed many of the old ways in language and custom.

Now Callum didn't completely forsake working his croft; he had rent to pay, which was usually expected in kind, and it would have proved suspicious if he always paid in gold, a supply of which was regulary coming his way through an arrangement with a butcher in the small town of Daviot. He found the work tiring and boring and wasn't helped by the fact that the only horse he had to work the land with was a weak, spay-backed creature with an evil temper. He had noticed that his neighbour over the river had half a dozen horses, and one of them, a fine, brown stallion about the same size as his own miserable nag, took his eye. Now he could probably have bought it from the man, even if it was his best horse, if he had been prepared to pay enough, but Callum, as ever, decided to use his cunning.

Secretly in his barn he killed his own miserable white beast and with his wife's help he carefully skinned it, and under cover of darkness they chopped up and buried the remains. That same night, in the wee small hours, he swam across the river to where he knew his neighbour kept the brown horse. Carefully he approached the beast and murmured softly in its ear. The beast came with him without any trouble and together they went back to Callum's. Here he and his wife spent much of the rest of the night sewing the brown horse into the skin of the white one! The creature didn't seem to mind at all. The next morning his neighbour found he had been relieved of his bonny brown horse and went off asking if anyone had any idea who had stolen it. For weeks he fretted over the loss unaware that the horse Callum was using to till his ground over the river was only white to the eye!

Cattanach of Bellastraid

Cattanach was a well-known cateran who lived at Bellastraid on the banks of the Logie in Cromar. Like many other local men he had been out in the '45 and had found it hard to settle down after the Jacobite defeat. Like so many others he took to the old raiding ways. However, he wasn't subtle about it and very soon he came to the attention of the authorities in Aberdeen for 'contraventions of the law'. However, he knew the Aberdeenshire hills very well and managed to escape being caught. Finally one Cuthbert, 'the terror of evil-doers' was sent to get him dead or alive. By now Cattanach was living in open defiance of the law, wearing Highland dress and permanently going around carrying weapons. Late one night a stranger arrived at the inn at the Milton of Logie, opposite Bellastraid. This was the famous Cuthbert whose intention was to surprise Cattanach in the morning. He knew exactly where Cattanach lived and had little doubt that he would either capture or kill the rebel when the time came. Although he was travelling incognito, any stranger was suspicious, and word got to Cattanach within hours of Cuthbert's arrival that there was a stranger at the inn who looked very much like a government man. Everyone was aware that the government could hardly let Cattanach away with his blatant behaviour. Being warned though, Cattanach rose very early the next morning, loaded the musket he had used at Culloden and hid it under his plaid over his back. He then crossed over the burn between him and the inn by the stepping stones there, just in time to meet Cuthbert coming out of the inn door.

'It's a sharp morning this, sir, and who might you be after today?' asked Cattanach.

'Who the hell are you that you demand a right to know that?' demanded Cuthbert.

'I am Cattanach of Bellastraid and I believe I have a right to know,' came the reply.

Cuthbert realised what was happening, drew out one of his pistols and fired straight at Cattanach. Luckily for him the pistol misfired, and Cuthbert went to draw his other pistol.

'Ha, ha, my man is that what you're after,' shouted Cattanach. 'We'll get you, Cuthbert, through the heart,' before calmly returning to his own house. He figured that he would have plenty warning if anyone else came after him.

Now even as late as the 18th century there was a strange superstition around the country, and it was this. If a man could 'see through beneath' the body of his victim he would escape unpunished – it had in fact led to several people being caught trying to do it! Now Cuthbert's body was carried to an outhouse in the village till it could be taken away for burial, and Cattanach saw his chance. By now he realised that this latest act would ensure the government would stop at nothing to apprehend him, so he figured he needed all the help he could get. He went to his neighbour, McCombie of Dovan, to ask for his help. Together the pair of them went to the outhouse and lifted Cuthbert's body for Cattanach to look under it. A lot of good it did him – a day or so later a whole troop of dragoons came looking for him and in the ensuing furore he could do no more than escape to France. Superstition was such at the time that people refused to live in the house at Bellastraid and it was demolished soon afterwards.

Morven Jamie

———⟫·◈·⟪———

Cattle-raiding in the Highlands continued even after the British Army left their garrisons in the glens in the late 1750s. One of the last of the cattle-raiders in Aberdeenshire was James Coutts, who operated from the area around Morven Glen on Deeside. He was a brave and somewhat reckless man who had been raised with no respect for the law. There was still resentment in parts of the Highlands, and elsewhere in Scotland, towards the British Government for what had happened after Culloden, and Jamie, like others before him, could rely on some support for the local population as long as he didn't steal from his neighbours.

An area of rich pickings for him was the Braes of Cromar where there were several large farms and wealthy farmers. One of these was a man by the name of McRobbie who kept on losing cattle and was sure that Jamie was the culprit. Undaunted by Jamie's reputation, McRobbie decided to approach him directly and asked his immediate neighbours for their support. None was forthcoming, but McRobbie persisted and finding out where Jamie was he came up to him one day. Now Jamie had a couple of local lads, brothers called McGregor, with him, who occasionally helped him out in his 'professional capacity'.

McRobbie boldly faced them.

'Right, Coutts,' he said, 'eethir gie ma back ma cattle or the full price o their worth. If ye dinnae I promise ye that I will bring doun the full force o the law on ye.'

'Is that so?' replied Jamie, stepping forward till his nose almost touched that of the farmer.

'Aye it is. Ye think that ye can get away wi oniethin but ye dinnae frighten me, Jamie Coutts,' McRobbie said, firmly standing his ground.

At this Jamie was about to hit the farmer, when the McGregor brothers came between them and pushed them apart.

'If ye ken what's best for ye mannie, ye'll jist gang awa hame an keep yer mooth shut,' Jamie spat at the farmer.

McRobbie gave him a glare, turned on his heel and walked off.

'Weel, that should sort him,' he said to the McGregors. 'I widna be sae sure,' the elder replied, 'that McRobbie doesn't seem the kind tae dae whit ither fowk tell him.'

'Aye,' interjected his brother, 'he's a lad wi a good sense o himsel an winnae be sae easy put aff.'

'Ach, havers,' snorted Jamie, 'he's jist a fat farmer. He'll no dae oniethin, ye'll see.'

However, McRobbie hadn't headed home. He went straight to the Earl of Gordon at Aboyne Castle and laid a complaint against Jamie. At this point in Scotland the aristocracy still had a grip on much of the process of law, and in the turbulent times of the late 18th century they were often called on to intervene in disputes. It didn't take long for Jamie, with his network of contacts among the local population, to hear what had happened, and by the time a messenger arrived from the castle summoning him to see the Earl, Jamie had taken to the hills. The upshot of this was all too predictable. The earl laid a further complaint against Jamie, and within a few days he was declared an outlaw at Aberdeen Sherrif Court. The two McGregors were summoned to the same court and only escaped the same fate by claiming that they hardly knew Coutts and had only intervened in the altercation with McRobbie to prevent trouble. They claimed they had in in effect been innocent passers-by.

Jamie was now a hunted man. He was safe as long as he stuck close to the Morven area but he would have to be careful from now on. It was only a few days after his declaration as an outlaw that a strange event occurred. McRobbie and his wife were awakened in the middle of the night by the smell of smoke. They scrambled from their beds to find that their farmhouse and their barn had been set alight. No one had any doubt as to who was behind this, but if Jamie was pressed on the matter all he would say was, 'Well, ye see nae good ever comes to anybody that's been ower hard on me, I'm just lucky that way.'

Sure enough his luck seemed to hold and he evaded capture while continuing to deplete local farmers of valuable stock. He had a wide range of contacts who were happy to buy cattle from him at a reduced price with no questions being asked on either side.

But he had to keep on the move. He had enough friends that let him sleep in their outhouses or barns and he actually began to develop a strict aversion to houses with doors, locks and bars. Many nights he slept under the stars and despite a few close shaves with officers of the law, he managed to continue a successful career as an outlaw. He had always liked the outdoor life and he had plenty of money for the luxuries he wanted. Now and again he would spend some time at the croft of the brothers, John and William Coutts, on the slopes of Morven itself. They were distant cousins of his and though honest, hardworking characters they had a soft spot for their wild relation – as long as they didn't see him too often!

As time went by Jamie became even more blatant in his robbery. He still limited himself to lifting cattle as his ancestors had done, but increasingly he acted as if he was uncatchable. Matters came to a head when he made the great mistake of lifting the cattle of the minister at Strathdon. Now in the years immediately after Culloden, Presbyterian ministers had been targeted by those who had fought in the Jacobite cause and stayed out. That however had been a good few years before, and the minister at Strathdon was a respected and well-liked man of the cloth. Enough was enough! The whole of the Strathdon area was raised against Jamie. He soon realised that many of those who had helped him in the past were now set against him, he had gone too far this time. The only place he thought he might briefly find refuge was at John and Willie's croft.

He arrived there in a state of exhaustion. He hadn't slept in three days and had hardly had anything to eat in all that time. The brothers took him in under cover of darkness, fed him and let him sleep in their barn, while keeping an eye out for his pursuers. Once he had had a good sleep and recovered a bit he told the elder brother, John, that he was having to leave the country, but because of their past kindnesses and support, he thought of the pair of them as close family and asked John if he would come to Aberdeen two days later. He then left and two days later John turned up at the appointed place, a dimly-lit tavern down by the docks.

He was sitting there having a drink when he was approached by a man dressed as a sailor. It was only when he sat down and spoke that John realised that this was Jamie himself. After having what was to be their last drink together Jamie handed John a small bag of gold and some papers for him to look after. His last words were, 'An' noo, John, I'm awa, but where I'll go or what I'll dae, I little ken, but the bonnie braes o Morven I'll see nae mair. I've enough siller to see me right for a while but, John, wherever I go, if I ever come tae onything I'll mak you my heir, mind that.' He then left the tavern to board ship and John returned home, relieved that the trouble was over and glad that Jamie had got clear. He knew he was a rogue but didn't want to see him end up transported to the West Indies or even worse, hanging from the end of a rope – one of which was sure to have happened if Jamie had stayed in the country much longer.

Ten years later a local man from Morven by the name of Duguid, was serving in the army in India. He was on his own, on foot, and travelling towards Madras, having been sent as a messenger to another army position. It was in the heat of the hot Indian midday sun when a large and ornate coach passed him by. It had just passed him when it stopped, and as Duguid came up to it he was asked if he would like to ride in the coach. In the gloom inside the coach he could see that the occupant was dressed in fine Indian clothes. He couldn't make out his features, not even if he was a European or an Indian. His accent however, sounded strangely familiar. Duguid was a bit suspicious, as there were stories circulating through the ranks that there were white men kidnapping soldiers for various Maharajahs who wanted intelligence about the British Army and its activities. He was standing there, unsure of what to do, when the man in the coach called him by name. He was astounded and at once got in the coach. It was Morven Jamie, whom he recalled meeting when he was young back in Aberdeenshire. Jamie plied him with questions about how things were back in the old country and asked specifically of the Coutts brothers and few other friends. The next few hours were pleasantly spent as they headed towards Madras, and it seemed as if Jamie couldn't hear enough about his homeland. When Duguid said he was soon to be discharged from the Army and would be going home, the former cateran asked him to take a message to the minister of Strathdon if he still lived. The message was, 'Tell him, whatever his intentions were, he did me the best turn I ever got in my life – tell him his haill stipend wouldnae keep shoes on the horses o' Morven Jamie these days. An' ye can tell fowk that there are some others thereabouts who micht hear o' me bye an bye, no to their disadvantage. But here our roads part. I wish ye a safe voyage, an mony happy days on our native heath.'

Duguid was set down just inside the city gates and watched as the resplendent coach disappeared into the thronging city. A couple of months later he returned home and the story of Morven Jamie and his great success abroad was the talking point of the entire Strathdon district for a while. It had been a long time since he had been forced to flee the country and there were only a few who weren't impressed by the tale.

243

Seventeen more years passed, the 19th century was about to dawn, when a notice appeared in the *Aberdeen Journal*: 'Notice is hereby given to the heirs of Mr. James Coutts who left the county of Aberdeen, North Britain [sic] in the year 1780, and in especial to John and William Coutts, now or then residing near the foot of Mount Mar, in said county of Aberdeen, them or their heirs, that they may hear of something to their advantage by applying to . . .' and there followed the name of a law firm in Madras. Now William had died childless, but John was survived by a daughter, Janet, who was by now the wife of a local farmer, and the mother of two lads herself. They heard of the advertisement and looking through her father's papers, Janet found the letters that Morven Jamie had given her father nearly thirty years earlier.

This seemed incontrovertible proof of their right to whatever the inheritance was, and their friends made much of the great wealth that was about to descend on them. At this time one of the local lairds was a partner in a leading Indian law firm and had come back for a few months to his home near Cromar. It was commonly known that he was due to go back to India, so Janet and her husband went to see him with a copy of the advertisement and the papers that Morven Jamie had left so long ago.

The lawyer had a good look at the papers and said he would be happy to approach the law firm in Madras on their behalf and find out about their inheritance – for a fee of course. He returned to India, and it was a few years before he came back again to Scotland, during which time Janet heard absolutely nothing from him about the supposed inheritance. They then heard that the laird had returned from India, very well off, and was living in a brand new house near Cromar. So Janet and her husband Charlie went to see him to ask if anything had come of the inquiries into Morven Jamie's estate. The words that he spoke suggest that the reputations that both Scottish lairds and lawyers in general have in certain circles, are probably well deserved.

'Well, Charles,' drawled the laird, 'I am sorry to say it came to nothing. You see there was some doubt about the identity of the person referred to in the advertisement with the man you mentioned; and it would have taken a great deal of proof to establish the point. Indeed it would have been necessary to send witnesses from this country to prove it, and that would have been very expensive; and then very likely on the back of that there would have been a long and costly lawsuit, for there were more claimants than yourselves; and altogether, when I considered the matter, it appeared to me not advisable to proceed. And the truth is, Charles that though you had made good your claim, you might never have got a shilling, for it is next to impossible to get money out of that country.' The last point of course is probably just why the laird actually practised law there!

The farmer accepted the laird's word though there were many in the area who remarked that the laird was no worse off than he'd been before he went to India. In fact it was generally considered that he had most likely used the letters, which would appear to have been proof enough of the case, to press matters to his own advantage, and that his bonny new house had been paid for by Morven Jamie!

A Cateran in Love

━━▶◆◀━━

Donald Donn MacDonald was a well-known man in the Braes of Lochaber. He had been on many a cattle-raid in his time and always took great pleasure in the activity. He was also known to be a man of generous heart and a noble soul and this might have had more than a little to do with his reputation as a poet. Poetry was a great delight amongst the people of the Highlands and Donald's talents were appreciated over a considerable distance from his home at Bohuntine in Glen Roy. In addition to being a well-loved poet he had the reputation of being a fair and honourable man.

A story was long told about a time when he was driving a herd of cattle home from a *creach* in the Braemar area. They had been active well before dawn and had managed to put many miles between the site of their raid and themselves when dawn came up. Looking over his catch as they came up the side of a hill Donald noticed that there seemed to be a queer shadow on one of the cows. He and his friends brought the herd to a halt and Donald moved amongst them towards the cow he had noticed. He was astounded to find that what he had thought was a shadow was in fact an old woman hanging on for grim life to the neck of the cow. She had obviously been hanging on for hours up and down hills and through rivers. Realising that she had been discovered, the old woman unclasped her arms from around the neck of her cow and stood to face Donald Donn. She was a poor-looking creature, her clothes were threadbare, and her lined face and white hair showed her to be of a considerable age indeed.

'Good heavens, mother,' said Donald, not knowing whether to laugh or cry at the sight of her, 'whatever do you think you are doing?'

'Well,' the old woman replied in a frail voice, 'it's always the same with you men. Raiding and fighting and showing off. Never mind poor old women like me.' At this she wiped the back of her hand across her eyes. 'This cow is all I have. I am a poor widow with no children to help me and this cow keeps me in milk and cheese. She is a great cow, Morag, and then you come along and just snap the poor beast up and away from me.' As she spoke she was gently rubbing the cow's back and Donald realised that the old woman saw more in this cow than just a supply of food. She was obviously fond of the beast. This was something that had never crossed Donald's mind – that someone could become attached to a cow! Sure, the children were often taken with wee calves just after they were born, but that never lasted once they had turned into cows, which he considered were pretty stupid creatures, even if they were valuable. It was then that his natural generosity came into play.

'Well then, mother, if you're like that to one cow, what do you think you would do with two?' he asked.

The woman looked at him with a puzzled look in her eyes. She shook her head as if to clear it and asked, 'What do you mean?'

'I mean,' said Donald, with a hearty laugh, 'that you can go back the way we have come, with your cow and this one as well.' At that he slapped the side of the cow next to him and carried on laughing at the look on the old woman's face. She had a look of utter amazement. This fierce Lochaber cateran had not only said she could have her cow back but was giving her another one as well!

'Now, Seumas,' he said, still chuckling, and, turning to one of his companions, went on, 'will you see this lady back on her way a bit, while we press on with the rest if you please? And you could keep a weather eye out for any of her neighbours.'

So later that day a crowd of Deeside men following the trail left by Donald and their own cattle, were astounded to be met on the hillside by the old woman walking slowly down the hill with her two cows before her. They never did catch up with Donald and his men and the upshot of the event was that the old lady was allowed to keep the second cow. The Deeside men reckoned that the time would come when they would raid Lochaber and get more than their own back. Meantime there were a lot of belts to be tightened. But hunger was nothing new for the Highlanders and they would always get by. The word of Donald's generosity soon spread throughout Lochaber and Deeside and he was ever after seen as a bit of a Robin Hood.

Now Donald didn't only go on raids to Deeside; he and his friends were also in the habit of raiding as far north as Ross-shire every couple of years. It was on their way to the north that Donald's fate passed from his own hands to another. He saw and immediately fell in love with Mary, daughter of Grant of Urquhart, the local chief who resided at Castle Urquhart. Now Mary was not unresponsive to the Lochaber man's advances and he paid a couple of visits to Glen Urquhart before Mary's father decided things had gone far enough.

Now virtually all Highlandmen considered themselves to be gentlemen; after all, were they not of the same blood as the chiefs themselves? But chiefs had a habit of seeing things a little differently. Donald was a noted poet and a skilled warrior with a considerable reputation, but Grant did not see him as a fitting match for *his* daughter, so he forbade them ever to meet again.

It wasn't long after this that Donald and a band from Lochaber carried out a *creach* in Ross-shire, and as they were heading homewards along the banks of Loch Ness, Donald decided to visit Mary. The rest of the band were a bit reluctant, but they all knew how much in love their poet was, so they camped in the hills above Glen Urquhart to allow him time to visit Mary. He managed to meet up with her at a mutual friend's house for a short while before returning to the camp. There in the night they were surprised by the men of Ross who had been on their trail. In the ensuing fight Donald and his friends escaped, but they lost all that they had lifted. What was worse was that the Ross men, knowing all about Donald and Mary, went to Grant and told him that the poet had been camped in the area and the only reason he would have slowed down his return home must have been to see Mary.

Grant was furious and sent a large party of men to try and catch up with the Lochaber MacDonalds. They were too late and the MacDonalds had got clean away. Well, all of them but one. Donald, after meeting Mary, had decided to stay in the area to lay plans for spiriting her away. Mary, however, was still hopeful of getting her father to change his mind about Donald. Grant was determined however to have Donald Donn hanged. Donald couldn't tear himself away from the area, so desperate was he to see his beloved, and he hid out in a cave overlooking the Altsaigh burn. The cave was well-hidden and nearly inaccessible, so he thought himself pretty safe there. However, this was Grant country and it was only a matter of time before his location was discovered. A frontal assault on the cave would have cost the Grants dear, as Donald was a fearsome warrior, so a stratagem was devised. One of the young herds who tended the cattle in the area was prevailed upon to take a message to the poet purporting to come from Mary. The message asked him to come to meet her at a certain house, whose occupant Mary trusted implicitly.

A day or so later Donald turned up from his hiding-place to meet his beloved Mary. The occupant of the house told him to make himself comfortable and that Mary would be along quite soon. He was offered whisky and in his excitement he may have drunk a little too much. At a given signal from his host a throng of Grants fell on the house. As Donald said in one of his last poems, there were 63 enemies sent to catch him – Grant was taking no chances of him escaping this time. Despite their numbers and his gun misfiring Donald used his weapon as a club and managed to get out of a window and run for it. He didn't get far before he was taken and dragged off to Grant's castle. There he was thrown to the floor of the great hall before the Grant chieftain. Of Mary there was no sign – she was being kept in another part of the castle far away from her suitor. 'Well, well, Donald Donn, will you make a poem of this, then?' Grant asked with a grim look. 'You have gone against my strict word. I told you to have nothing more to do with Mary; she is far too good for the likes of you. But you have bothered me long enough, and tomorrow you will hang.'

Donald, on his knees, with his arms tied behind him, looked up at Grant and rattled off a poem, the last two lines of which translate as 'The Devil will take the Laird of Grant out of his shoes and Donald Donn will not be hanged.' He was defiantly referring to the fact that hanging was normally the fate of people whose actions were truly criminal, and this, plus the high regard he was held in as a poet, caused the Grants to suggest to their chief that beheading would be a more fitting end for a man of his stature. That night he composed his last poems, one of them being a direct statement to Grant, which goes:

> Tomorrow I shall be on a hill
> Without a head
> Have you no compassion for my sorrowful maiden
> My Mary, the fair and tender-eyed.

But Grant had no compassion, and the following morning Donald Donn was beheaded on a hill beside Castle Urquhart, in front of the assembled Grants and the grieving Mary. According to legend, after the axe fell, severing his head from his body, a miraculous thing happened. The head opened its eyes, its lips moved, and Donald's voice could be clearly heard saying the fateful words. 'Mary, lift ye my head.' It seems that even death could not dim the love of the Highland poet for Mary Grant.

A Spirited Defence

Now raiding didn't take place only on the mainland. There were men who followed the way of the cateran on the islands as well as on the mainland, and raiding from one to the other was something that happened regularly. Now it so happened that the Mackenzies of Kintail were in the habit of raiding the Isle of Lewis before they managed to take over the island itself from the MacLeods in the 17th century. It came about one time that a group of the Mackenzies decided to take the chance to go to Aignish a few miles to the east of Stornoway on the Eye peninsula. It was quite late in the year, but when the Mackenzies left Kintail the weather, though cold, was quite clear. Under the cover of night they had sailed up the Minch and crossed over to come down into Broad Bay. By the time they got close to Lewis the weather had changed and there was a stiff wind blowing mist in from the Atlantic with odd squalls of sleet and snow.

On the machair, the beach composed of crushed seashells that covers so many Hebridean coasts, an old woman was out looking after a herd of cattle early that morning. She had gone out just after dawn with the herd but the weather was so coarse that she decided she would be better finding some shelter. She was quite close to the ancient burial ground of the MacLeod chieftains near the (even then) ancient church of St Columba. She was huddling down behind the wall surrounding the graveyard when she heard the crunch of footfalls on the machair between the burial ground and the sea. She listened intently and realised that there were quite a few people coming along the beach. Now she knew that with the weather most of the local folk would be staying indoors and that if anyone was coming towards Aignish, there would be only one or two. Her suspicions were aroused. Slowly and carefully she raised her head to look over the wall. There, around the cattle she was in charge of, were a bunch of Mackenzies, just ready to start moving the beasts off to the east, where she realised they must have landed their boats. The mist was swirling and no one from the village would see them. The wind was blowing from the west too, so if she cried out her voice would do no more than warn the raiders, and her life would be in peril. What should she do?

Now it is often said that old women tend to be wise. They have seen much in their lives and learned from most of it, but she was sore tested. She knew she couldn't let these thieving Kintail cateran run off with the village's cattle, but how could she, a lone old woman, hope to stop a bunch of armed and determined men? Then she had it, and a wee smile came across her lined face.

Out on the machair the Mackenzies were beginning to move the cattle as quietly as they could. They had seen no one about and reckoned this was going to be an easy day's work. Then suddenly through the swirling mist came a high-pitched cry. It came from the ancient burial ground. They all turned to look. There, through the swirling mist they saw a ghostly creature rise, a dark heavily muffled shape right in the middle of the burial ground. They were rooted to the spot. Was it a wraith, the ghost of one of the ancient chiefs? As they hesitated the figure gave a great piercing cry that struck them to their very marrow, 'Children of Clan Leod, will ye not rise, the enemy are amongst ye. Strike them down.' Now they had no doubt. The dead were rising to resist them. As a man they bolted, leaving behind the cattle they had so wanted to lift. Off into the mist they scattered as the old woman sat down in the burial ground and began to laugh. A short while later some people from the village had arrived, having heard something going on but unsure what it was. They were greeted by Old Morag calmly sitting on the dyke of the burial ground looking calmly over the cattle she had saved, a wee smile playing around her lips.

A Winter Raid

As we have seen, raiding for cattle did not only take place overland. Sometimes cateran raids originated in the Hebrides and in other instances mainland clans would raid the islands. One year, a couple of weeks before Christmas, seven men of the Clan Maclean set out from Crogan on Mull to carry out a raid on the Braes of Muckairn to the south of Oban. They came ashore from their birlinn, the traditional boat of the islanders, and landed at Gallanach Beag Bay, two and half miles to the south of Oban. They headed inland with the intention of lifting all the cattle they came across. The procedure of the cateran was often to pick up beasts in ones or twos, cattle that were the property of people whose life was not that different from the later Highland crofters. Essentially they were living in a subsistence economy, growing all they needed for their own use. Many of the clanspeople throughout the Middle Ages, and their earlier predecessors, would have no more than one or two beasts. However, picking up beasts in ones or twos could soon lead to dozens. Or so the Macleans were hoping that time on the Braes of Muckairn.

Their first success was in taking the single cow from a man called MacCallum at Larach-a-Chnodail in Glen Lonain. They then headed down the glen, picking up cattle wherever they could. The weather was bitterly cold and most of the local people were content to stay indoors, unconcerned at the possibility of any cateran raiding in such weather. So the Macleans went on their way and soon had another seven beasts. No one had even noticed them. They thought they had got clean away with their booty, but one of the last locals they had 'visited', had come outside and seen the tracks of the small herd and at once realised what was happening.

At once he sped round his neighbours and soon there were five men tracking the Macleans and the cattle through the snow. The Macleans reached their beached boat without incident. If they tied the feet of the cattle and laid them in the birlinn there would be just enough room for themselves and the beasts. All in all they thought, a good day's work. They had just got the second beast tied and lifted into the boat when the Glen Lonain men arrived. Caught up in lifting the beast into the birlinn, the Mull men were at an immediate disadvantage, as the Glen Lonain men attacked them with swords. The fight on the beach at Gallach Beag was short, and within minutes five of the Macleans lay dead on the sand. The Glen Lonain men drew back, three of their own lay dead there too. It was a stand-off, two against two. Taking their chance the Mull men grabbed the sides of their birlinn and shoved it into the water, leaping aboard as soon as the boat was free of the beach. The two Glen Lonain men simply stood and watched as the men in the boat rowed out to sea. It was hardly a success for either side. Only two of seven Macleans returned home to Mull, with a single cow to show for their companions' lives. The Glen Lonain men had restricted the cleansers to taking just one beast, but at a high price, three of their own. All in all it was a bad day all round. The following year at the same time of the year Niall MacCallum, one of the survivors of the previous year's fight, was awakened in his bed at his home at Larach-na-Chnodail in Glen Lonain. He nudged his wife. 'I am sure I was just hearing the white cow mooing, listen,' he whispered as she came awake.

The sound came again. They knew the sound of their own few beasts well enough and it was definitely the white cow. The sound was clearly moving away. It could only mean one thing.

Someone, most likely the Macleans from Mull, was lifting the glen cattle, again. Now this happened at a time when firearms were just becoming generally available, and only a few of the Highlanders had acquired them. Niall had been given one by the clan chief only a couple of weeks before, and had been spending a great deal of time practising firing the gun. It only took a few seconds for him to leap out of bed, get dressed and load his new gun. He then carefully removed the heather in the window at the front of the house – glass was still a luxury – and looked out. There in the moonlit night was a group of men heading west up the glen with half a dozen beasts, his own white cow amongst them.

Niall let the raiders turn round a crook in the glen and ran from his house up the side of the hill that the men were skirting. He knew just the place. Running as fast as he could in the dim light he soon reached the boulder. Below him, at a distance of about sixty feet, was the closest of the raiders, walking alongside the white cow. Kneeling down and resting his gun barrel on the rock, he sighted on the cateran. A shot rang out. The man beside the white cow let out a cry, raised his arms and fell head first into the snow. The others didn't hesitate. They knew well enough about firearms – they even had a couple of pistols, but being shot from a distance by an unseen enemy did not appeal. Off they ran, leaving their comrade in the snow.

At once Niall came down and began to herd up the cows. He was helped by his wife who had followed him at a careful distance. Soon they had their own three beasts and those of their neighbours safely back at the Larach. The following morning Niall went back to get the body of the fallen Maclean. He was a man much like himself and the least he deserved was a decent burial. He got to the spot, and there in the snow was a great splurge of blood. But no Maclean. He never did find out if the man had died or not, but he understood what had happened. The Macleans had run off from his gun but had soon stopped, and once realising they were not being pursued, had come back to see to their fallen comrade. Even if he was unsure of the man's fate, Niall built a small cairn on the spot, just in case it had been the place where the Mull man had breathed his last.

A Bag of Meal
and a Pair of Shoes

In 1689 a group of fifteen men from Lochaber came over the hills to Aberdeenshire. They managed to lift a total of one hundred and twenty fine, well-fed cattle from the area around Kildrummy and headed homeward. As usual, they came in the night and left with first light. A couple of them had been hiding in the area, working out how best to make their move. So when the rest of them arrived there was already a plan and the raid went like clockwork. In the morning when the raid was discovered, a large group of men from the immediate area was brought together. It took some time for the men to organise themselves, get horses and provisions and weapons. This gave the cateran a good start, but the Kildrummy men reckoned they would be able to catch them on horseback. By the time they left there were fifty of them and each one was carrying provisions not just for their own use but also to offer in ransom for the cattle, if peaceful negotiation with the caterans could be arranged. They also had a couple of dozen pairs of shoes that a local farmer had received as part of a debt.

Over the years the death toll in struggles between the Lowland farmers of the north-east and the cateran raiders had been growing, and these Kildrummy men were prepared to do anything to avoid further bloodshed. They weren't cowards, but unlike their Highland contemporaries they hadn't been raised with the notion that battle and the possibility of death were integral parts of life. So they hoped that the extra bags of meal and the shoes they were carrying would allow a trade with the Highlanders. It would be an expensive transaction but anything was better than more men being killed. The Lochaber men had headed into the mountains via the slopes of Morven and eventually came along the Rathad na Mearlaich into Strathspey. Here they headed south and passed through Glen Truim and down along the western side of Loch Ericht.

The cateran had been driving the cattle almost continuously for nearly three nights when they decided to stop to eat just after dawn, near the side of the loch, before heading through the Bealach Dubh to Loch Ossain, then on to their homes in the west. Here, at a spot called Dalunchart, they had stopped and slaughtered a cow, which they were roasting over an open fire when the Aberdeenshire men came upon them. At once the cateran drew their weapons and readied themselves for fighting. They were outnumbered three to one, but with the Highlanders' contempt for what they thought were soft Lowlanders, they reckoned they had a fair chance of driving them off. After all, weren't they the cream of the warriors of their clan?

The horsemen drew up just out of pistol shot as the Highlanders formed a line. Then one of the Aberdeenshire party, a middle-aged, grey-bearded man called Moir on a big black stallion, rode forward, both hands held up to show he had no arms. The leader of the cateran, Angus MacArthur, waited till the horseman was well clear of his own men before striding through the heather towards him, putting his sword and pistol down a few paces before he stopped. The horseman approached.

'Ye hae our cattle,' he said.

'Well, we were thinking that they were our beasts now.' The cateran replied with a grim smile, 'and we are prepared to fight to defend them.'

'We thocht ye micht feel that way,' said Moir, scratching his chin through his beard, 'so we hae a proposition for ye.'

'And what would that be?' asked MacArthur.

'Weel nou,' Moir said, 'ye can see we outnumber ye three tae ane, but we are quite ready tae mak ye an offer for the peacable return o' our cattle.'

'How much?' demanded the cateran,

'Right, then,' Moir said, 'we will gie each o' ye, you an' yer men here, a bag o oatmeal, an we also will pit in a pair o' brand new shoes each. How's that?'

Angus MacArthur threw back his head and let out a great laugh.

'You think we will hand over a hundred-and-twenty fine cattle for a bag of meal and a pair of shoes. You are as soft in the head as you are in your heart, you Lowland coward,' he spat out. 'If you want these beasts you will have to take them.' And at that he turned and ran back towards where he had laid down his sword and pistol.

Now the Aberdeenshire lads with Moir might have been keen to avoid bloodshed, but cowards they were not. Moir raised his hand and signalled them forward. MacArthur ran back to join the line of his companions as the horsemen thundered down on them. The Highlanders had pistols and a couple of guns and thought the Aberdeenshire men would scatter at the first shots. They managed to shoot a few of their opponents out of the saddle but the rest came onwards. The Highlanders were well versed in fighting men on horseback when they were on foot, but they did not realise that the first of the men attacking them were well seasoned themselves. Several had served as soldiers and others had met with cateran before. The numbers were just too much for the Lochaber men. Some of the Kildrummy lads dismounted to attack on foot, while others stayed on their mounts. A couple of the horses were hamstrung by the Highlanders, but within a matter of minutes there were just three of them left, standing back to back, their swords dripping blood. Not one of them was unmarked. They were surrounded by a ring of swords.

Moir stepped forward and said to his companions, 'Pit up yer swords.'

He turned to face the Highlander nearest him. 'Ye too. Pit doun yer swords. There's been enough killing here this day. An aw because o yer damned Hielant pride. We'll help ye bury yer dead an then ye can gang hame. It is over.'

The remaining Highlanders realised that here was a man of honour himself. Offering to help bury their dead was an honourable thing to do, and of course he was offering them their lives. They accepted. An hour or two later the Kildrummy contingent headed home, with half a dozen of their horses carrying the bodies of their riders and quite a few with injured riders. Behind them at the side of Glen Ericht were twelve freshly-dug graves. And all because MacArthur thought a bag of meal and a pair of shoes too low a price!

Epilogue

The Battle of Culloden on 16 April 1746 saw the end of a form of society that had survived for hundreds and hundreds of years. The clan system of the Scottish Highlands had developed from earlier tribal societies that harked back to at least the Iron Age. While Culloden can be clearly understood as the last battle in what was a Civil War in Great Britain between two contesting Royal dynasties, in terms of Highland society it was also a case of a modern society destroying an essentially ancient one. The extreme brutality of the British Army after Culloden has been extensively documented in *The Lyon In Mourning* and to modern eyes what took place in the Highlands in the aftermath of the last battle has all the hallmarks of present-day ethnic cleansing. From the point of view of the Duke of Cumberland, still talked of as a butcher in Scotland today, and the British establishment, the clan system was simply a collection of anachronistic savages who had had the temerity to support an attack on the modern British State, involved at this point in its first real surge towards a global empire.

It is important to understand that a considerable amount of the obscene brutality of the process was carried out by Scots: the Jacobite rebellion was never simply a matter of Scotland versus England. The '45 was a Civil War with a strong underlying religious component with the Highlander Jacobites, who were mainly Catholic and Episcopalian opposed by other clans who were primarily Protestant. For centuries before the Union of the Crowns in 1603 and the subsequent Treaty of Union of 1707 (which incidentally is the written constitution of the United

Kingdom despite the ongoing waffle from politicians, journalists and academics who should know better) Scottish kings had been attempting to subdue the clan areas. Their kin-based societies, their habit of turning every male into a warrior and their addiction to raiding, particularly for cattle, made them anachronistic in a modern nation-state. Their language and dress were different and until the romanticisation of the Highlander in the early 19th century, they were perceived in England and in many Lowland Scottish areas, as little more than barbarous savages. Their literature, both written and oral, their music, still tell us of a complex, sophisticated and remarkably long-lived society, but they were seen as little more than essentially foreign thieves by their countrymen.

And it is in this portrayal of them as thieves that the last of them have been so ill-served by history. Such men as Serjeant Mor and his cousin Duncan Ban Leane Cameron knew that after Culloden the only fate that awaited them at the hands of the British Army was death. They had two choices: leave the country or fight on. It is in their decision to 'stay out' after Culloden that we can see their actions for what they were. They must have known after the brutality of the British army's spread throughout the Jacobite Highlands, that they had no hope of eventual victory for their cause. Iain Dubh Cameron, the Serjeant Mor, had already served abroad in the French Army, and we can only assume it could have been possible for him to escape there. Yet he, and a few hundred other Highlanders returned to the ways of The School of the Moon to continue the fight. Because of their reversion to the raiding behaviour of their ancestors they have been almost totally ignored by historians, and their representation as nothing more than thieves by the British government has tended to go unchallenged.

The behaviour of Serjeant Mor towards the Army quartermaster in the Mamore mountains shows something of his attitude, but it is in the behaviour of the British army that we see that what these desperate Highlanders did has all the hallmarks of a limited, and essentially hopeless, guerrilla campaign. In the period from 1746–53 there was hardly a glen in Scotland outside Argyll that did not have a garrison of British Army troops. These are clearly delineated in the Cantonment Records of the British Army of the period. Some of these were substantial, as at Aviemore and Dalwhinnie, Ruthven, etc., while others in places like Glen Clova in Angus, Glen Feshie, Glenalmond, Glen Urquhart, Inchrory, Locharkaig, Morven, etc., could be as little as half a dozen men. The point is that they were in virtually every glen, and there were also riding parties moving through the hills between these garrisons. At the same time there were substantial garrisons in such places as Aberdeen, Alloway, Balfron, Banff, Blairgowrie, Crieff, Dalkeith, Dumfries, Dundee, Elgin, Findhorn, Fochabers, Forres, Inverness, Nairn, Peterhead, Stirling and Stranraer, apart from garrisons in such places as Edinburgh, Fort William and Glasgow. There are some mentions of trouble in the cities at the time, and the picture appears to be that of a country under occupation.

The fact that the cities too had to be garrisoned underlines this, and the number of Lowland towns that were considered to need garrisoning shows how widespread dissent was in Scotland. It is possible that the actions of the British Army troops after Culloden could have set off such dissent, though there had been considerable support for the Jacobite cause in many Lowland areas as well as in the Highlands. Scottish Episcopalians, many of whom were Lowlanders, had joined the Jacobite Army in considerable numbers.

The situation appears to have been virtually a wholesale occupation of Scotland by the British Army in the face of a guerrilla campaign that may have included a few hundred men. It is difficult to be certain as there has been so little published about this period, and even the casualties among the British army for the period, are included in the overall figures for all campaigns. These figures include those from other parts of the world as the British Empire began to spread. Luckily a few of the situation reports from commanders in the field have survived and have been published. Here I quote some of these sources, but first, here is the declaration that was pinned to every church door in Scotland in June 1749, three years after Culloden. It comes from the unpublished *Cantonment Registers*, p. 91:

> In order to prevent Depredations, as much as possible, this is therefore to give notice to all concern'd that whenever any cattle are stolen, the owners are immediately to cause the Track to be followed, at the same time acquainting the nearest party of soldiers who have orders to give all possible assistance for the recovering of the cattle and apprehending the thieves. The Country People are directed to be very Cautious in giving false Alarms, to prevent the Troops being harassed unnecessarily.
>
> Tis recommended and Expected that the Gentlemen and principal Tacksmen in the neighbourhood of each Party would meet and concert the most proper measures for rendering this service effectual and that they would be so good as to transmit their opinion in writing to the Commanding Officer that he may give the necessary Instructions to the officers under his command to take the most Effectual Measures for the publick Service.

Because they had resorted to the traditional practice of cattle-raiding the Government simply designated the rebels as thieves. However, the fact was that these rebels had support within the Highland community. Though this might have occurred anyway, the atrocities committed by the British Army, and some of its Scottish soldiers, must have reinforced people's resentment, thereby making it more likely that they would support those who continued to fight against the government. On p. 26 of the *Cantonment Registers* we have the following instruction regarding a garrison in Lochaber:

The proper place for this Camp (to keep the country in Awe and good of troops) is Fort Augustus, which, lying in the neighbourhood of the Frazers, Camerons, McDonalds, McKenzies, McPhersons is at hand to prevent any Insurrection of these Clans and likewise to put the Disarming Acts in force.

Here it is clearly shown that the government feared further rebellion and thus it appears that they clearly understood that the Jacobites who 'stayed out' were, at least potentially, a lot more dangerous than mere cattle-thieves. On page 89 we again see that the 'thieving' is clearly understood as part of a bigger picture:

The Lt. Governors of the forts to have a Warrant or Power sent to them. To act as Justices of the Peace, there being none in the neighbourhood to commit persons taken up by the Parties for having arms, wearing the Highland Dress, or Stealing.

The Disarming Acts were particulary enforced against those whom the government considered rebels and they clearly believed that in many areas of the Highlands the local magistrates could not be relied upon to act against their own people. This would appear to be in fact the implementation of direct military rule. Other comments in the *Cantonment Registers* seem to be disingenuous at the least. On page 90 there is a reference to the Moving Patrol covering the area between Dalnacardoch and Rannoch where it is said to be

For preventing the Depredations and Thefts usually committed by the Highland Thieves, to the great prejudice of His Majesty's honest subjects and of all industry in such parts of the country as are exposed to these pernicious practices.

The surviving situation reports from officers in the field make it abundantly clear that many, if not all of them, considered the entire Highland population to be thieves and criminals. This following piece is from a situation report from a Captain Desclouseaux in Braemar, dated the 15 June 1752. It was published in *Glasgow Past and Present*, p. 614:

When my corporal was going to take the prisoner before a Justice of the Peace, by my order, the mob rose; on which my corporal secured Allan Coats, and brought him to me at Braemar; on which I sent Ensign Butler with him to Mr. Gordon, who I was informed was a Justice of the Peace, but he refused acting as not being qualified. One Shaw, a half-laird, who came in with my corporal and party to Braemar, has given his note for Coats' appearance. He pretends to say the soldiers were in fault: but by all accounts I can receive, this Shaw was the occasion of the riot, calling to the men in Irish [Gaelic] to secure the soldiers; and now I find that Coats is his servant. I long to know your commands. We want magistrates that will, or dare, exert themselves. This is a nest of rogues and rebels.

A communication from Captain Johnston at Invercomrie in September of the same year again underlines the widespread support for the rebels. It is from the same published source, p. 617:

In my last, Sergeant More and his gang brought into this country a drove of cattle. They remained here at grass, not three miles from Invercomrie for a month, and there was not a man in the whole country honest enough to give me the least intelligence of it. Their keepers, the thieves, even lay in the shielings of Invercomrie and Finart, and in lurking places about.

What is clear is the total incomprehension of the soldiers regarding the fact that they were dealing with people who saw the world differently from themselves. They accepted the notion of the Highlanders as thieves, effectively as barbarians, people who were outside the norms of what they saw as civilised society. By adopting the tactics of the cateran, Serjeant Mor and the others were emphasising the differences between Highland society and the rest of British contemporary society. What we do not know we often fear and there is little wonder that some of the Army officers display what would nowadays be considered paranoia. This can hardly excuse the viciousness with which Highlanders were treated after Culloden and later, and it is hardly surprising that another Captain Johnstone, writing on 10 November 1752 showed a remarkable degree of cynicism towards the inhabitants of the Highlands in general and those around Rannoch Moor in particular. He wrote then, *ibid.*, p. 622:

It is a truth well known, that the inhabitants of Rannoch in general, but especially upon the estate of the late Strowan [Robertson], are notorious thieves. If there are a few who are not actually concerned in theft, they all know of it, and think nothing so scandalous as informing against the thieves, or even acknowledging that they know any of the guilty. This they pretend is for fear of the thieves, who never fail to revenge themselves by plundering the cattle of such as do give the least intelligence; but this is all pretence, for they know they would be protected. It is no great wonder that they are thieves, since from the earliest settlement the Camerons, McDonalds, Kennedys, McGregors, Robertsons, which are the prevailing names here, thieves have always been protected by the gentlemen of estates, who kept them to join in every rebellion, as the most desperate, the most hardy, and most proper to be made officers of, or give lesser commands to, as may be demonstrated here . . . the inhabitants of this country are all or mostly notorious thieves, it is next to be considered what method is best to root out thieving and turn the minds of people to industry. Some say, turn out all the old inhabitants of the estate, late Strowan's, together: and others say that if you do turn them out, you make desperate a set of poor wretches who are not actually offending, and force them to plunder, and so create continual work to yourselves to destroy them; therefore turn them out by degrees; a family this year, another the next, and every person who commits an act of theft immediately.

A clear and explicit call for ethnic cleansing. That this was the ongoing attitude of the British Army can be seen in the following excerpt from a letter written by General Wolfe in 1755, quoted in J.T. Findlay's *Wolfe in Scotland*, p. 268. Wolfe, who had served in the Highlands after Culloden, is referring to Cluny MacPherson, a noted Jacobite, when he writes:

Mr, McPherson shou'd have a couple of hundred men in his neighbourhood with orders to massacre the whole Clan if they show the least symptom of Rebellion. They are a warlike tribe, and he's a cunning, resolute fellow himself. They shou'd be narrowly watch'd; and the Party there shou'd be well commanded.

This from a British general who has gone down in British history as a great hero.

Other situation reports regulary refer to men being arrested for wearing banned Highland dress or for carrying arms, but the tone throughout is the same. The officers writing these reports clearly despised the people amongst whom they were living and made no attempt to come to terms with the linguistic and cultural differences between them. The Highlanders are seen as virtually sub-human, an attitude that no doubt had a lot to do with the atrocities that happened after Culloden, recorded in *The Lyon in Mourning*.

By the mid-1750s things seem to have quietened down considerably, though, as Wolfe's letter shows, there was still a fear that the Highlands could rise again. The work of opening-up the Highlands that had begun with the building of roads by General Wade in the 1730s had progressed considerably, the destruction of Highland society being greatly advanced by the slaughter of 1746 and the subsequent execution and deportation of so many Highland men. With the execution of Serjeant Mor in 1753, following that of his cousin Duncan Ban the previous year, the cateran raiding seems to have begun to fizzle out and at least with the defeat of the French invasion fleet at Quiberon. Certainly there was continuing sympathy in Scotland for the Jacobite cause, but with the destruction of the clan system, with its hundreds of available fighting men on call, there was no real power base that the Stuarts could depend on.

Politically, the brutality of the Duke of Cumberland's army and the subsequent occupation of the Highlands ensured that never again would an army of kilted warriors stream south from the Scottish Highlands. The ancient way of life of what was still essentially a Celtic-speaking, warrior society, that had survived for centuries beyond counting, was over. The way was now clear for the institution of a modern cash economy that within a few decades would see sheep as of more value than humans in the Scottish Highlands. The ancient practice of lifting cattle that had been so central to the culture, and the stories, of the people of the Highlands was no more.

Appendix – Blackmail

—⟫•◈•⟪—

Nowadays the idea of blackmail is pretty straightforward. It is generally accepted as the extortion of money by threatening to disclose information about the targeted victim. However the definition of 'Black Mail' in the Oxford English Dictionary tells us something slightly different about how the term originated. It refers to blackmail as 'a tribute formerly exacted from farmers and small owners in the border counties of England and Scotland, and along the Highland border, by freebooting chiefs, in return for protection of immunity from plunder'. Even this definition, however, is open to interpretation. The suggestion is clearly that, even if the perpetrators of blackmail did provide some sort of protection against raiders, they were effectively extorting or 'exacting' the money paid.

This attitude towards blackmail has a long history. An act of the Scottish Parliament of 1507 has the following passage, 'That none sit under the assurance of thieves, or pay them black-mail under the pain of death, and escheat of their moveables'. In 1587, the year of the institution of justices of the peace, it was further pronounced

It is statute and ordained that the justice-clerk and his deputes, and the kingis commissioners, constitute to further justice, quietness, and gude rule in all schires, sail diligently enquire and take up dittary of the uptakers and payers of black-muiill, and to make rentals of the quantities thereof, and to person alsweill the takers, as payers thereof, at justice aires,

271

and particular diettes, and do justice upon them, according to
the lawes, and receive soverty, under great pains, that they sail
abstaine in time coming.

As we have seen, the attitude of central government towards
Highland society was that the clans were little better than
barbarians. For centuries the Scottish kings tried to exercise
control over the fierce Highland clans with varying levels of
success. The presentation of the Highlanders as little more than
thieves came to a head in the years after Culloden, but the idea
itself was well-established long before then. The mutual incomprehension between the increasingly modern Lowlands and the
society of the Highlands, rooted as it was in ancient traditional
behaviour patterns, was considerable. It is this ancient antipathy
that has given rise to the modern idea of blackmail, as in truth it
was something much less criminal.

Given the problems and stresses inherent in the situation
where what were effectively two different types of society living
side by side, there was need for solutions to those problems. The
Highland clans did not live in isolation, but their society was still
that of a tribal, pastoral, warrior society. Although there was no
definitive border between the two societies, the majority of the
lowland rural population were, by the 17th and 18th centuries, a
part of a modern nation state. They thought of themselves as
Scots, while the Highlanders, perhaps having some sort of
loyalty towards the nation, were still essentially bound by the
kinship ties of clan society. The carrying of arms was becoming
less common in the lowland areas while every Highlander
thought of himself as a warrior, and what kind of a warrior
would go anywhere without his weapons? In those times the
administration of law in the Lowland areas adjoining the Highlands was still very much in the hands of local magistrates, who
were almost unanimously local landowners. The modern institution of the police had not yet come into being.

As Highland society came under increasing economic, political and social pressure the raiding habits that had long been integral to their existence began to change. While there had always been instances of raiding into the Lowlands this was not the norm – most of the cattle-raiding took place between the clans. Increasingly, some of the clans began to see the lowland areas as easy pickings. The male population was not trained to fight, few of them carried arms and the development of agriculture meant that there were more, and fatter, cattle to be had in a raid on the Lowlands than in any Highland glen. Highland cattle were traditionally sturdy, small, black beasts as opposed to the shaggy red Highland cattle we see today. In the Lowland areas the land was more fertile, farming was more intense and particulary by the 18th century agriculture was being improved. This meant the Lowland cattle were larger, fatter and thus more valuable than the cattle in the glens. With the additional complications of the disputed monarchy and the Jacobite leanings of many of the clans the situation was clearly unstable.

However, the Lowland and Highland peoples had lived alongside each other for centuries. There were intermarriages, trade and all levels of social intercourse among the contiguous peoples. It is obvious that deeper into the Highlands there would be clans who had little to do with the Lowlanders and might not have much knowledge of them at all, other than as a potential source of income. It would appear more than likely that it was from amongst these clans that most of the raiders came.

In order to try and combat the incursions it no doubt appeared eminently sensible for some of the Lowland landowners to turn to their Highland friends who lived nearby for help. And this help came in the form of blackmail. It would hardly be likely that anyone would write down the terms of extortion, but we do have extant contracts of blackmail. Here is one originally published in Nimmo's *History of Stirlingshire*:

Copy of an original Contract for Keeping a Watch on the Borders of the Highland, anno 1741

It is contracted, agreed, and finally ended betwixt the parties underwritten, to witt James and John Graham, elder and younger of Glengyle, on the one part, and the gentlemen, heritors, and tenants within the shires of Perth, Stirling, and Dumbarton, who are hereto subscribing, on the other part, in manner following:

Whereas, of late years, several persons within the bounds aforesaid have been very great sufferers through stealing of their cattle, horses, and sheep; for preventing whereof the said James and John Grahams, with and under the conditions, provisions, and for the causes after specified, hereby bind and oblige them, conjunctly and severally, their heirs, executors, and successors, that the said James Graham shall keep the lands subscribed for, and annexed to the respective subscriptions, skaithless of any loss, to be sustained by the heritors, tenants, or inhabitants thereof, through the stealing and away taking of their cattle, horses, or sheep, and that for the space of seven years complete, from and after the term of Whitsunday next to come; and for that effect, either to return the cattle so stolen from time to time, or other wayes, within 6 months after the theft committed, to make payment to the persons from whom they were stolen, of their true value, to be ascertained by the oaths of the owners, before any judge-ordinary; providing always, that intimation be made to the said James Graham, at his house in Correilet, or where he shall happen to reside for the time, of the number and marks of the cattle, sheep, or horse stolen, and that within 48 hours from the time that the proprietors thereof shall be able to prove by liable witnesses, or their own or their herds' oaths, that the cattle amissing were seen upon their usual pasture within the space of 48 hours previous to the intimation, as said is; and declaring, that it shall be sufficient if the heritors or tenants, be-south or be-east the town of Drymen, make intimation in writing at the house of Archibald Strang, merchant in Drymen, of their losses in the before mentioned, to a person to be appointed by the said James Graham of Glengyle to attend theire for that purpose, and in his absence to the said Archibald. And further, it is specially condescended to and agreed upon, that the said James Graham shall not be bound for restitution in cases of small pickereys; declaring that an horse or black cattle stolen within or without doors, or any number of sheep above six, shall be constructed to be theft, and not pickerey. And with regard to horses and cattle stolen within the bounds aforesaid, and carried to the south, the said James Graham obliges him, that he shall be as serviceable to the gentlemen subscribers in that case as he possibly can; and if he cannot recover them, he submits himself to the discretion of the heritors on whose ground the theft was committed, whether he shall be liable for their value or not.

And it is hereby expressly provided and declared by both parties, that in case of war within the country, that this present contract shall henceforth cease and become void; for the which causes, and on the other part, the heritors and tenants hereto subscribing, with and under the provisions and declarations above and underwritten, bind and oblige them, their heirs, executors, and successors, to make payment to the said James Graham of Glengyle, or to any persons he shall appoint to receive the same, of the sum of four pounds yearly during the space foresaid, for ilk hundred pound of ye valued rent of the lands annexed to their respective subscriptions, and that at two terms of the year, Whitsunday and Martinmas, by equal portions, beginning the first term's payment thereof at the said term of Whitsunday next, for the half year immediately following, and so further, to continue at the said terms during the continuance of these presents: providing always, like as is hereby specially provided and declared, that it shall be leisome and lawful for both parties to quitt and give up this present contract at the end of every year as they think fitt, intimation being always made on the part of the said James Grahame at the respective kirk-doors, with the bounds aforesaid, on a Sabbath day, immediately after the forenoon's sermon, a month before expiration of the year; and on the part of the heritors and other subscribers, by a letter to the said James Grahame from them, and another from him, acknowledging the receipt thereof, or the attestation of two witnesses, that the letter was left at his house, or was delyverred to him two moneths before expiring of the year; it being always understood, that any subscriber may quitt and give up the contract for his own part, whether the rest concur or not, at the end of each year, as said is. And both parties bind and oblidge them and their foresaids to perform the premisses licinde to others under the penalty of £20 sterling, to be paid by the party failzier to the party observer, or willing to observe their part thereof, att our performance. And moreover for the said James Grahame's farther encouragement, and for the better restraining the evil practices above-mentioned, the subscribers hereby declare, that it is their intention that all such thieves and pickers shall be apprehended by the said James Grahame of Glen-gyle, or occasionally by any other person within the bounds aforesaid, against whom there is sufficient proof, shall be prosecute according to law, and brought to justice. And for greater security, both the saids parties consent to the registration hereof in the books of council and session, or others competent, that letters of horning on six days, and other executorials needful may pass hereon as effeirs. And to that effect they constitute, their procurators, etc. In witness whereof, both the saids parties have subscribed these presents, consisting of this and the preceding sheet, written on stamped paper by Andrew Dick, chyrurgeon in Drymen, at Balglas, the twentyeth day of Aprill Im vije. and fourty-one years, by Robert Bontein of Mildovan, before William MacLea his servant, and Mr. William Johnston, schoolmaster at Balglas, the; said Robert Bontein having filled up his first date, and witnesses names and designations. At Ballikinrain the tuintie-first day of foresaid moneth and year, by James Napier of Ballikinrain, before Alexander Yuill his servant, and Gilbert Conan, tenant in Ballikinrain, the said James Napier having filled up this second date, witnesses names and designations. Att Boquhan the twenty-second day of Aprile, moneth foresaid, and year by Hugh Buchanan of Balquhan, before these witnesses, John Paterson and Robert Duncan both tenants yr. Att Glins, the tuenty-seventh day of moneth and year foresaid, before those witnesses, Walter Monteath of Keyp, and John Buchanan younger of Glins. Att Easter Glins, the tuenty-seventh day of moneth and year foresaid, before these witnesses, Walter Monteath of Keyp, and Thomas Wright younger of Easter Glins, subscribed be Alexander Wright of Pensid. Att Arnmere, the first day of Mey seventin hundred and fortie-one years, befor thees witnes, Arsbelt Leckie of Arnmere, and Walter Monteath younger of Keyp, Walter Monteath, att above place, day, date, year, and witnesses, by James Key portioner of Edinbelly, moneth, date, place, and year aforesaid, before these witnesses, Walter Monteath therein, and Walter Monteath younger of Keyp, and by Robert Galbraith of Fintrie, fourth May, before Robert Farrie of Balgrochan, and James Ure, tenant in Hilltown of Balgair.

William Johnston, witness.
William M'Lea, witness.
Gilbert Cowan, witness.
Bontein of Mildovan, for my lands of Balglas in the paroch of Killern, being three hundred and fifty pound of valuation; and

hinds of Provanstoun in the paroch of Balfron, ninety-seven pound seven shilling valuation.

Alexander Yuill, witness. John Paterson, witness. Robert Dunn, witness. Walter Monteath, witness. John Buchanan, witness. Thomas Wright, witness. Archibald Leckie, witness. Walter Monteath, witness. Alexander Wright, witness. Archibald Leckie, witness.Walter Monteith, witness. Walter Monteith, witness. Robert Fame, witness. James Tire, witness. John Buchanan, witness. James MacGrime, witness.

James Napier of Ballikinrain, for my lands in the paroch of Killern, being two hundred and sixtie pound of valuation. And for my Lord Napier's lands in said paroch, being three hundred and twenty-eight pound of valuation. And for Culcreuch's lands in the paroch of Fintrie, being seven hundred and twentie-seven pound of valuation. And for said Culcreuch's lands in the paroch of Balfrone, being one hundred and ten pound valuation.
Hugh Buchanan of Balquhan, for my lands of Boughan and Brunshogle, in the paroch of Killearn, being one hundred and seventy-three pound of valuation.
Moses Buchanan of Glins, two hunder sextie-two pund valuation.
John Wright of Easter Glins, sixtie-six pound valuation.
Alexander Wright of Puside, one hundred and foure pound and six shilling and eightpenny Scots valuation.
Walter Monteath of Kyp, three hundred pounds valuation.
James Key, portioner of Enblioy, for sixty-six pound Scots valuation.
Robert Galbrath, portioner of Enbelly, for thritie-three pound Scots valuation.
Alexander Buchanan of Cremanan, for my land of Cremanan, in the paroch of Balfron, and . . . being two hundred and sixty-eight pound of valuation. valuation ; yet I now agree

with you for three per cent, for the lands you have contracted for; and that the first term of Whitsunday, and in time coming during the standing of the contract. And I am, sir, your most humble servant. *JA. Grahame.*

The following receipt granted by Mr Grahame of Glengyle, to Mr. Robert Galbraith, for the payment of 'watch-money' is probably, the last of its kind. By the time of its issue, just before the beginning of the following year (1745), the plans for the Jacobite Rising were well under way, and by July, Prince Charles had actually embarked for Scotland. By the back end of the year, Glengyle's hands must have been filled with more important concerns:

Hill, 12th Dec., 1744.
Then received by me James Grahame of Glengile from Robert Galbraith, portioner of Enbelly fourtie shillings Scots money in full payt. of all bygone watch money due to me out of his portion of Enbelly proceeding Martinmas last as witness my hand place and date above written.
JA. Grahame.

Nimmo also tells us of a contract that existed between the father of Rob Roy MacGregor and the heiress of Kilmarnock, known as Lady Cochrane. For the protection of her property he was to receive sixteen bolls of meal yearly. Contracts of this kind were generally paid by agricultural produce, that commodity being very scarce north of the Forth. For some time Lady Cochrane paid her annual tribute with considerable regularity, and by the stern watchfulness of MacGregor and his clansmen thieving became less and less frequent on her ladyship's property. Thinking herself secure, she refused to pay her dues until she had fallen considerably in arrears. By and by MacGregor led her to understand what would be the result if her obstinacy continued, but to this message something like a threat of defiance was returned. MacGregor now summoned his retainers, and assisted by his son-in-law, Macdonald of Glencoe, swept the banks of the Leven of all its valuable stock. Sitting down beside Lady Cochrane in her own parlour, he told her that if she did not feu off her lands to enterprising 'tacksmen', he would take the estate from her altogether. At this time the plundering of stock was not regarded as theft, but simply 'liftings'; and unless the loser could stake his lost cattle or sheep in fair fight, there remained no other alternative than to be content with the loss.

The Highland way relied fundamentally on the force of arms, as it had always done, while the Lowland society of the 18th century was increasingly peaceful, and, certainly by its own lights, modern. In the instance quoted it was the Lowlander, Lady Cochrane, who effectively 'welshed' on the deal.

The use of blackmail to curtail the worst abuses of cattle-raiding seems to have been a relatively efficient business. The existence of contracts like the one above shows how formalised the relationship between landowner and protector eventually became, though one has to wonder how things went when the 'claims adjuster' was armed to the teeth and surrounded by his henchmen!

The payment of watch money that Grahame refers to above suggests quite clearly that what we are seeing is an effective and localised form of policing, with the added attraction for the landowner of having a built-in insurance component.